Empowering Science and Mathematics Education in Urban Schools

Empowering Science and Mathematics Education in Urban Schools

EDNA TAN AND ANGELA CALABRESE BARTON
WITH ERIN E. TURNER AND MAURA VARLEY GUTIÉRREZ

THE UNIVERSITY OF CHICAGO PRESS CHICAGO AND LONDON

Edna Tan is assistant professor of science education at the University of North Carolina at Greensboro. **Angela Calabrese Barton** is professor of science education at Michigan State University. She is the author of *Teaching Science for Social Justice* and *Feminist Science Education*, coauthor of *Rethinking Scientific Literacy*, and coeditor of *Teaching Science in Diverse Settings: Marginalized Discourses and Classroom Practice.*

The University of Chicago Press, Chicago 60637
The University of Chicago Press, Ltd., London

Printed in the United States of America
21 20 19 18 17 16 15 14 13 12   1 2 3 4 5

ISBN-13: 978-0-226-03797-4 (cloth)
ISBN-13: 978-0-226-03798-1 (paper)
ISBN-10: 0-226-03797-5 (cloth)
ISBN-10: 0-226-03798-3 (paper)

Library of Congress Cataloging-in-Publication Data

Tan, Edna.
Empowering science and mathematics education in urban schools / Edna Tan and Angela Calabrese Barton with Erin E. Turner and Maura Varley Gutiérrez.
pages ; cm.
Includes bibliographical references and index.
ISBN 978-0-226-03797-4 (hardcover : alkaline paper) — ISBN 978-0-226-03798-1 (paperback : alkaline paper) — ISBN 0-226-03797-5 (hardcover : alkaline paper) — ISBN 0-226-03798-3 (paperback : alkaline paper) 1. Science—Study and teaching (Middle school) 2. Mathematics—Study and teaching (Middle school) 3. Critical pedagogy—United States. 4. City children—Education. 5. Educational equalization. I. Calabrese Barton, Angela. II. Varley Gutiérrez, Maura. III. Turner, Erin E. IV. Title.
Q181.T35 2012
507.1—dc23

2012011666

♾ This paper meets the requirements of ANSI/NISO Z39.48-1992 (Permanence of Paper).

Contents

CHAPTER ONE

Changing the Discourse on Equity and Math and Science for All

"Mmmmmm! Now That's Science!"

It was late morning on a sunny but brisk November day. The students in Mrs. Tiller's classroom had been engrossed in a science unit focused on dynamic equilibrium and the human body. One of the goals of the unit was to support students in learning how to bring scientific evidence and reasoning to bear on making healthy eating and activity choices. The curriculum was introduced to Mrs. Tiller's school as part of a much larger federally funded project. Along with all of the material resources needed to teach this unit, Mrs. Tiller had weekly access to professional development and classroom support.

Mrs. Tiller had been a teacher at Jefferson Middle School for many years, with a long-standing reputation for caring deeply for her students but also for being a no-nonsense kind of teacher. While her background was not in science, a typical situation in underresourced urban districts, she did have a background in nutrition and home economics, giving her a particular knowledge base to bring to a unit on dynamic equilibrium in the human body.

The first unit of the curriculum focused closely on the complex system of influences on young people's food and activity choices, which are biological, environmental, personal, and cultural in origin. In the second unit, students learn about how taste influences food choices. They learn about the biological taste preferences that humans have for fats and sugars, and how stores, fast food establishments, and food advertisements take advantage of our innate taste preferences, making it challenging to achieve health-oriented goals.

The curriculum instructs the teacher to begin the lesson by telling students that they are to close their eyes and listen to the following scenario:

> You are walking down the street and smell French fries cooking at a fast food restaurant. They smell hot and delicious [please add any relevant descriptors]. You and your friends are hungry so you decide to go in and order some food. The French fries smelled so good you decide to order some with your meal. When you get the fries, they are exactly what you wanted. They taste even better than they smelled! Each one is crispy and satisfying. You eat all your fries.

The teacher is to read the scenario out loud, and then, after listening to the scenario, the students are to individually answer questions on a five-point scale (from never to always), about whether the smell of French fries makes them want to buy some, whether they order French fries in fast food restaurants after smelling them, and whether French fries taste good to them. After students discuss their responses in groups, the teacher tallies up the student responses and uses that to help students build initial theories about the biological preferences of taste.

Mrs. Tiller was excited to teach this lesson! In our professional development sessions with her before the implementation of the unit, she was never short of a story on how her students lived on a diet of fast food. However, she was not satisfied with a simple visualization, especially given her background in home economics. As she said,

> I know what I'm going to do for this lesson. I'm going to get some potatoes and cook up in my classroom some home-made French fries. Just imagine how the smell of those fries will linger in the hallway as they walk to my classroom. I'm even going to let them eat the fries. Savor their taste. Enjoy them. They are going to have to answer those questions honestly with the fries right there in front of them! (Field notes, professional development session)

True to her word, Mrs. Tiller made the fries and the smell wafted down the hall just as predicted. In the class periods before lunch, the smell for many of her students was irresistible. As she anticipated, her students entered her class curious, excited, and hungry. The hot fries sat in the front of the room, and getting her students to step away from the fryer and back toward their seats proved somewhat challenging. One student seemed to get the whole class laughing when he said rather loudly, "Mmmmm . . . Now that's science!" However, Mrs. Tiller used her students' excitement to engage them immediately in the lesson:

> OK, who wants fries? Hot, crispy fries? Hmmm. Don't they smell good? Sit down and raise your hand if you want fries!

As she passed out the plates of French fries, she re-created the initial visualization scenario for them, inviting her students to think about how much the smell of the fries made them want to eat them. As she enticed the class, "The smell is just making my mouth water. How about you?" she asked them to record their observations in addition to their scores to the questions on taste and preference. After she finished passing out the French fries, she directed her students to answer the questions on smell, taste, and preference while she made a chart on the board, which she used to tally student responses (see Table 1.1).

Using the students' tallies, Mrs. Tiller worked to get her students talking about the patterns in the table. Did students like French fries? Did they want to buy them? The students seemed to key in more to what they liked about French fries and whether Mrs. Tiller's French fries were good. After turning their table into graphs, she was able to get her students to notice that most of the students in class liked fries and would buy them because they smelled good. When one student said, "Well, just about all of us picked 4 or 5 for all of the questions," Mrs. Tiller capitalized on the comment, telling her students, "That's right! Our bodies are naturally inclined to want fast food and we are hardwired to want to eat fries!"

Whereas Mrs. Tiller initially intended to spend most of the class period talking about the pattern of taste preferences, talk about French

TABLE 1.1. **A representation of how Mrs. Tiller tallied her students' responses on the board.**

	Never	------------	------------	------------	Always
5-point scale	1	2	3	4	5
Q1 (want to buy fries?)	1	2	2	6	12
Q2 (buying fries)	1	2	0	3	17
Q3 (taste)	1	2	0	0	20

fries led the students to insist on a more complex and perhaps realistic discussion about the social and cultural influences of taste and healthy eating. As one student said, "Why say fast food is bad if we are *supposed* to like it?" Another student wondered why one student in the class actually voted that French fries do not ever taste good if the human body is supposed to prefer fatty food. Creating lots of laughter was a student comment about how businesses make their money off their smells. Compared to normal discursive patterns in Mrs. Tiller's class and around Jefferson more generally, students were loudly engaged in debating the value and relevance of the science of taste and its sociopolitical connections. They began to build evidence-based claims not only around the intended focus (i.e., the biological preferences of taste) but also around unintended ideas and experiences central to making healthy eating decisions in everyday life (i.e., the role of the complex environment in food choices) and the limits of scientific ideas (i.e., not everyone has the same preferences for sweet and fatty foods).

While the entire activity (estimated in the curriculum to take about 10–15 minutes) took her entire class period, Mrs. Tiller felt satisfied with the results. Later Mrs. Tiller justified her pedagogical decisions:

> It was a little chaotic in there. Everyone wanted fries, seconds and thirds. It was the perfect set up. I know that my students will just want to give the "right" answer. But there is no right answer. I just want an honest answer. How else can I get them to really use their knowledge to make healthy choices if they don't know what they know? (Interview)

Mrs. Tiller wanted her students to answer "honestly," rather than in a fashion that parroted back the content. She believed that her students had rich, personal experiences directly relevant to this science topic and creatively engaged her students in activities that allowed those rich experiences to emerge as valuable threads in the classroom discussion. Even though her classroom looked and sounded unconventional, Mrs. Tiller was committed to helping her students engage in authentic inquiries that are essentially messy in nature. Mrs. Tiller told us that while the science of dynamic equilibrium in the human body, or "energy in and energy out," is "pretty straightforward," making healthy choices is not, because "science mixes with all of the things in kids' lives." She viewed her task as the teacher of this unit as helping her students use science to reason through good choices and helping her students see that the question of healthy eating, like many science questions, is not neatly "answered by a textbook."

Unpacking Equity, Access, and Empowering Science and Math Education

What Constitutes Equitable Opportunities to Learn Math and Science?

Math and science hold uniquely powerful places in contemporary society. These domains open doors to high-paying professions; provide a knowledge base for more informed conversations with health care workers, educators, and business and community leaders; and demystify issues of global importance, such as air and water quality standards, population density, toxic dumping, and the economy. Despite the interconnectedness of science and math with global sustainability, Western culture has a history of limiting access to the influential discourses that shape decision making in these areas (Buckingham, Reeves, and Batchelor 2005; Newman 2001; Gutstein and Peterson 2005; R. Gutiérrez 2007; Powell and Frankenstein 1997).

Schools play a crucial role in mediating access to math and science. Yet schools have also been complacent in the reproduction of the demographic trends of who has access to science and math and who does not (Gilbert and Yerrick 2001; Oakes, Joseph, and Muir 2003). While access to science and math actively occurs through tracking and the course-taking patterns allowed or supported by a school or district, it is almost always amplified by the ways in which classroom practices maintain norms and routines that depict science and math as "objective, privileged way[s] of knowing pursued by an intellectual elite" (Carlone 2004, 308), and as discontinuous with the ways of knowing and doing held by students from nondominant backgrounds (Martin 2000; Turner and Font Strawhun 2007; Warren et al. 2001).

When schools equate teaching science and math and learning with "knowledge acquisition" (at best) and "doing school" (more likely)—rather than with scaffolding participation in a community of practice of which knowledge is only one dimension—students have few, if any, school-based opportunities to develop the kind of mathematical and scientific literacies necessary for broader societal engagement (Gutstein 2006a). Such focus on "what" students learn to the exclusion of "why" or "how" they might learn to participate in science- or math-related communities of practice delimits the possibilities for understanding why students opt out of science and math, and why these trends noticeably manifest themselves along racial, ethnic, and socioeconomic lines. It should be no surprise that research continues to indicate that not only do students from urban and nondominant backgrounds lose interest in learning science and math as early as middle school but also that this trend has not changed in the past 15 years (Atwater, Wiggins, and Gardner 1995; Barmby, Kind, and Jones 2008).

The need to address equitable access to science and math education dates back several decades, even centuries (Spencer 1859; Wilkinson 1857). While the reason and scope for the call for science and math education "for all" has shifted over time from legitimizing the core courses in the standard school curriculum in the late nineteenth century, to national security in the mid-twentieth century, the call to make equitable math and science instruction has tended to reside in the policy sector with extension into curricula, rather than in any systematic line of inquiry into what this should look like and why. Further, and relevant to our course of inquiry, there has been no attempt to examine how equitable experiences might also be empowering experiences, especially for those students from nondominant backgrounds. There has also been scant attention to the specific needs of urban learners in the effort to promote science and math for all, despite decades of research outlining the inequities present in urban communities.

Bill Tate (2001) has argued that high-quality science and math education is a civil right for all students, and that this right is especially significant for those from nondominant groups. He rests his case on the mounting evidence that science and math education has been and continues to be mired in inequality. That is, children of racial and ethnic minority backgrounds and from high-poverty backgrounds living in high numbers in cities and rural communities disproportionately lack access to opportunities to learn science or math, even though they may have gained the physical space in schools to do so. In fact, he argues that to address fundamental issues of equity in science and math education, the research community must shift from arguments for civil rights as shared physical space in schools to demands for high-quality academic preparation that includes opportunities to learn. We concur with Tate in his call for equitable opportunities for all learners in math and science. And yet, we wonder, what exactly do these equitable opportunities to learn science or math that Tate and others rightly demand for our children look like? What are their outcomes?

Equity as Equality

The lines of reasoning around equitable opportunities to learn are anything but straightforward. In the immediate post–civil rights and post–women's rights eras, equity-driven concerns in math and science education, as instantiated in educational policy and practice, tended to draw upon a focus on equality, or in other words, an understanding or measurement of either "equal treatment" or "outcomes," usually based upon comparisons of demographic groups (Secada, 1989, 68). The focus in science and math education, therefore, has centered on whether opportunities to learn exist for all students (i.e., equal treatment) or on whether all students are achieving in science and math, and if not, where the achievement gaps exist (i.e., equal outcomes).

Studies of equal treatment and equal outcome have played, and continue to play, powerful and historically important roles. Most researchers are generally familiar with the chilling statistics that describe high-poverty and minority urban and rural students' differential access to resources in US schools, and are aware that these trends have changed little in the past three decades. Students attending zoned schools in low-income urban and rural communities by and large continue to have limited access to updated science and math books, equipment, and extracurricular activities (Oakes, Joseph, and Muir 2003; Campbell and Silver 1999). They also continue to have limited access to certified teachers or to administrators who support high-quality science and math teaching, such that either students are denied high-level courses (because they are not offered) or they take courses with uncertified or unqualified teachers (Allexsaht-Snider and Hart 2001; Darling-Hammond 1999; Ingersoll 1999; Spade, Columba, and Vanfossen 1997). High-poverty, urban students are disproportionately tracked into low-level classes where educational achievement typically focuses on behavior skills and static conceptions of knowledge (Oakes, Joseph, and Muir 2003). In fact, some studies have shown a complete absence of science in low-track science classes (Page 1990; Gilbert and Yerrick 2001).

While equity as equality has provided a rich look into the basic landscape of access and opportunity, more socioculturally and critically oriented approaches to equity argue that such a view does not account for how participation and achievement in science and math are mediated by a complex set of sociocultural and systemic factors. For example, why is it that students with access to the same resources can have radically different learning outcomes that often pattern along gender and ethnic lines? Embedded within a discourse of equality of input and outcome is the assumption that science and math are objective and universal knowledge bases, and that with adequate access to these knowledge bases students can become successful in these areas. Without consideration of the sociocultural and systemic factors that shape science and math education, all students are viewed as homogenous, promoting a reform agenda best described as "one science [or math] fits all" (Calabrese Barton 1998, 531). Gutiérrez (2002) further critiques the notion of equity as equality, noting that "it is not clear that having all students reach the same goals represents 'justiceí for studentsí own desires or identities" (p. 152). Instead, she proposes a definition of equity that assumes neither equal approaches (e.g., teaching strategies or resources) nor equal outcomes, but instead focuses on the goal of being unable to predict student achievement and participation patterns solely on the basis of characteristics such as race, language, gender, or class. In short, sociocultural and critical perspectives bring the social, political, and economic realities that students grapple with daily into sharper focus and take an integrated view of how the daily contexts in which children live, play, and learn should matter and critically inform opportunities for all to learn science and math.

Dynamic Communities and Transformations: A Basis for Empowering Education

Our stance on empowering education is informed by the contexts in which we work, in addition to the theories that inform our thinking. We work closely with youth in urban settings from low-income families who are also predominantly of ethnic and racial minority backgrounds. Learning within and across communities must always call to question the sociopolitical dimensions of participation within community. The reasons and the ways that communities enact and sustain various networks of power are important for understanding learning, because they shape how communities develop a history of privileging particular discourses, identities, and forms of participation over others (see also, C. Lee and

Majors 2003; Moje et al. 2001). While such privileging may often be the result of the nature of the practice (i.e., science communities valuing science discourse over other discourses), they are often just as much the result of gender, race, class, and other cultural-historical structures that shape how and why people relate to one another (Bell et al. 2009). How such histories are disrupted is something we are keenly interested in as we seek to advance our understanding of student learning in math and science.

Our stance on empowering science and math classrooms is deeply informed by critically oriented sociocultural perspectives on schooling, learning, and society. Critically oriented sociocultural lenses draw attention to how the culture of classrooms is dynamic and activity based (K. Gutiérrez and Rogoff 2003; O. Lee 2002). K. Gutiérrez and Rogoff (2003) argue that an activity-oriented understanding of learning suggests that culture can be understood only through its context development, and never as a set of definable, measurable traits. Instead of expecting students to "cross over" into the culture of school science and math, where one's primary discourse is viewed as discontinuous with that of school science or math, the process of enculturation should attend to how outside discourses and practices can productively transform a community.

Math and science classrooms are replete with practices that are culturally grounded and sit at "the junction of cultural artifacts, beliefs, values and normative routines" (K. Gutiérrez 2002, 313). Indeed, it has been argued that "success and failure in school is contingent upon one's ability to regulate and situate identities, utilize culturally-developed semiotic tools and negotiate models of meaning in shared social activity" (C. Lee and Majors 2003, 49). However, we have few stories in the literature that help us to see just how much teaching and learning math and science are cultural processes. Notable exceptions are the work of scholars such as Beth Warren and her colleagues.

For example, Beth Warren and Ann Rosebury (1995), in rich ethnographic detail, illustrate how youth from nondominant backgrounds have cultural knowledge and experience that is highly relevant to doing science, and that can be leveraged toward developing a kind of practice in science that attends to both the discipline and the home. They show us how, in bilingual classrooms, students often *imagine themselves a part of science*, and of the scientific phenomenon they are trying to understand, even when they feel marginalized by norms and practices of school science. Their work serves as a foundation for a growing tradition in science education to identify the ways in which discourse mediates engagement in science, including not only what one learns but also how and why one comes to participate in science-related communities of practice.

Similar studies have been documented in math with analytic attention paid to the microprocesses of the classroom community. For example, Stinson (2008) described how four highly successful African American math students, in addition to persisting with math in school, were skillful in knowing how to negotiate the discourses that surround African American male students learning math. It is precisely this meta-level knowledge of how discourses operate in classrooms described by Warren and Stinson that supports teachers and students in co-opting classroom practice to allow for a more authentic merging of everyday and disciplinary discourses.

Learning is not only about what learners know, but also about how what they know is part of a larger system of practices, norms, and values (Brickhouse and Potter 2001). Getting involved in new activities, performing new tasks, and mastering new understandings also means becoming a different person with respect to the possibilities associated with being able to participate differently within a community (Wenger 1998). In this process, a person's beliefs become crucial in shaping the kinds of practices they decide to undertake. Thus, providing students with opportunities to become aware of the norms and practices of math or science includes developing a meta-level knowledge of how they are expected to participate through discourses, ways of knowing, and practices (D. Anderson and Gold 2006; Esmonde 2009; Hogan and Corey 2001).

Little attention outside of equity-driven research has focused on how learning is informed and transformed by the sociopolitical dimensions that shape everyday activity and living. It is therefore important to note that instead of viewing learning as changing participation within a community of practice as individuals move from novice to more expert positions, critically oriented sociocultural theorists point out that learning also involves a process of cultural production. As an individual joins a community, he or she brings resources in the form of particular historical and cultural experiences, which by their activation can transform the discourses and practices of the community. As novices leverage resources from outside the community to develop expertise within the community, they create new discourses and practices that can—

depending upon the dynamics of that community—transform its culture, discourse, and practices.

We argue in this book that instead of taking the view of science and math for all in which the "all" must be appropriately conditioned to receive the discipline—that is, "one science or math fits all"—science and math for all needs to be recast to be emergent of the interests, needs, concerns, locations, and conditions of those who participate (see also, R. Gutiérrez 2007). Similarly, Allexsaht-Snider and Hart (2001) have called for more to be done and for the complex issues of equity to be critically examined in the contexts of "financial, human, leadership, curricular, and evaluative resources" (p. 99) if the goal of "math for all" is to be accomplished. Current research on multicultural science and math education has revealed the complexities of developing science and math instruction that meets the needs of the diverse students while actively recruiting them as legitimate members of the science community. Students face hurdles of linguistic discord (O. Lee and Fradd 1998; B. A. Brown 2004; Secada 1992), conflicts of gender and ethnic identities (Brickhouse 1994; Calabrese Barton 1998; Boaler 2002), as well as alienating instruction (Rosebery, Warren, and Conant 1992, Oakes 1990).

It cannot be overstated that without access to the content, practices, and discourse of the disciplines, youth may not have opportunities to develop rich repertoires of science and math knowledge and practices that open the door for access to the professions. This is not our question. What we question is the process by which access is made available and what the agreed-upon outcomes for learning should be. Literacy in math and science should aim for more than functional literacy. As we discuss in chapter 2, in addition to providing an understanding of scientific and mathematical concepts, science and math education should build upon or be integrated with youths' everyday knowledge and practices, so that they may be equipped for participation in public life toward a more just and democratic society through the development of critical understandings about their lives (Freire 1973; Giroux 1988). Science and math education should aim for critical literacy in ways that account for the sociopolitical dimensions of learning, for what it means to use science and math to engage one's life and the world in empowering terms, and for the students' development of a sense of efficacy in the classroom and in society. In our own work in low-income, urban settings, we have noted how youth consistently assemble both traditional and nontraditional resources in non-routine ways: they craft hybrid practices that merge their social worlds with the worlds of science and math in order to inscribe new meaning into both the cultural and scientific symbols that frame their participation and position across a range of communities. In this sense, learning is less about practicing the routines of knowledgeable others than it is about re-creating those practices in socially and culturally situated ways that confer the student with more agency with which to participate across communities.

Returning to Mrs. Tiller's Classroom

We began this chapter with a short vignette about Mrs. Tiller in order to stress how complex working toward "equitable" science and math education is. Mrs. Tiller teaches in a school that is strapped for resources, and the vast majority of her students receive free or reduced-price lunch. But resources alone—or the lack of them—do not account for why her students struggle or what Mrs. Tiller might do to make her class more empowering for her students. Sixty-four percent of her students are African American, 21% are white, 8% are Hispanic, and 7% are "other." Jefferson Middle School's reputation is that it is a tough school, and on the basis of its test scores, Great Schools had given Jefferson a "quality" rating of "2 out of 10."

Limited resources, low scores on tests, and teachers who are teaching out of field potentially limit students' opportunities to learn science. Yet Mrs. Tiller, like many of her teaching colleagues at Jefferson, put in the extra effort to acquire curricular materials, such as the reform-based inquiry science unit on dynamic equilibrium referenced above, for her students. She invested herself in learning the new content so that she could teach it well by coming into school an hour early once a week for the months of November, December, and January—months in which mornings in her geographic region are very cold and dark. She designed activities that made explicit how learning science was a "way of knowing and talking" that connected to their lives, but asked them to think about "evidence" and "reasoning." She did not shy away from the complex social system in which knowing/doing science is situated, but she also admitted to not really knowing what to do when these conversations emerged. While not officially "highly qualified" to teach science, given her lack of academic preparation in the domain, she brought a background in nutrition that she used to enrich her teaching of the unit. She traded out some lessons in the curriculum to expand other lessons, as we saw with the French fry visualization. She cared deeply about her students and wanted them to care about the health of their bodies. While she wanted to create a setting that would get her most challenging students to wonder, in her words, "what's up with science," she simultaneously made her class "a little more chaotic" and "not exactly what the principal wants to *hear*." Still, she clung to the notion that "doing science," especially in a unit focused on helping students to make healthy food and activity choices, had to focus on their cultural practices—that is, what students cared about (actually eating French fries) and what they did—on a day-to-day basis.

Mrs. Tiller's classroom highlights just how much building equitable opportunities to learn science (or math) "*is at once about accessing the world as it is about transforming it*" (Freire and Macedo 1987). Mrs. Tiller's classroom may not have changed the way that Jefferson Middle School youth eat and exercise day in and day out. However, she did purposefully seek to create teaching and learning moments for her students that went beyond the science at hand, to consider how science can be both a tool for and an object of critique. She also used her love of nutrition to reposition the students as coauthors of the investigation. Thus, to frame movement toward equitable science instruction as only about "access to high-quality teachers and curricula" limits our understanding of what may be most transformative in Mrs. Tiller's classroom. Meaningful learning and engagement in science (and math) is about more than access to the resources for teaching science or crossing boundaries into the world of science. It is about transforming science and math education "in ways that uphold the identities of diverse students, work against social inequalities, and help students develop tools of critical literacy" (Gutstein et al. 1997).

While both resources and being able to cross boundaries were important in Mrs. Tiller's classroom—you need to be able to talk and do science as part of engaging in critical dialog—Mrs. Tiller's classroom presents us with a set of conundrums about equitable and empowering science instruction. Mrs. Tiller's class allows us to consider the distinction between *equitable* classrooms and *empowering* classrooms, and how clarifying the differences between the two ideals might help us uncover social justice pedagogies and methods. Her teaching further demands that we answer questions: Was Mrs. Tiller's teaching of the dynamic equilibrium unit really empowering? If so, how do we know? Is the evidence in the unit test scores, state level test scores, classroom performance, or personal practices with respect to food and activity choices? As science and math teachers and researchers, how do we describe, document, and seek to enact empowering science and math instruction for all learners?

As we explore in depth in the next chapter, we use the phrase "empowering learning environments" intentionally to capture a vision of education that engages youth in learning and using science and math as both a tool and a context for change. This means that one both views the world with a critical mindset and imagines how the world might be a more socially just and equitable place, and views oneself as a powerful scientific and math thinker and doer. We argue that an empowering science and math education is one where authentic hybrid spaces are created, which allow students to merge their worlds with the worlds of science and math education in support of learning and agency. While many have written about the need for creating such hybrid spaces (or third spaces) in classrooms, especially in light of the increasing achievement gaps between white and minority students (e.g. Moje et al. 2004; K. Gutiérrez, Baquedano-López, and Tejeda 1999), we do not as yet have many images of what these hybrid spaces look like, how they may be connected to students' lives and what they need to learn, how they might be measured, and how they can fit into the current policy and practice climate. This book offers a set of images of hybrid spaces in action as well as a discussion of what hybrid spaces are, and how they may be connected to the teaching and learning of middle school science and math and the transition to high school. We also pay special attention to the cultivation of student critical science and math agency as an essential outcome of student engagement in hybrid spaces.

We focus primarily upon middle school–aged youth (and the transition to high school) because middle school is a crucial time to examine how youth take up math and science in ways that matter to them. Middle school is when youth's choices for peer groups, mentors, grades, and afterschool programs play a pivotal role in the high school trajectories they pursue and in the support they seek to become and remain engaged in math and science (AAUWEF 1999; O. Lee 2002). Middle school is also a time when attitudes toward schooling and achievement drop precipitously (Atwater, Wiggins, and Gardner 1995). Arguably the transition years between middle and high school may be the most important, because it is at this time that youth move into schooling tracks that significantly impact their career trajectories.

This book examines the following questions:

- What do empowering learning environments in urban math and science look like, and what meaning do they carry for urban youth and their teachers?
- How are such environments constructed inside and outside of the school building?
- In what ways are empowering learning environments made possible through the hybridization of youth's Discourses[1] and funds of knowledge alongside the Discourse and culture of schooling as well as the disciplines of math and science?
- How do these empowering learning environments help students cultivate a sense of critical math and science agency?

Engaging in Research Critically

Each of the chapters in this text draws upon research conducted within a "critical ethnographic" framework (Carspecken 1996). Critical ethnography is a methodology for conducting research focused around the goals of participatory critique, transformation, empowerment, and social justice (Trueba 1999). Critical ethnography is rooted in the belief that exposing, critiquing, and transforming inequalities associated with social structures and labeling devices (i.e., gender, race, and class) are consequential dimensions of research and analysis. Given that urban education is marked by layers of inequalities from how schools are staffed and funded to the kinds of courses and resources available to students, the analysis and transformation of inequalities is particularly important in urban science education research. Critical ethnography also calls us to search for and to use tools that will enable us to examine and transform inequalities from multiple perspectives, and in particular from the "perspective of the oppressed" (Trueba 1999, 593). This point about perspective is consequential because the majority of youth in urban schools live

1. We use Discourse with a capital D to reference communication patterns that reflect ways of being and knowing, that are related to one's identity, as opposed to discourse with a small d that references conversation or talk that one uses without its strong connection to identity (Gee 1999).

in poverty at some point in their childhood, and more than half belong to an ethnic minority group. Critical ethnography also demands that the purposes, tools, and outcomes of research be co-imagined and produced by the researcher/researched, in order to break down such a binary and to allow the toils and fruits of research to be informed by a range of perspectives.

The authors of this book are also teachers and researchers in many of the settings we describe, and we work closely with the teachers, school leaders, parents, and youth who also participate in planning and research. We meet frequently with our coparticipants to discuss the goals of our project and to work toward new and different spaces for youth to author our research with us. Therefore, the stories in this text rely both on traditional forms of ethnographic data—such as lesson plans, field notes, and classroom artifacts—and on interviews. We also conducted interactive conversations and worked with teachers and youth to create products that reflected their curiosities and desires. We folded these products into our database as well, offering us an opportunity to engage in content analysis over a range of student works. More details on the methodology relevant to each study will be presented in the chapters.

The Chapters in This Text

Chapter 2 sets the stage for our text by accomplishing two goals. First it offers images of what hybrid spaces in real classrooms look like in ways that account for the possibilities they present. Second, this chapter provides a theoretical framing for the stories we tell in the remainder of the text. This chapter goes on to give a brief overview on the theory of constructing hybrid spaces in learning.

Chapters 3 to 6 describe hybrid spaces in action, in both science and math classrooms and after-school clubs. Hybrid spaces in middle school math is described in Chapter 3 by Erin Turner. This chapter presents a series of vignettes about how students use math to solve real problems in their lives in school related to overcrowding. The author describes how students displayed critical mathematical agency through four different ways: asserting intentions, authoring, improvisation, and critique. The author also discusses how the math teacher, Ms. Font, enacted specific pedagogical strategies to foster students' interests and agency, thereby creating learning environments that encouraged students to take up agency-enhancing mathematical learning and identities.

Chapter 4 focuses on Mrs. Davis' seventh-grade science classroom in a Midwestern city and describes how she and her students use storytelling as a pedagogical tool to promote narrative inquiry in school science while learning about nutrition. Through telling stories, students and teacher were able to open up new curricular spaces for new content threads, affirm science-related student identities grounded in their out-of-school lives, and position students with more power to negotiate for both the science content they were interested in and the inquiry activities to engage in.

Chapter 5 investigates the development of agency in science among low-income urban middle school youth as they participate in a voluntary year-round program on green energy technologies conducted at a local community club in a Midwestern city. Focusing on how youth engaged a summer unit on understanding and modeling the relationship between energy use and the health of the urban environment, the authors discuss how the youth asserted themselves as Community Science Experts in ways that took up and broke down the contradictory roles of being a producer and a critic of science/education. Findings also suggest that youth actively appropriate project activities and tools in order to challenge the types of roles and student voice traditionally available to students in the classroom.

How fifth-grade minority girls in an afterschool math club were able to prevent the closure of their school through the use of math is presented in Chapter 6 by Maura Varley Gutiérrez. The author describes how the girls strategically used their math skills to lobby the school board to keep their school from closing and sending all the students to another school further away. Varley Gutiérrez describes how the girls exhibited functional and critical math literacy by conducting rigorous mathematical investigations and enriched their findings with the social contexts of their lives and their local knowledge about neighborhood safety issues to build up their case to keep their school open. This chapter emphasizes how multiple funds of knowledge are integrated in a hybrid learning space.

In chapter 7, we discuss the learning outcomes both to the individual student and to the learning community as a whole that result from hybrid-space science and math learning. Attention is paid to the new resources that are made available in hybrid spaces, the new practices validated through the use of such resources, and how students and teacher are afforded new positionings as a result. We propose the notion of critical science and math literacy and agency as crucial components of hybrid-space learning in terms of both its enactment and its sustenance. We reiterate the main tenets of the book and pay attention to the implications that hybrid-space learning has with regard to educational policy, teacher preparation, and teacher professional development.

CHAPTER TWO

Empowering Teaching and Learning in Math and Science Education

"You're Out. You're Playing with Pictures of Eyeballs, and That Doesn't Look like Weather to Me!"

In the spring 2009, I (Angie) was teaching a fifth grade science unit on "weather" along with one of my colleagues (David) at a small urban school at the request of one of the teachers. The school was a public charter school known around the district as the school of "second chances" for youth struggling to succeed in the regular public system. The teacher's request was loaded. We were originally at her school to work on a project related to parental engagement in science. However, her school had just gotten a new principal who had declared a moratorium on science and social studies instruction in order to devote more instructional time to literacy and math to help advance student scores in these tested subject areas. She had hoped that by asking us to teach science, her students could still get science and she would not (as an untenured teacher) put her job in jeopardy. Further, she was exhausted from a long school year with a large class, few resources, and a limited science background.

In preparing for the unit, we were not surprised to learn that most of the students thought weather was boring—they would rather be outside playing in the warmer spring weather or socializing through digital technologies (i.e., Myspace or instant messaging) with their friends. In our own efforts to build a unit that was oriented toward teaching science for social justice, we opted to integrate literacy (a clear need, felt deeply at the school level) and technology (a strong youth interest) into our unit. Specifically, we engaged students in gathering and reasoning with real world evidence that they could use to build a case, in a digital story format, for how young students (K-4) might stay safe from weather events while on the playground this summer. The end goal for the fifth grade unit was to put on a science conference, where they premiered their digital stories with the K-4 students at their school.

One of the school leaders who initially approved our project visited the children several times, encouraging them to work hard, and appearing excited with their progress in the unit. The classroom teacher provided us with additional time in the computer room at school. She used her literacy block to work with the children on their storyboards for the unit. Yet, we were consistently disheartened by the explicit and implicit messages the students received from some (but not all) adult leaders at the school. The computer room teacher, Mr. Flato, said many times that he was sure the students could not make digital movies. The students themselves were excited about making movies but were afraid to show them to the third or fourth graders for fear of being made fun of—for taking science seriously, for presenting personal work, and for taking an academic stand.

We conducted lessons and experiments on how storms form and how approaching frontal systems can be predicted using data gathered at home and in school. We assembled barometers with materials easily gathered in the home (balloons, straws, plastic cups, etc.), we conducted cloud observations and examined the role that different cloud formations play in weather, we interviewed each other and parents about weather "rules of thumb" and "old wives' tales," and we used graphs and charts to represent data (see Table 2.1). Then the students began work on their digital movies. The first task was to prepare a storyboard to outline their main ideas, and to brainstorm what kinds of images, music, and text they would like to include. The next step was to begin to assemble the needed images in a desktop folder so that they could be easily imported into Movie Maker, the program we were using for these movies.

Maurice, one of the students in the class, had completed uploading 14 images into Movie Maker based on his storyboard. He had carefully scoured the web for pictures that illustrated dangerous thunderstorms, damaging hail, and pouring rain and wind. He also located pictures of different cloud types, and a graph demonstrating a typical weather pattern for the upper Midwest. Following my instructions, he, like the rest of the students, saved all of his pictures in a folder on the desktop called "Weather Project."

TABLE 2.1. **Weather Unit Outline**

Session	Description
1	Introduction to weather and storms. Show one or more short video clips of severe weather. Have students discuss prior experiences with and knowledge of severe weather. Ask students what causes severe weather. Discuss recent storms in the news.
2	Describe types of severe weather. Discuss the characteristics of tornadoes, hurricanes, thunderstorms, blizzards, drought, etc.
3	Introduce MovieMaker and storyboarding.
4	What causes storms? Discuss the sun as the source of energy and the greenhouse effect. Air pressure and wind.
5	Devices for weather data collection. Students build a simple measurement/data collection tool such as a hygrometer, barometer, anemometer, or dew point tool.
6	Thunderstorms. Describe the formation of thunderstorms. Optional activity: Have students build a simple dew point tool.
7	Understanding clouds. Discuss the formation of clouds and differentiate between cloud types.
8	Weather and folklore. Explore the origins of various local and distant myths, proverbs, and activities related to weather and seasonal phenomena.
9	Connect with math skills. Students graph data about storms using damage caused, category of storm, location, risk assessment, etc.
10	Living with severe weather. Discuss and describe the hazards of hurricanes and how to prepare for them.
11–13	Digital storytelling.

Note: Due to block scheduling, multiple sessions were covered on the same day.

The next week when we returned to the computer room to continue work on our project, the students noticed that their Weather Project folders were missing from their desktops. I thought they must be mistaken and painstakingly searched a couple of computers for the files, but I could not find them either. I had a choice in the moment—track down the computer teacher and ask what happened to the folders, or take a gamble and ask the students to search for new photos. I opted for the latter, hoping that they would not feel too discouraged in having to search again. I figured that it would take too long to find the computer teacher, precious class time would be wasted, and we still might not find the folders, and searching for new photos might offer the students a chance to refine their thinking about what pictures they really wanted. I also knew that several students had not finished the task the previous week and more time searching would have been necessary anyway. While a few students grumbled, most got on right away with the task.

Maurice, however, was particularly frustrated because he could not locate the violent hailstorm photo he was so proud of the previous week. He complained to me, to his friends sitting near him, and to no one in particular. While a little louder than I might have liked, Maurice still was on task, searching for new photos, images, and charts on the Internet. While I did not know Maurice well, as I was only a guest teacher in the school for the weather unit, I did know that Maurice was a handful. Not only did several teachers "warn" me about Maurice—with the regular classroom teacher telling me not to think twice about sending him to the office—but also we had experienced our own frustrations during a lesson building barometers. He kept wanting to play with the balloon rather than to build his barometer, and he seemed not to care during the lesson about why or how these instruments worked. Still, Maurice struck me as a sincere youth who struggled with what it meant to be a good student. Some days he would easily get into a class conversation, making thoughtful comments, and urging others to pay attention. Other days he seemed to decide he either did not like the activity or did not want to do school, and would resist any meaningful engagement. All in all, his inconsistency worked against his efforts to succeed in school. "He's one of my IEP[1] students," his classroom teacher told me matter-of-factly, clearly viewing him as someone who struggles and who needs extra support in order to succeed.

While Maurice was grumbling away, the computer room teacher, Mr. Flato, had walked into the room. I pulled him aside to ask about the problem with the weather folders, but before he could answer me, he was admonishing Maurice for being off task and sent him immediately to the office. Besides my own frustration—this was my classroom, after all, and I do not appreciate other teachers coming in and trying to take over!—Maurice's frustration was palpable. He screamed back at Mr. Flato, insisting his innocence—"I am working. You don't know what you're talking about!" This, of course, did not help matters, and Mr. Flato responded, "You're out. You're playing with pictures of eyeballs, and that doesn't look like weather to me!" Mr. Flato personally walked Maurice to the office, ensuring that Maurice did not return to class that day.

1. IEP stands for Individual Education Plan.

Because I was a guest teacher, my hands were tied somewhat. However, after class I told Mr. Flato that I would handle my classroom myself, to which he said, "If that is what you really want." I made a point of going to the office after class to talk with both Maurice and the principal, but I wondered whether the damage could be undone. Would Maurice engage with this project again? Would he make a movie? Would he learn more about weather? Would he prove his antagonist wrong?

When I had the chance to ask Mr. Flato about the weather folders, he told me that once a month he "purges" the desktop. Students know they are not allowed to save items on the desktop, and such procedures are necessary to rid any of the computers of potentially inappropriate material. As a guest teacher, I had not known this and felt it was my fault the students lost their folders of work; still, I was frustrated because the computer teacher knew we were working on a weather project. That the students were punished instead of me for this mistake seemed to further position them as outsiders to success.

The next week Maurice was back in science class but found himself behind his peers. Rather than working on text and transitions in his movie, he was back searching for images. The regular classroom teacher, however, began to use her literacy block to allow the students to work on their digital stories in the computer lab. With that little extra time in class that week, Maurice was able to finish his movie. When he stood up to present his film to the second, third, and fourth graders during our science conference at the end of the unit, the normally carefree student struck me as nervous, as he clutched his written explanation and read his introduction:

> MAURICE: This is a movie about weather, and it's for you kids, yo [laughing]. There are lots of kinds of clouds and they, uh, they do different things. I say, stop, look, and listen.

Maurice's movie was a short 45 seconds in duration, and as noted in the first scene, he assumed the identity of Kobe Bryant, the basketball star, as author of the movie. Maurice's movie began with the title fading in by line against a clear blue sky backdrop:

Weather safety . . .
For kids . . .
By Kobe Bryant

The title faded away into an image of farmland with thin wispless clouds moving in from the west (or left-hand side) of the image. Text then floated into the center of the screen, which read, "This is a picture of cirrus cloud."

While it is not clear whether Maurice intended to suggest that cirrus clouds often signal an approaching frontal system as discussed in class, about 5 seconds into this scene, the sound of wind and rain came into the scene. The picture then slowly transitioned into an image of a large cumulonimbus cloud, deeply gray and casting rain over some low mountains. The wind and rain then gave way to a thunderous roar. Text then rolled across the screen, stating, "If you see this cloud, it will most likely rain. . . . Do you know why?" Another crack of thunder roars, and new text moves into the screen shot that reads, "pressure drops/cause clouds to form/and lightening . . . and damaging wind." The screen transitions with a blast effect into an image of a tornado, a violent rotation of air that connects cumulonimbus clouds with the ground. The text reads, "if you hear or see one of these, it would be safe to go to the basement." The tornado image transitions using the twisting effect into a bright red STOP sign, which then transitions to an image of large disembodied eyeballs while the text reads "Stop. Look. Listen." This transitions into the last screen shot, which is an ear, and which includes the same text. A final credit is given at the end scrolling down the screen, "The End. . . . By Maurice."

Despite Mr. Flato's own grumblings, Maurice had a movie to share, and while his movie lacked some of the sophistication of some of his peers, he managed a clear content focus, and provided the second, third, and fourth graders with sound advice about keeping safe from storms. Moreover, he spoke in a scientific language younger people can understand: Stop, look, and listen. Most young people have learned about using their five senses to make good scientific observations. Maurice's point that looking and listening provided good cues on weather were not lost on the students. He used digital effects to exaggerate key ideas: the wind blowing in a storm, the tornado twisting away. He provided visual representations of the cloud formations that one might look for. From his sound selection to his word and image choices, science—as a content, a discourse, and a way of knowing—became a tool Maurice could use to engage others about their world.

We begin with this short vignette because we believe that it highlights just how much social justice is about accessing the world and transforming it. The youth at Maurice's school clearly lacked access and opportunity (some more than others) to engage science in any meaningful way in their school for reasons beyond their or even their teachers' control. Without intense out-of-school compensatory experiences, they held little hope either for achieving on the statewide science exam or for gaining the knowledge to identify questions, to determine answers, or to explain scientific phenomena in ways that might matter in their daily living or for meaningful civic participation (NRC 1996). The youth consistently received messages about what they could accomplish. They could have walked away from the school year believing that they were not capable—or worthy—of doing science or that science held no real meaning in their lives.

It has been argued that socially just science teaching differs from teaching science for social justice (Moje 2007). On the one hand, socially just science teaching is about access and opportunity—all children deserve the right to good teachers, to adequate materials, and to a chance to succeed on society's terms, whether that be a grade or a test score. Teaching science for social justice, on the other hand, "not only provides access to mainstream knowledge and practices but also provides opportunities to question, challenge, and reconstruct knowledge. Social justice pedagogy should, in other words, offer possibilities for transformation, not only of the learner but also of the social and political contexts in which learning and other social action take place" (Moje 2007, 4). What should science and math education look like so that students can be equipped with the knowledge, skills, and agency—that is, empowered—to critically redress the inequalities in their lives and communities by drawing on what they are learning from math and science classes? The rest of the chapter is to provide the conceptual basis for what "empowering math and science education" might entail in the middle grades.

Transformative Third Spaces and Empowering Math and Science Education

Challenging the Script

Empowering math and science education supports youth in appropriating canonical knowledge and practices of science and math but also provides opportunities to question, challenge, and reconstruct knowledge, practice, and the contexts in which youth live and learn (Moje 2007). To unpack empowering math and science education, we therefore have to look both at how science and math learning communities in classrooms operate and at how notions of learning frame the goals and outcomes of science and math education.

In the teaching episode described earlier, Mr. Flato assumed that Maurice was "off task" because it was not clear to him how pictures of disembodied eyeballs could be connected to a movie on weather. How much of who Maurice is as a young man, or the encounters he has had with Mr. Flato over time, played a role in Mr. Flato's assumption? What might have happened if he had asked Maurice for an explanation? Would their already tenuous relationship have pushed Maurice to resist another time and refuse an explanation? Or would he have explained how the picture connected to his thesis? We will never know the answers to these questions. However, what we can learn from that moment is just how much science (and math) classroom communities are loaded with a script ("dominant cultural values") and counterscript ("formed by those who do not comply with the teacher's view of appropriate participation") that can position students and teachers in oppositional ways (K. Gutiérrez, Rymes, and Larson 1995, 445).

The script, in this case, reflected Mr. Flato's authority in school and his efforts to position Maurice's work on the digital movie as off task. Maurice had a history of noncompliance at school, and his efforts in a unit on weather did not fit with Mr. Flato's vision of what it meant to be a good student at that moment. The counterscript, reflected in Maurice's rejection of Mr. Flato's reality, emerged in his defense of his actions as well as in his own efforts to craft a movie that would connect with young people but not look like school science. While Maurice used the tools of science, he selected nontraditional images and a storyline that was very child-centered. As the guest teacher, I felt caught in the middle, wanting to reject the script imposed by Mr. Flato, and also wanting to connect with Maurice's nontraditional attempts at his movie. Yet, while I concurred with Maurice's dissent, I also did not want to suggest it was appropriate for youth to scream at teachers during class. Later Maurice would tell me that those eyeballs were "cool" and "creepy," and that was "what you want" in a movie. For me, the teacher but not the real teacher given my guest status in the school, there was an additional script/counterscript playing out. Mr. Flato took it upon himself to discipline my students, without my consent, and his disciplinary tactics clearly opposed my own approaches. There was jockeying for hierarchies.

Mrs. Tiller's classroom (chapter 1) likewise exposes the tensions emergent when studying a science content area that is loaded with social, political, and cultural value. Mrs. Tiller believed it was not enough for students to understand that human bodies are regulated through dynamic equilibrium, and that such dynamics need to be considered when making food and activity choices. She also wanted her students to be able to take this knowledge to bear as they navigated the highly complex and economically driven environment that mediates all food and activity choices. And yet, the process of bringing that knowledge to bear was rife with controversy in Mrs. Tiller's classroom: Why do fast food establishments take advantage of the biological preference for fatty foods? What can youth do about the food environment when so much of it is out of their hands? Take, for example, youth growing up in Detroit, Michigan, today. There is no nondiscount grocery store operating within city limits. Access to high-quality produce (not to mention organic produce) is essentially nonexistent. The process through which residents learn to have a voice in when, how, and why these decisions are made is the acquisition of critical science literacy.

Third Spaces

K. Gutiérrez, Rymes, and Larson argued back in 1995 that the gap between script and counterscript can be bridged by building "third spaces," or hybrid spaces, in classrooms. As we discuss in more detail later in this chapter, third spaces are places where the script and counterscript *productively* intersect, creating the potential for authentic interaction to occur:

> In the face of a rigidly monologic teacher script, the relevance of students' counterscript to the processes or topics discussed in this classroom has little influence on the teacher's script. The only space where a true interaction or communication between teacher and student can occur in this classroom is in the middle ground, or "third space," in which a Baktinian social heteroglossia is possible. Conceiving the classroom as a place for social heteroglossia reveals the potential for the classroom to become a site where no cultural discourses are secondary. Acknowledging the inherent cognitive and sociocultural benefits that come from the multiple discourses is of particular importance, especially in classrooms populated largely by African American, Latino, and mixed race students. (K. Gutiérrez, Rymes, and Larson 1995, 447)

As K. Gutiérrez and her colleagues point out, third spaces are important because they connect the worlds of youth with the world of school learning through social heteroglossia. Discourses and forms of participation and activity, as mediated by "the tools of talk and interaction" of the classroom, are socioculturally situated and imbued with relationships of power. It matters whether the discourses and practices of youth in schools run counter to the teacher and the social institutions of schooling, and it is often the case that the local knowledge and resources of youth are not recognized or valued in the classroom. With Maurice, it was certainly viewed as "off task" at best, and possibly deviant. Without ignoring the power of counterscript as opportunity to challenge the societal and classroom discursive norms (and therefore also sociocultural beliefs and practices of broader society, which give rise to discursive norms), third spaces call for a rewriting of script/counterscript in the classroom, making legitimate space for how youth participate in the world.

The idea of third space has its history in hybridity theory, which "recognizes the complexity of examining people's everyday spaces and literacies, particularly in a globalized world" (Bhabha, 1994; Soja 1996) (quoted in Moje et al. 2004, 39). Indeed, culture, discourse, and identity are always heterogeneous (Roth 2006). When confronted with differences or challenges to the discursive norm, individuals continually engage in "cultural bricolage," or "taking from here and there to make do," producing new, heterogeneous, hybrid knowledges and identities (Roth 2006, 6). While it can be argued that everyone enacts hybrid discourse practices all of the time, it is important to recall how the kind of hybridity that gives rise to third spaces works to "ruptur[e] metanarratives" that provide the structure and meaning to everyday activity (McFarlane-Alvarez 2007, 44). Hybridity thus reflects a place of negotiation, an "in-betweenness" that is as much ambiguous as it is productive, as it allows for alternative histories, discourses, and positions to emerge (Bhabha 1990). Such moments are also subversive in their stands against the rigidity of dominant ideologies and "entrenched essentialisms" (Wade 2005, 602).

Acts of creating hybrid spaces, discourses, and identities are always political and of higher risk for those whose knowledge, discourse, and identities are positioned as lesser. For example, many of the youth in the settings where we work are marginalized because their hybrid practices are punished by symbolic violence— a kind of oppression brought about by the imposition of systems and meanings in which only particular systems and meanings are granted legitimacy (Bourdieu 1977). Third spaces refer to those moments when the enactment of hybrid discourses, practices, and identities disrupts how communities enact and sustain various networks of power and their histories of privileging particular discourses, identities, and forms of participation over others. In other words, third spaces—spaces that are "multiscripted, multivoiced and polycontextual" (K. Gutiérrez, Baquedano-Lopez, and Tejeda 1999, 287)—work against this violence, allowing for the coexistence of diverse discourses and identities that "resist and transform signs and symbols" by "open[ing] them up to multiple interpretations" (Rahm 2008, 102).

Moje et al. (2004) shows that three different, although related, views on third space have been taken up in education research. One view defines third space as a bridge between academic and traditionally marginalized knowledges and discourses (e.g., K. Gutiérrez, Baquedano-López, and Tejeda 1999). A second view defines third space as a navigational space, or a way of crossing and succeeding in different discourse communities (e.g., New London Group 1996). Finally, third space has been defined as a space of cultural, social, and epistemological change where competing knowledges and discourses challenge and reshape both academic and everyday knowledge (e.g., Moje et al. 2001). Moje argues that all three views are important contributions because they shed light on how youth cross borders in school settings, allowing them to maintain or to build upon their knowledges and identities from outside of school while finding or creating ways to succeed within the school setting.

In the work presented in this text, we specifically draw upon Moje's third orientation of third space, or the kind of space that allows for cultural, social, and epistemological change. This kind of "transformative" third space offers a way of understanding how learning in these disciplines involves learning to negotiate the multiple texts, discourses, and knowledges available within a community as well as learning particular content and processes. A transformative third space allows one to examine not only how practices travel through contradictory contexts and activities, but also how those practices at once are transformed by those communities and transform communities themselves. Transformative third spaces not only allow for the transformation of practices but also of identities—who one must be to engage in a community of practice. As K. Gutiérrez (2008) explains, a transformative third space is a "particular social environment of development" in which "students begin to reconceive who they are and what they might be able to accomplish academically and beyond" (p. 148).

The power of the transformative third space resides in how it posits the horizontal dimensions of learning as integral to the more traditionally understood vertical dimensions of learning. K. Gutiérrez (2008) explains that unlike a focus on the vertical dimensions of learning—on movement from "immaturity and incompetence to maturity and competence"—horizontal notions of learning focus on expertise that develops within and across practices and communities (p. 149). In horizontal learning, the focus is on both the distributive nature of learning and the repertoires of practices that individuals cultivate as they move through space and time. Such a focus considers a more expansive range of learning outcomes that stretch beyond learning content as pure academic exercises, or even as discipline specific. Gutiérrez's point is particularly important because little attention outside of social justice–driven research has focused on how learning is informed and transformed by the sociopolitical dimensions that shape everyday activity and living, or in Gutiérrez's words, "how poverty, discrimination, exploitation, anti-immigrant sentiment, language ideologies, and educational and social policies gone awry complicate current understandings in the learning sciences about learning and development" (p. 149).

We believe that using the framing lens of a transformative third space challenges how we think about the sociocultural-physical space of science and math classrooms as well as how that space mediates learning. Such a critical orientation to the transformation of the spaces of learning offers a mechanism for resisting the binary between home and school, formal and informal, and pays attention to the "cultural dimensions of learning and development that occur when people, ideas, practices of different communities meet, collide and merge" (K. Gutiérrez 2008, 150). The value of the third space, which is a kind of hybrid space, offers insight into how learning science involves the negotiation of the multiple texts, discourses, and knowledges available within a community alongside developing understandings of the content and processes of science or math. It suggests that learning science or math is an *embodied* activity—one that takes place within context and involves not only coming to know but also coming to be. Learning science or math, in short, involves learning the content of the discipline, how to participate within the negotiated boundaries of the discipline, and how to take a stance through discourse and action within the discipline.

Expanding the Goals of Math and Science Education

Moving beyond Function

What should be the goals and outcomes of an education in math and science, and why should that matter in how learning environments are constructed? As discussed in chapter 1, the reforms of the late 1980s rewrote the goals and outcomes in both of these domains to explicitly target mathematical and science literacy for all. While science and mathematical literacy have pushed the education community to consider the role that knowledge, practices, and discourses of these disciplines play in learning, the reforms remain fairly knowledge-centered and focus on functional literacy. The term functional is meant to imply that individuals gain the knowledge, skills, and habits of mind of science and math necessary for "personal decision making, participation in civic and cultural affairs, and economic productivity" (NRC 1996, 22; see also Ryder 2001; Shamos 1995). However, functional science and mathematical literacy attend to participation in the world as it is now, without explicit critical attention to how or why scientific or mathematical ways of knowing or being might bring about a more just world for individuals or communities, or themselves be transformed by broader and more diverse participation.

While such a stance has advanced the debate around reasons to learn science and math, it also leaves uncontested what it means to "function" in society. Take the case of science education, for example. A glance at the most recent literature in science education reveals that this phrase takes on different meanings on the basis of the theoretical stance it inhabits; however, in mainstream policy and practice circles, the meaning of "Science for All" has deviated little from what was intended when first introduced in the late 1980s. As written in Project 2061,

> Science education should help students to develop the understandings and habits of mind they need to become compassionate human beings able to think for themselves and to face life head on. It should equip them also to participate thoughtfully with fellow citizens in building and protecting a society that is open, decent and vital. America's future—its ability to be a truly just society, to sustain its economic vitality, and to remain secure in a world torn by hostilities—depends more than ever on the quality of education that the nation provides its children. (AAAS 1989, v)

The meaning and boundaries of "Science for All" are manifold but intersecting: Knowledge of science is both necessary and important for national security and economic vitality. The kind of economic vitality intended by such legislation refers to the vitality of the nation-state, not to individual economic advancement. Individuals have both the right and the responsibility to engage science to take up the challenges of the day. Science as a way of knowing and doing can solve our problems. National legislation in the United States over the past decade has amplified these meanings. Standards documenting what students should know and be able to do in order to be scientifically literate have been written. High-stakes tests for holding students accountable for learning such knowledge have been implemented, with wide-ranging economic implications that include loss of funding to schools whose students do not score well.

While a growing body of research has attended to the challenges faced in meeting science for all, especially among low-income urban youth, English Language Learner students, and underrepresented ethnic and racial groups, the national policy attention has been focused on how these findings translate into better achievement scores (O. Lee and Luykx 2006). For example, the most recent science education reform efforts have attended to the challenges of fostering "Science for All" through a concerted effort, both financially and intellectually, to focus on the design and development of the "next generation of curriculum materials," with much attention given to implementing these materials in "high needs" districts. The vast majority of these efforts are grounded in the belief that all students can learn science if they are appropriately scaffolded. Primary attention has been paid to how these materials have been shown to improve student learning as evidenced by standardized test scores in science (Schneider et al. 2001).

Yet, little attention has been given to unpacking the meaning of scientific or mathematical literacy in current policy and practice. Achievement scores, tightly aligned with content standards, remain the gold standard for documenting the impact science and math education has on learners, allowing other potentially powerful constructions of what it means to learn science and math fall away to the side as less important. Does science and math for all equate to all students achieving adequate test scores around a particular body of content? What implication does this stance have for other ways students may demonstrate knowledge and practice in math or science content, or how or why one might choose to engage in their classrooms, communities, or society scientifically or mathematically? Is national economic vitality and security the crux of an education in math and science? Should attention be given to promoting a core student identity as a future productive member of the labor market?

Until *Project 2061* (founded by AAAS in 1985) in science education and *Everybody Counts* (NRC 1989) in math education, the United States had no wide-reaching reform initiatives that encouraged inclusion of *all* students. The 1960s reform initiatives focused only on the "best" students who were needed to move on into science, math, and engineering in colleges for purposes of economic vitality and national security. These earlier reforms advocated the position that those who wanted or needed to learn science and math needed to come and to learn these subjects on scientists' and mathematicians' terms. This stance is akin to requiring students to audition for the right to learn science and math on the basis of a set of predetermined dispositions and intellectual abilities, sending the unmistakable message that "people either have mathematical [and scientific] ability or not, and that people who are good at mathematics [and science] are 'really smart'" (Allexsaht-Snider and Hart 2001, 96).

The science and math reforms of the late 1980s contributed to the expansion of the discourse on equity in two important ways. The concerted effort to engage in debate on what it means for "everyone to count" rather than only the elite made room for consideration of how the culture of schooling, the home, and the disciplines of science and math all contribute to how or why students have opportunities to learn in ways that spanned more broadly than physical access to a course. Additionally, the goals of the reforms repositioned math and science as ways of understanding the world rather than as mere content domains that set up higher-level work in college.

Schoenfeld (2002) writes that before these reforms, "In K-12 mathematics there was little emphasis on the kinds of mathematics that would enable students to make sense of the world around them—neither statistics nor mathematical modeling was part of the traditional curriculum. There was also little or no emphasis on communicating and using mathematical ideas" (p. 14). Instead, the goals of these reforms have been to promote all students in becoming "literate" in math and science. As the American Association for the Advancement of Science explains, "Science literacy requires understandings and habits of mind that enable citizens to grasp what those enterprises are up to, to make some sense of how the natural and designed worlds work, to think critically and independently, to recognize and weigh alternative explanations of events and design trade-offs, and to deal sensibly with problems that involve evidence, numbers, patterns, logical arguments, and uncertainties" (AAAS 2009, para 3).

At the same time that calls for science and mathematical literacy for all were broadly circulated through reform-based activity, broader critiques of the nature and practice of the disciplines as represented in schools were gaining traction (Brickhouse 2001; Nasir, Hand, and Taylor 2008). Informed by the influx of feminist and critically oriented sociological studies within the disciplines, school science and math were described as advancing a dominant narrative that was neither objective nor value free, thereby selectively discriminating by disallowing some but not all of the perspectives that youth bring to engaging math and science (Wiest 2001; Stanley and Brickhouse, 1994). For example, the social studies of science cast light not only upon the idea that the knowing and the doing of science are historically, socially, and politically situated processes (Haraway 1989) but also upon specifically how the subjective Western boundaries around what constitutes the content, process, rules for participation, and discursive practices of science positioned it as an objective, value-free practice (Harding 1991). Stanley and Brickhouse (1994) argued that the science curriculum should be, in part, about addressing such questions as "Whose knowledge are we teaching?" and "Whose knowledge is of most worth?" (p. 387). Similarly, Reyes and Stanic (1988) argued for a close examination of classroom processes to uncover procedures and discourses that define what math is and who is allowed to learn it. Thus, questions on the cultural nature of knowledge production—and access to that knowledge production—openly challenged the nature of science and math as reflected in the traditional curriculum and how all students were scaffolded and expected to take it up. Equity-minded researchers were charged with figuring out not only how to provide access to all but also how the microprocesses of life in classrooms provided opportunities to develop scientific and mathematical literacies.

Little consensus has emerged, however, on how all students are to acquire or to develop these literacies in math and science. However, two interpretations of mathematical and science literacy have prevailed, significantly shaping the equity agenda. The "knowledge-centered perspective" foregrounds the "knowledge and understanding of scientific concepts and processes required to be a scientifically literate person" while the "sociocultural-centered perspective" considers "the modes of interaction and sociohistorical contexts brought into play in the construction in how and why individuals within communities take up science" (Brown, Reveles, and Kelly 2005, 780).

The knowledge-centered perspective, which Anderson (2006) has also argued can be viewed as "scientific literacy for conceptual understanding," is arguably the tradition with the "longest history and the most influence within the science education community" (p. 7). At the heart of this stance is the idea that learning science involves developing deep conceptual understandings of the big ideas of science. Undergirding this position is the notion that science is inherently conceptual and theoretical, and that students are protoscientists. It is not surprising, then, that both the American Association for the Advancement of Science and the National Research Council put forth a set of recommendations "spelling out the knowledge, skills, and attitudes all students should acquire as a consequence of their total school experience" (AAAS 1989, 3) if they are to be regarded as scientifically literate. This stance aligns more with the equity-as-equality stance, framing opportunities to develop science and math literacy as a function of access: access to good curricula, good teachers, and good resources. The reform efforts which have grown out of this stance focus on developing national standards and designing standards-based curricular materials and professional development to support teachers in understanding and teaching from these materials.

The sociocultural perspective, while also concerned with what students learn, takes on the complex system that mediates why, how, and for whom access makes a difference, and the nature of that difference. Focusing instead on how sense-making in science and math is a negotiated process (Warren et al. 2001), the norms, values, and practices of particular communities of practice are viewed as playing a significant role in shaping one's learning, identity, and patterns for participation (Enyedy and Goldberg 2004). Researchers holding sociocultural perspectives have criticized the knowledge-centered perspectives for maintaining an assimilationist view toward promoting science and math for all. Citing claims such as "teachers should . . . make it clear to female and minority students that they are expected to study the same subjects at the same level as everyone else and to perform as well" (AAAS 1989, 151), some socioculturally oriented researchers argue that equal access, while important, alone does not necessarily equate to equitable opportunities to learn because such a stance assumes that all students should "cross over" into the worlds of science and math without respect for their home and everyday communities and discourses (Calabrese Barton 2003; Turner and Font Strawhun 2007; Moje et al. 2004).

Consideration of "the modes of interaction and sociohistorical contexts brought into play in the construction in how and why individuals within communities take up science" (Brown, Reveles, and Kelly 2005, 780), transforms the goal of promoting science and math for all from assimilation to enculturation. Science learning, when viewed as enculturation, can be understood as involving a process of making explicit and supporting learners in taking up the discourses and practices of science and math (Ladson-Billings 1997; Lave and Wenger 1991; Moje et al. 2001). This stance positions the learners in relation to the learning community (Kafai and Ching 2001; Lineham and McCarthy 2001; Roth and Bowen 1995). As students learn science or math in their classroom communities, they are also developing certain ways of being in the science classroom while engaging in activities and tasks, and in relating to the teacher and their peers.

Enculturation into the discourse communities of science and math has greatly expanded the equity debates. Referring to the process of developing science or mathematical literacy as becoming "bicultural" or "bilingual" puts the spotlight on how access alone cannot account for how or why one may opt in or out of science or math. It emphasizes how learning to participate in a community of practice involves more than learning content and even more than acquiring a discourse; it requires an ability to move between one's primary discourse and that of school science and math with relative ease. As Okhee Lee argues, "equitable learning opportunities" occur when "school values and respects the experiences that students bring from their homes and communities, articulates their linguistic and cultural knowledge with respect to the disciplines, and offers educational resources and funding at the same levels as mainstream students" (O. Lee 2005, 493).

Teaching and Learning as Enculturation into Communities of Practice: Advances and Limitations

Enculturation expands the equity agenda because it makes concrete the complex challenges that many youth face as they are expected to cross borders between the "home-based cultural worlds" and the "world of school science and mathematics." Moje and her colleagues (2001) show us that learning science and math involves movement across at least three discourse communities: disciplinary discourses, home and everyday discourses, and school discourses. Enculturation is therefore not only a process of acquiring a new secondary discourse but also a process of figuring out how to merge the various discourses that make up life in classrooms. Hogan and Corey (2001), for example, describe how the process of enculturation in science classrooms is mediated by the intersections of the experiences that students bring to the classroom, the pedagogical ideals of the teacher, and the teacher's explicit understanding of how to bring together the dimensions of professional science practice and her own pedagogical ideals. Teachers and students must therefore figure out how to negotiate common understandings of science (and math) across what are sometimes vast cultural differences between home, school, and science, and that these differences create poignant tensions. Science, for example, has "particular social conventions and modes of discourse and exchange through which knowledge claims are collectively generated and sanctioned, that differ from social interactions in everyday life" or "in classrooms" (Hogan and Corey 2001, 215).

The process of enculturation is thus fairly complex and fraught with many equity-related concerns. Crossing over into the worlds of science and math, with their attendant discourse and practices, is a highly political and dynamic process, especially when the ways of knowing and being that youth bring to school are constructed as "barriers" to or "discontinuous" from math or science learning. Equity research must account for how math [and science] classrooms are "non-neutral" places "where issues of power and identity play out in teaching and learning processes" (Hodge 2006, 373). The process of enculturation is uniquely political in how teachers (and students) take seriously "issues of equity in the form of power" and what becomes constituted as legitimate math [and science] and mathematical [and science] identities in practice (Hodge 2006, 373).

Identity studies in both math and science education offer insight to these particular challenges. Several influential studies in math education unravel the processes by which sociohistorical context and community norms play a formative role in African American students' mathematical identity development (Cobb and Hodge 2002; Martin 2000 and 2006a). Developing an identity as a mathematical person, for many African American students, is linked to broader social narratives that intimate that African American students cannot do math and are not part of the math elite, making crossing the border into mathematical expertise both an intellectual and a sociological challenge (Martin 2006b). However, Martin also asserts that this narrative is under constant negotiation in classrooms as youth assert individual agency, carve out goals for themselves, and engage in explicit talk about the multiple and conflicting narratives that shape one's participation and identity development in math in schools.

Similar findings exist in science education. While Brown's (2004) study on discursive identities is meant to demonstrate a process by which urban youth become enculturated as full members of a science learning community, his study simultaneously reveals how, for some ethnic minority students, participation in the cultural practices of science classrooms created intrapersonal conflict, yielding four domains of discursive identities: Opposition status, Maintenance status, Incorporation status, and Proficiency status. Ethnic minority students code switch within this continuum of discourse identities in response to peer pressure and cultural conflicts, manifesting substantial resistance toward endorsed scientific discourse, which "implicated the value of conceptualizing discourse as an artifact of individual identity" (p. 830). Brown's study highlights the intrapersonal conflicts ethnic minority students experience as they grapple with the cultural politics that motivate the shifting of discourse genres. Studies such as Brown's reveal the convoluted negotiations involved in student development of a scientific or mathematical identity, suggesting that for students for whom the culture of math and science is vastly different from their home culture, the process of enculturation can be highly political as well as intellectual.

Similarly, Brickhouse and Potter (2001) describe minority girls' struggles in forming a scientific identity in an inequitable playing field where prejudice and stereotyping were leveled against them. The African American girls in their study were not expected to excel in science, and when they did, they were treated as anomalies whose success was not acknowledged by their science teacher because their science identity did not reflect that of the traditionally good female student. The girls' performances were hampered by the "stereotype threat . . . [of] being at risk of confirming, as a self-characteristic, a negative stereotype about one's group" (p. 973), and they received extensive pressure to "blend in." While one of the girls who was highly successful in science succumbed to normative expectations by switching to a vocational track, the other managed to create an authentic space for authoring her science identity, largely because of extraordinary parental support in her subject area.

While a focus on enculturation vastly shifts the discourse on equity because it calls attention to the sociocultural dimensions of learning science, it may also work indirectly to increase the barriers between youth of underrepresented groups and math and science. Enculturation, to some extent, emphasizes to students that science and math are *not* their domain, which is precisely why they have to learn particular ways of being and talking in order to have the chance to succeed. Carlone (2004) criticizes this narrow vision of scientific literacy as a product of "prototypical science education" (p. 394), characterized by a pedagogical and curricular approach that promotes objective, impersonal discourse that censures student knowledge and experience. In the same vein, math educators call for moving away from viewing math as a "sieve that filters out the less able and towards mathematics as a 'net that gathers more and more students'" (Allexsaht-Snider and Hart 2001, p.96; Ladson-Billings 1997, 699).

In short, viewing enculturation as a discontinuous process of trading in one's home discourse for that of school science and math sets up learning as moving from one discourse to another. Many are sensitive to the culture positioning of learners and understand the "conflict" they might experience (cf. Brown 2004; Brown, Reveles, and Kelly 2005) and the extra scaffolding they might need (cf. O. Lee and Luykx 2007). However, the stance that one could and should "trade off" home discourses, practices, and identities for those of the culture of power ignores or diminishes the ramifications in how this positions learners socioculturally as either in or out, as well as the cultural production that inevitably occurs when outsiders enter into a new community. Indeed, studies intended to provide insight into how to support learners in crossing the borders into scientific and mathematical communities also uncover the limitations presented by this framework. In a way, undergoing the process of enculturation in science and math for many students is analogous to the experience of colonization.

Critical Science and Math Literacy for Social Justice

In this text, we argue that empowering science and math education is built on critical rather than functional science and mathematical literacies. Critical science and mathematical literacy not only expands upon but also challenges functional literacy in several important ways. Science and math literacy for all is grounded in a public image of "illiteracy," which presupposes that the public should understand science or math on scientists' and mathematicians' terms. Critical science and math literacy, however, moves beyond monolithic narratives of school science and math to incorporate how individuals in their everyday lives appropriate scientific and mathematical ideas and thinking, and to merge them with other understandings, personal knowledge, and practical experience. While functional science and mathematical literacy emphasizes gaining the knowledge and skill for participating in society as it is now, critical science and mathematical literacy emphasizes developing the knowledge, practices, and discourses for transformative purposes. By transformative we draw upon Freire's (1970) notion that education ought to provide opportunities to understand, challenge, and re-create understandings of the self and the world.

Critical science and math literacy is built on three main ideas: transformation of discourses and practices, transformation of identities, and transformation of spaces for learning/doing science. We take up each one of these points below.

First, critical science literacy embraces the call for all to develop understandings of and facility with the big ideas and practices of science and math. However, it also prioritizes critical engagement with text, ideas, and ways of knowing and being that frame the discourse and practice of science and math. Classroom practices often represent science and math in its "final form," yielding descriptions of content that appear complete and stable rather than as knowledge-in-the-making. Critical engagement with the text of science and its concomitant ways of knowing and being deprivilege the authority of text and teacher, thereby expanding opportunities to more fully define and situate mathematical and scientific problems, describing methods, and posing limitations to knowledge claims.

Critical engagement with the text of science and math spans many activities, including the narratives of what science and math are, who can do science and math, the materials and symbols that give structure and meaning to the discipline, and the norms for participation. Take, for example, the investigation in urban youth's experiences in the urban northwest (Tzou, Scalone, and Bell 2010). These researchers followed a group of students who were involved in an after-school environmental science program housed at a community center that served a significant Latino population. On one particular day, they were going to the local farm to do community service and to learn about the role the farm played in the community. Upon arriving, they noted people planting and tending to gardens. However, when they were greeted by one of the garden leaders, he spoke to the group in Spanish (positioning them with a particular identity) and explaining to them that their job that day was to use the wheelbarrows to haul manure. While fertilizing a garden is an important task in the ecology of the garden, it was clear to the youth that they were positioned as "other"—as the hard laborers. One of the participants, however, commented on how the youth were positioned in the "stinkiest jobs," expressing a dominant cultural-historical narrative that "linked Mexicans to doing hard labor—not only hard labor, but the 'stinkiest jobs'—and the power dynamics that accompany that societal role" (Tzou, Scalone, and Bell 2010, 18). For the youth in this study, having the opportunity to critically read the narrative of what it means to do science across racial and class lines was a powerful learning opportunity for challenging and changing these dynamics.

Gutstein (2003) places an even sharper focus on "reading the world" through math. In making the case through his teaching that youth are a "part of the solution to injustice," Gutstein describes how students began to understand complex issues involving justice and equity using math (p. 37). This approach, he argues, supported students in simultaneously developing mathematical power, changing their orientations to the value and purpose of math, and critically challenging and expanding their understanding of their place and voice in the world. An important note here is that Gutstein argues that while a standards-based curriculum is important, because this theoretically promotes equity, it was the real-world project that was fundamental to bringing about change.

Second, critical engagement with science and math also calls into question who can do science and math and what it means to author and challenge scientific and mathematical authority. The subjectivities that youth bring to doing science and math shape how they seek to access the domain and the roles they take up. When the learning community fails to legitimize the identities that one brings, then opportunities for critical engagement are shut down. Take, for example, the recent work of Nasir and Hand (2008). In this study, the authors argue for the importance of practice-related identities in when and how youth engage in basketball and math. They make the point that classroom math compared with the basketball team yields lower levels of engagement and thus less meaningful learning because youth have limited access to the domain, constrained opportunities to take up integral roles, and fewer legitimate modes of self-expression. Who one is and who one has the opportunity to become—as made possible or not through access, role-playing, and expression—fundamentally shape the process of learning.

Opportunities to develop and draw upon practice-related identities for meaningful learning can be productive when they take shape in the context of youths' worlds and are formed through youths' subjectivities. In our work, we have noted that youth often play with new and different identities in science class in order to bring fun, to establish stronger peer relationships, or to reduce the risk of taking up science. Take the case of Amelia, widely known as a bully and a failing student, who leveraged her identity as the "field trip girl" to author a space of powerful science learning in her sixth-grade science class. While her desire to be loud and in constant motion bumped up against the norms of the classroom, both she and her teacher crafted roles and activities that allowed these very aspects of herself to be important contributions to the science learning community. When she discovered the "worm poop" during a lesson on the role of composting in the larger ecosystem, her movement around the classroom and her loud engagement pushed a class of 32 students forward in vivid discussion of the cycling of matter in nature (Calabrese Barton, Tan, and Rivet 2008).

Third, critical engagements with math and science can serve as robust contexts and tools for participating in a democratic society in fair, just, and transformative ways. As a context, science and math act as a set of conditions that allow youth the space to take up new identities and practices for tackling questions normally constitutive of other people with more power. We have worked with youth, for example, who have experienced environmental injustice because of the location of diesel bus terminals or the selection by the city of certain abandoned lots to renovate. These environmental injustice contexts presented, in part, a science narrative that allowed students the space to bring their visions for a better neighborhood as a mode of critically engaging with science, as we saw with youth who turned an abandoned lot into a community garden (Fusco and Calabrese Barton 2001). In other words, science and math become the objects upon which they act through their lived experiences.

Yet, by engaging in the knowledge, practices, and identities in science and math in embodied ways—using engagement as a tool—youth can also transform the worlds they traverse, which includes the worlds of science and math. Take, for example, the PrisonPolicy.org initiative, which, in part, uses the tools of survey and mapping to re-read criminal public policy in cities, thereby calling into question dominant crime narratives. One particularly interesting example is the organization's review of a Massachusetts' law requiring "a mandatory sentence of at least two years for certain drug offenses committed within 1,000 feet of schools" (http://www.prisonpolicy.org/news/pr07262008.html 2009, para 1). Critically re-reading sentencing data using GIS technology, Prison Policy.org revealed how the legislature "erred in setting the zones' size at 1,000 feet":

> "The zones are so large that they overlap and cover the majority of urban areas," said Prison Policy Initiative Executive Director and report co-author Peter Wagner. "When you move out of one zone, it's very easy to accidentally step into another. So drug dealers have no incentive to move." (http://www.prisonpolicy.org/news/pr07262008.html 2009, para 4)

In this case, mathematical tools were used to rewrite the context.

The lines between context and tool are porous, and as the last two examples revealed, they are also intimately connected. However, the "point of entry" into critical engagement of the world with and in science and math is multipurposed, and how youth are positioned with respect to science and math can make a difference.

Looking across these three elements of critical science literacy, we can see that critical mathematical and scientific literacy implies that students use the knowledge, practices, and context of these disciplines to develop empowering identities, to advance their positions in the world, and/or to alter the world toward what they envision as more just. By way of example, take the study presented by Varley Gutiérrez in Chapter 6. In this study, she shows how upper elementary school youth drew upon the practices and tools of math, such as graphs and line plots, to make a compelling case to the school board that their school should not be closed down. The youth were able to use expertise gained from an after-school math club to engage in sociopolitical discourse with adult members of the community who wield more power than they do. Critical mathematical literacy that was grounded in robust mathematical knowledge and skills (i.e., functional mathematical literacy) and informed by the youth's deep sense of belonging across communities that matter to them—as members of the mathematical community in math club, as members of their school, and as members of their local community—empowered the youth to become deeply engaged in learning and using math to study, analyze, and solve a very real and urgent problem that affected the students' and their community. The youth in Varley Gutiérrez's study experienced social justice pedagogy in math and were both equipped and empowered to leverage their mathematical expertise to bring about real and significant changes in their lives. This is an example of what teaching math for social justice can look like (see Figure 2.1).

The youth in the studies of both Turner (chapter 3) and Varley Gutiérrez were beneficiaries of both an *equitable* and an *empowering* math classroom. Teachers who ran the after-school math club were highly

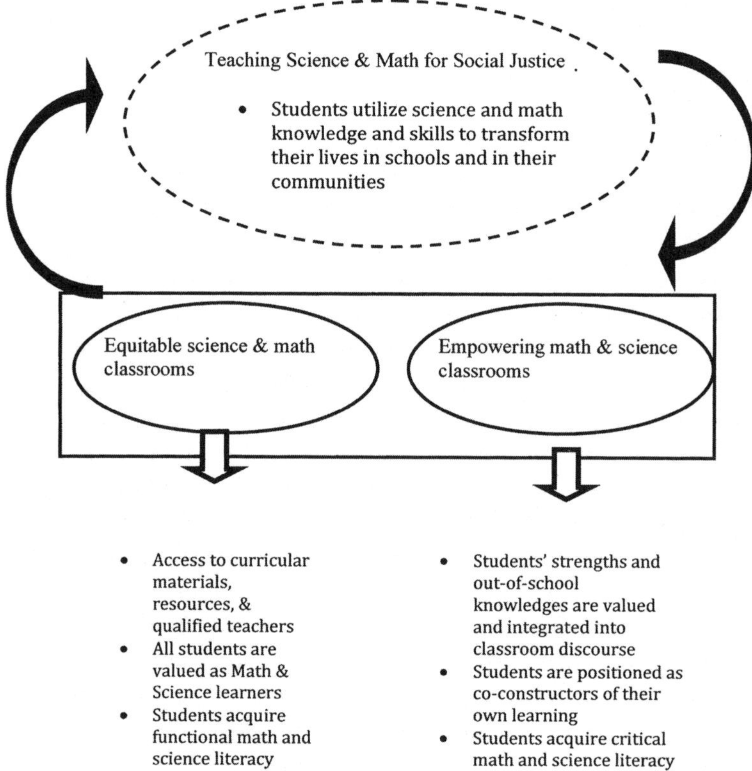

FIGURE 2.1. How teaching science and math for social justice is dependent on and in turn reinforces the dual components—equitable and empowering science and math classrooms

qualified in math and had access to rigorous curricular materials. They held the youth to high mathematical standards and encouraged all members to participate fully in the club's activities, scaffolding access to the ways of thinking, knowing, and doing dominant in the discipline. Thus, the youth had access to an equitable mathematical learning community in terms of resources and opportunities to learn and to participate in the discourse of math. In addition, the teachers valued the students' membership in other communities as they engaged in the math club, so that when students were concerned about the impending closure of their school, it became a *legitimate mathematical problem* for the math club to discuss and investigate. The boundaries of math club were expanded and made porous to the concerns, knowledge, and texts that matter to students outside of math club. Social justice was enacted when the students successfully argued their case with the school board.

Our point here is that for math and science teaching and learning for social justice to become a reality, the terms of both equity and empowerment need to be enacted. As discussed in chapter 1, the history of research in equitable opportunities to learn in math and science education points out the importance of access to resources and to robust opportunities to develop a metalevel awareness of the discourses and practices in math and science. However, as we have pointed out in this chapter, empowering science and math education is made possible when students' life-worlds are valued as legitimate sources of knowledge, and when youth have opportunities to use science and math as contexts and tools to bring about a more just world. With this case of how young people sought to "save their school" through math, we see how critical engagement with math offered a space for transforming how district-wide decisions are made.

There is mounting evidence that critical math and science literacy greatly expands opportunities to learn math and science in ways that make a difference in one's life, both at the personal level and at the social level. Buxton (2010) describes a project in which middle school–aged youth engaged in the study of local environmental challenges and the implications for human health and well-being. During an intensive summer investigation, students considered environmental risk factors in a series of structured activities to develop background knowledge on environmental health issues. Pairs of students then worked together on a relevant topic of their choosing to create and share "public service announcements" in the form of posters, to educate their peers, family, and community members about one of the public health topics they had studied. Using a mixed methodology, his study showed that participation enhanced students' science content knowledge while also engaging them in a process of decolonization and reinhabitation of their places as members of society.

The studies described in this section are important because they demonstrate that the goals of critical mathematical and scientific literacy can be achieved while not compromising the reform goals of developing the knowledge, practice, and discourse of science. Far too frequently, critically oriented scholars in math and science education are criticized for a lack of rigor with respect to content. However, Buxton, Gutstein, and the authors of the chapters in this text demonstrate in clear terms how this is simply not the case. Empowering math and science education provides opportunities to engage the disciplines deeply while developing the knowledge and practices to critically examine and evaluate them as well. In short, the outcomes of science and math education are broadened to include how student identities and agency in math and science should matter, in addition to test scores.

Looking ahead: Learning from Elías, Giselle, and Zara

In this book, we focus on third spaces precisely because of what they allow us to "see" in terms of learning and how they make possible the challenge of critical science and math literacy and empowering education. Let us take one more example from an after-school program where we (Erin and Maura) were facilitators, to draw out this point in more detail. In this example, we offer a narrative about Elías, Giselle, and Zara, and their investigation of the math practices of a custom auto shop in their community.

Elías, Giselle, and Zara, all fourth graders, were participants in an after-school bilingual math club that was part of the Center for the Mathematics Education of Latinas/os (CEMELA), an interdisciplinary, multi-university consortium focused on the research and practice of teaching and learning of math with Latina/o students in the United States.[2] The

2. This research was supported by a National Science Foundation award to CEMELA, The Center for Mathematics Education of Latino/as (grant number ESI-0424983). Any opinions, findings, and conclusions or recommendations expressed in this manuscript

math club took place at Agave Elementary School,[3] which is located in a primarily Mexican and Mexican American neighborhood of a Southwestern US border city. The math club met twice a week, and participants included approximately 20 third- through sixth-grade students, most of whom were Latina/o (some part Native American), Spanish-English bilinguals with varying levels of proficiency in each language. Similar to many after-school programs that have proven successful for low-income, nondominant students (e.g., Vásquez 2003), the program was nonremedial, centered in students' lived experiences, and characterized by extended group projects that often involved interactions with community members.

During one project, students worked in small groups to investigate the mathematical practices of several community businesses, including a *panadería* (bakery/donut shop), a *dulcería* that sold piñatas and party supplies, and a custom auto shop that specialized in converting standard automobiles to lowriders. Students visited each setting multiple times. They took photographs, interviewed employees and observed their practices, posed their own mathematical problems related to the setting, and then created digital stories to document what they learned. This project was aimed at expanding students' views about math, including understanding math as a tool to solve authentic, real-world problems, and at helping students to recognize the rich and varied mathematical activity in their community.

Elías, Giselle, and Zara, who all had family members who were skilled mechanics, decided to visit a custom auto shop that specialized in lowrider car conversions, a source of pride and artistic expression in this community and in many urban areas across the United States. As facilitators, we knew very little about the art and mechanics of car customization. In contrast, the students brought prior knowledge and experience related to customizing cars, which they drew upon to pose interesting questions and to dialog with shop owners and employees about their work. For example, after an initial visit to the shop, students were particularly impressed by the airbrushed artwork they had seen, and wanted to learn how images were designed and then transferred to the hood of a car. Elías alluded to the need to be precise in asking, "How

are those of the author(s) and do not necessarily reflect the views of the National Science Foundation.

3. School and all student names are pseudonyms.

do they make the paintings- are they sure . . . How are they sure is it big enough?" Giselle asked about the process of transferring designs to the hoods of cars.

> GISELLE: ¿Cuando hacen el diseño en el papel, como saben de que tamaño va a ser en el carro? *(When they do the design on the paper, how do they know what size it will be on the car?)*

The auto shop owner explained the math involved in the process, namely measuring the car hood and calculating the area for the design, thereby refining Giselle's understanding.

> SHOP OWNER: Lo que hacemos es medimos la área donde va a estar el diseño y luego de las medidas esas, hacemos el diseño para que le queda al carro. Primero medimos el carro y que tan grande puede ser el diseño. *(What we do is that we measure the area where the design will be and then from those measurements, we do the design so that it will fit on the car. First we measure the car and how big the design can be.)*

Also significant in this exchange is the fact that Giselle was able to articulate her question in Spanish, her first language, which supported her active participation in her group's investigation. In fact, students and community members frequently communicated across languages, which validated students' home languages and expanded the resources students could draw upon to articulate their understanding and make sense. This was in stark contrast to the students' classroom-based experiences, where state legislation that effectively eliminated bilingual education (Proposition 203 2000) constrained their ability to use Spanish. Giselle reflected on this, noting that whereas people would sometimes laugh at her in school because she did not speak fluent English, she felt accepted and comfortable in the math club, and actually enjoyed learning math because she was able to explain her ideas in her stronger language.

In a subsequent visit to the auto shop, lowrider artists explained to students that they began with small designs in a sketchbook, and then scaled up the designs to the needed size, often with the assistance of computers and copy machines. In response, Elías, Zara and other members of their group decided to reenact the practices of the lowrider artists, sketching a small image for the hood of a car, and then using proportional reasoning to transfer their drawings to a larger piece of paper, similar to the transfer process used by the artists. This reenactment helped students to understand how math was involved in practices (i.e., lowrider artwork) that were typically undervalued and even seen as nonmathematical in dominant discourses. In the excerpt below, taken from the group's digital story, Zara summarized her design process.

> ZARA: The city that I live in is famous for lowrider cars. . . . and I'm also interested in cars because my dad works on cars. . . . This picture [digital story shows picture of a woman with long braids, wearing a cowboy hat] helped me pick a design that I wanted to draw on the hood. And that is how I started designing my own design on a piece of paper. The design helped me measure and draw my own picture [digital story shows scanned image of her design]. I just guessed how many times bigger the small design would need to be and then I did the real measurements and figured out that my guess was the right answer to make the exact drawing, only bigger [digital story shows picture of Zara working on design]. I really worked hard designing my own design for the hood and designing how big is gonna be the girl's arms, face, legs [picture of Zara smiling as she works]. I learned about how artists design the car's hood . . . that nobody knows [picture of Zara with her completed, enlarged design] and only the artists of the lowrider shop really know how to do the design on the hood or on the sides. But I actually got to do it too! (text from digital story)

Throughout the project, all three students, who were reluctant participants in traditional school math activities, were actively engaged, posing questions to shop employees, measuring and scaling up their designs, and contributing text, photos, and artwork to the group's digital story. One difference between this project and typical school math lessons was that it positioned the unique knowledge and experiences that students brought as resources that could support their opportunities to learn math (i.e., their knowledge about cars and their fluency in Spanish, the language spoken in many community businesses). Whereas school math tasks were often decontextualized or reflected contrived or unfamiliar situations, thereby rendering students' out-of-school–based knowledge and experiences irrelevant, the auto shop project was grounded in a familiar activity. Students' knowledge of the activity then positioned them as experts with important knowledge and experiences to share. We find these contrasts between the auto shop project and typical school math lessons important because they highlight the power of hybrid learning spaces to bridge school and out-of-school contexts, and in doing so, to position youth and their communities as valuable resources for math learning.

Additionally, the digital stories Elías, Giselle, and Zara created about this experience served as counternarratives (Giroux et al. 1996) to dominant deficit perspectives related to Latino/a students doing math and to the lack of mathematical activity in urban Latina/o communities. The students' work challenged metanarratives about who can do math, what it means to do math, and the role that math plays in low-income, Latino/a communities. While we do not often equate math with the worlds of low-rider artists, in the third spaces authored by Elías, Giselle, and Zara, the auto shop employees, and the math club facilitators, these visions were possible.

K. Gutiérrez (2008) suggests that third spaces are accomplished by a range of "mediating tools" that "privileges and is contingent upon students' sociohistorical lives, both proximally and distally" (p. 149). Science and math classrooms configured as third spaces allow students a hybrid platform to be positioned with more power to engage with the content material in authentic ways while leveraging out-of-school–based knowledge and resources. In the following chapters, the authors share stories on what such math and science spaces look like, how they empower youth to participate more critically and agentively in math and science, and how youth apply their expertise in math and science to address sociopolitical issues in their lives.

CHAPTER THREE

Critical Mathematical Agency in the Overcrowding at Francis Middle School Project

Erin E. Turner

Introduction

During a conversation about overcrowding at their diverse, urban middle school, Naisha[1] and Cristina, two sixth-graders in Ms. Font's math class, spoke critically about connections between the situation at their middle school (Francis) and broader educational inequities. Specifically, the girls compared the space at their school to the space occupied by Longmore, a smaller and clearly better-resourced technology magnet school housed on the fourth floor of the same building. They noted that in contrast to most district middle schools, including their own, Longmore had a highly selective admissions process and was populated primarily by white students. Cristina commented, "There are more white people than anything at that school. I mean a few, a few Hispanics. I am not saying that no black people can get in, but . . ." For Naisha and Cristina, the overrepresentation of white students at Longmore was consequential, and directly related to educational enrichment programs; enhanced school facilities, such as wider hallways and larger classrooms; and modern resources, such as laptop computers for all students. Naisha summarized the disparities between the two schools as she stated, "It's

1. All student names and school names are pseudonyms.

Agency in Math Classrooms

Cobb, Gresalfi, and Hodge (2009) argue that when math classrooms construct mathematical competence to include enacting conceptual agency (Pickering 1995)—that is, when students are expected to select and generate solution methods, justify ideas, and articulate connections—students are more likely to develop positive dispositions toward the subject and to see themselves as capable mathematical thinkers. I concur with math education researchers that advocate attending to student agency as a way of promoting more meaningful engagement in discipline, productive mathematical identities, and enhanced student learning (i.e., Allexsaht-Snider and Hart 2001; Boaler and Greeno 2000; Cobb, Gresalfi, and Hodge 2009; Empson 2003).

But I also take a more explicitly political stance. I link student agency—in particular agency that goes beyond students' sense of themselves as math learners to also include students' understandings of themselves as people who can critique and act transformatively on situations in their lives and communities—to notions of empowerment and social justice (e.g., Ernest 2001; Gutstein 2003 and 2007; Pruyn 1999; Valero 2002; Varley Gutiérrez 2009). This perspective links agency to equity, in that as students develop agency, they not only position themselves as competent mathematical learners but as contributors to ongoing struggles for justice. As Pruyn (1999) notes:

> Through taking agentive stances and actions, individuals begin to see themselves . . . as potential socio-political actors. . . . Through participation in agentive acts, individuals begin to recognize, and struggle against, attempts by hegemonic cultural institutions to position them as passive followers and conformists.(p. 20)

Applying this broader notion of agency to the math classroom, Gutstein (2007) reports on a series of real-world projects that afforded opportunities for middle school math students at an urban, predominantly Latino/a school to use math as a tool to critically investigate issues of fairness and injustice. He describes how students use math to understand the complexities of an important issue in their community: how rising rents and property taxes due to development and gentrification was forcing long-standing community members out of the neighborhood. In this project, students enacted agency as they used mathematical arguments to critique city development plans, and as they generated alternate plans that would support their community. Gutstein notes that students' opportunity to link their own mathematical analyses to larger community-wide struggles was critical to the development of agency. Consistent with a perspective that links student agency to equity and empowerment, Gutstein argues that denying students "opportunities to develop the knowledge and dispositions with which to analyze, critique and change the conditions of their lives and society as a whole" is essentially perpetuating inequity (p. 440).

Unpacking Critical Mathematical Agency

I refer to the kind of agency described by Gutstein (2007), agency that has both mathematical and critical/sociopolitical components, as *critical mathematical agency* (Turner 2003; Turner and Font Strawhun 2007; Varley Gutiérrez 2009; see also Gutstein 2006a). To begin, critical mathematical agency (see Table 3.1) implies students' capacity to view the world with a critical mind-set, to imagine how the world might be a more just and equitable place, and to engage in action aimed at transformation (*critical agency*). Additionally, this sense of agency includes students identifying as powerful mathematical thinkers, who construct and use math in meaningful and even transformative ways (*mathematical agency*). In classrooms that foster *critical mathematical agency* (versus just conceptual mathematical agency as described by Cobb, Gresalfi, and Hodge [2009] and Pickering [1995]), what matters is not only students' mathematical understanding, but also how students make use of what they know, and how what they know facilitates the possibility for transformative action.

TABLE 3.1. **Critical Mathematical Agency Defined**

	CRITICAL MATHEMATICAL AGENCY
Is Critical	Involving students' capacity to: • View the world with a critical mind-set • Imagine how the world might become a more socially just, equitable place • Engage in action aimed at personal and social transformation
Is Mathematical	Involving students' capacity to: • Understand mathematics • Identify themselves as powerful mathematical thinkers • Construct and use mathematics in personally and socially meaningful ways

In the remainder of this chapter, I use vignettes from students' participation in the Overcrowding at Francis Middle School project to highlight the various ways in which students enacted critical mathematical agency (i.e., through critique, through improvisation, etc.), and how their mathematical and critical understandings seemed to support and inform one another. Given that agency is a rather elusive construct, and that as a field we are just beginning to understand what it might mean for students to enact critical agency in math classrooms, highlighting different ways that students demonstrate agency is important. Throughout the vignettes, I also discuss aspects of Ms. Font's pedagogy that seemed to engender a transformative, third-space learning environment (K. Gutiérrez 2008) that supported the development and enactment of agency. I begin by describing the context of the overcrowding project, as well as the methods that guided the research.

The Context: Overcrowding at Francis Middle School

Francis Middle School, located in a predominantly working-class African American, Puerto Rican, and Dominican community in a large city in the Northeast, opened in 1990 following a district call to increase the number of "small schools" for middle grade youth. At the time, the school's founding principal faced the near impossible task of finding vacant space for the school within the district's existing structures. As in many urban districts, space was limited. The only viable option was to use the vacated fifth floor of an elementary school that was no longer in use because of repeated problems with a leaking roof and pigeon infestations. Francis's principal claimed the space, repairs began, and the new middle school opened shortly thereafter.

During the year of this study, Ms. Font was the sixth-grade math teacher at Francis. Like all the teachers at the school, she experienced considerable curricular autonomy. As long as she addressed state standards and drew upon the school's math text as appropriate (*Connected Mathematics*[2]), Ms. Font was encouraged to adapt and create her own lessons, implement extended projects, and collaborate with other teach-

2. *Connected Mathematics* is a National Science Foundation–funded reform-based middle-school math curriculum.

ers on interdisciplinary units. Moreover, the Francis staff shared a commitment to educational experiences that were personally and socially relevant. Along these lines, Ms. Font, her students, and I (Erin) negotiated a series of project-based units in which students used math to investigate issues in the school, local community, and broader global context.

This chapter highlights one of those projects—Overcrowding at Francis Middle School—which, as previously noted, arose from students' concerns about limited space at their school. Although Francis' enrollment was small, a recent district-wide enrollment surge resulted in an increase from 145 to 213 students, and an additional 15 to 20 percent increase was projected for the following year. Thus, when Ms. Font asked students to discuss issues related to the school and community that concerned them, how their school's limited space could accommodate an increasing student population was at the top of the list. Students posed questions, such as "*Why are our classrooms so small?*" "*Why does Longmore have bigger hallways?*" "Why do we have less space than Longmore?" To help students connect their concerns with relevant mathematical tools, Ms. Font posed questions such as, "How can we show them [the district] how much space we have? What kind of information would we need to collect? How can we prove that we are more crowded than Longmore?" Students quickly realized that measuring and quantifying the school space would be useful and began to pose problems that could be investigated mathematically.

To support students' understanding of mathematical concepts and skills relevant to their investigations (i.e., area of irregular spaces, perimeter, measurement), Ms. Font began the 5-week unit with a series of minilessons. Next, students spent two weeks measuring classrooms and hallways, and collecting relevant information about district building codes and space regulations. Toward the end of the unit, students worked in small groups to investigate different aspects of their school space, such as the ratio of bathroom stalls per students at Francis and Longmore, overcrowding in the hallways during the seven-minute passing period between classes, and whether the area of classrooms was in line with district building codes (see Table 3.2). The unit involved a range of mathematical concepts, including perimeter and area, use of ratios to express relationships and compare data, adding and multiplying mixed numbers and fractions, and conversions between metric and standard units.

TABLE 3.2. **Focus of Small Group Projects in the Overcrowding at Francis Middle School Unit**

First Period	Comparison of total hallway area at Francis vs. Longmore Analysis of hallway width against district building codes Ratio of students to hallway space at Francis vs. Longmore Bathroom space per student at Francis vs. Longmore Ratio of classroom space to students at Francis vs. Longmore
Second Period	Comparison of total hallway area at Francis vs. Longmore Ratio of gym space to students at Francis Analysis of fire hazards created by hallway width and area Analysis of gym use by students at Francis vs. Longmore Safety hazards created by poles in classrooms and the gym

While Ms. Font and I collaborated on the design (and in a few instances, the implementation) of the overcrowding project, my primary role in Ms. Font's classroom was that of a researcher. I videotaped class sessions on a daily basis, interviewed selected students about their experiences and learning, and collected examples of students' classwork, journal entries, and presentations. In addition, Ms. Font and I met regularly to discuss recent lessons, plan upcoming activities, dialog about the progress of particular students, and reflect on emerging patterns and tensions related to students' participation, learning, and agency. All of these meetings were audiotaped and included in my analysis. Analysis attended in particular to interactions and conversations that evidenced some aspect of critical mathematical agency. I then constructed a set of four case studies that reflected the range of ways that students in Ms. Font's classroom enacted agency during the project. The vignettes that follow come from these case studies. While each vignette evidences multiple ways of enacting critical mathematical agency, for the purpose of clarity, I focus on one aspect in each vignette.

Critical Mathematical Agency in the Overcrowding Project

Critical Mathematical Agency as Asserting Intentions: Angel's Story

One way that students enacted a sense of critical mathematical agency during this project was by asserting personal and collective intentions. By intentions I refer to desires, needs, plans, hopes, interests, and goals that are grounded both in what an individual (or a group of individuals) brings to a particular situation, and in how that individual perceives a set of possibilities for the future (Skovsmose 1994b). Skovsmose has argued that providing opportunities for students' intentions to shape and inform the learning process is "a condition for productive teaching [and] learning" (p. 184). I argue that intentions are also linked to agency. As students assert intentions in an effort to impact their experiences in a particular figured world (e.g., the classroom, the community), their expressions of intention are enactments of agency.

In this project, asserting intentions engendered acts of critical mathematical agency as students defined personally and socially meaningful mathematical problems, advocated for collecting particular forms of data or for representing their findings in a particular way, and articulated their ideas about how their message about overcrowding should be communicated (e.g., a student-led strike, a fact sheet that delineated all the "illegal" aspects of the school space) and to whom (the Board of Education, the mayor, other neighborhood schools). That students asserted their intentions as a way of enacting agency is not surprising, in that Ms. Font's classroom and this project in particular were designed to foster student decision-making and ownership. What is more interesting is that for many students, asserting intentions seemed to be an entry point, a way to begin to develop and enact critical mathematical agency in their classroom.

Consider the following example. Angel, a tall and rather quiet African American student, was extremely concerned about the size of the schools' bathrooms. Angel expressed frustration that she often entered the girls' restroom and found it difficult to navigate among the other 10 or 12 people in the tight space. She was especially bothered that all females in the school, including teachers and administrators, had to share one small facility. She worked with a group of peers to sketch a floor plan of the restroom, measure its dimensions, and calculate the area (which was a challenging task due to the irregular dimensions of the room). She also collected information on the number of stalls, the number of females in the school who may need to use the facility at any given time, and the space available for waiting.

It is important to note that Angel's capacity to investigate questions that mattered to her (i.e., to assert her intentions), or in her words, "to go deeper into the project," was supported by multiple aspects of Ms. Font's pedagogy. Ms. Font encouraged students to pose questions of personal importance (e.g., "What's your issue?"), she validated their concerns (e.g., "Yes, bathroom space is a really important issue"), and she then supported students with the resources needed for their investigations (e.g., class time to measure the bathroom, data about number of females in the school). Moreover, Ms. Font encouraged students to think critically about the data they generated and how they might draw upon that data to create convincing arguments (e.g., "How can you prove that point? How can you show that it is too small?").

As Angel allowed her intentions (i.e., proving that the girls' restroom was too small) to guide her participation, her intentions generated an authentic need for a range of mathematical concepts and skills, such as linear measurement, working with fractions and ratios, and approximating the area of irregular spaces. In fact, Angel, who prior to this project had been a reluctant participant in math, worked intensely to make sense of ways of multiplying mixed numbers so that she could figure out the area of the bathroom (see Figure 3.1).

Angel believed that math would support her investigation, referring to math as "one of those things that helps you solve your problems" and "gives you more defense because you know more stuff that they [whoever you are arguing against] didn't even know about." Angel's new mathematical understandings enhanced her capacity to contribute in meaningful and even transformative ways to the work of her group. In Angel's words, her developing understanding (i.e., her mathematical agency) afforded her "more defense" in her efforts to engage in transformative action (i.e., her critical agency).

During the final days of the project, Angel expressed frustration as her group struggled to pull together all of the variables they had considered to construct a compelling mathematical argument that "proved"

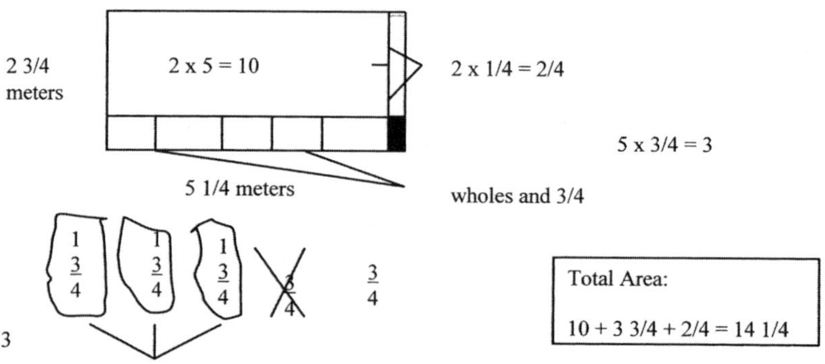

FIGURE 3.1. Angel's strategy for calculating the area of the girls' restroom

the bathroom was too small. While they could have calculated a space per student ratio, like many other groups, Angel resisted this idea, because her primary concern was the number of stalls available, and for how long and in what conditions girls and women at the school had to wait to use those stalls. As Angel continued to allow her intentions to guide her participation, this meant that her project was driven not by a certain mathematical concept (i.e., area or ratio), but by her personal experiences waiting to use the restroom, and at times entering and deciding that she didn't even have time—or space—to wait based on the number of people already in line. In this way, by asserting her personal intentions Angel not only "figured" herself as an active and consequential participant in the figured world of Ms. Font's classroom (which in itself is an act of agency), but also challenged and added complexity to traditional ways of using math to evaluate crowding (e.g., space per person ratios). Angel's story alludes to the potential power of students negotiating their intentions into the curriculum to not only transform their experience with and relationship to the math, but also potentially challenge the mathematical content that they investigate. In summary, by suggesting a more complex, and I would argue more meaningful, mathematical analysis (one that went beyond a single measurement like area), Angel evidenced critical mathematical agency, in that she considered how to use math as a tool to critique what she viewed as substandard conditions at her school.

Critical Mathematical Agency as Authoring: L. J. and Joel's Story

In other instances, students enacted critical mathematical agency through *acts of authoring.* As students respond to the positions cast upon them and/or to the circumstances of their lives, they simultaneously make meaning of the world and themselves, a process which Holland (2003 and 2001) has referred to as self-authoring. As Holland et al. (2001) state, "In answering [the world] (which is the stuff of existence), the self 'authors' the world—including itself and others" (p. 173). In this way, acts of authoring, to the extent that they are aimed at transforming individuals themselves and/or the conditions of their lives, are expressions of agency. In the Overcrowding at Francis Middle School project, students enacted critical mathematical agency through acts of authoring as they contributed (authored) their own unique perspectives about overcrowding at their school, and as they imagined (authored) more just and equitable ways to allocate the school space, among others. For example, consider the story of L. J. and Joel.

For L. J. and Joel, the most pertinent aspect of the school space were the numerous large columns (i.e., "poles") that jutted from floor to ceiling throughout the school gymnasium. Both boys were avid basketball players, and although the columns were heavily padded to minimize injury, they still posed significant challenges during basketball games, obstructing players' view, blocking passes, and creating frustrating obstacles as players tried to move from one end of the court to another. Thus, after several classmates shared about a meeting with district administrators in which they described various aspects of school's overcrowding, L. J. interrupted, positioning (i.e., authoring) his perspective on the school space as an important part of the story. He asked, "Did you all talk about the gym to the Board of Education? . . . Like how we can't have [basketball] tournaments because of the poles in the gym?"

In response to L. J.'s question, the principal, who was visiting Ms. Font's classroom at the time, stated that they chose not to talk about the columns in the gym because "there is nothing [the district] can do." She proceeded to explain that when the building was constructed, steel beams were not available, and thus large weight-bearing columns were installed all over the top floor to support the building's tile roof. When the floor was converted into a school, it was constructed around these poles, which now lie in middle of classrooms and throughout the gym. In spite of the principal's decisive statement that the poles were not removable (thereby negating the possibility of action that would result in change), L. J. and Joel maintained that the poles posed a significant safety issue, and positioned (authored) their perspective on the school space as an integral part of the class investigation.

Ultimately, L. J. and Joel shared their perspectives via a short video that they scripted, produced, and presented to their peers. In the following excerpt, Joel describes their initial plan for the video.

JOEL: Yeah, "The Poles in the Gym," by Joel Productions. [In the video] we would be like walking in the hallway to the gym, and we would be like, man, those hallways are small. So then when we finally get into the gym, we are like, ah'ight, let's play some basketball. And we are playing and we keep getting hit by the poles because they are all over. And then we are like, "We should move these poles," and then Ms. Williams comes and she

> is like, "Yes, we should. And are gonna try." And she is talking about how dangerous the poles are and people could really get hurt.

Striking in this excerpt is how Joel used authoring the video to imagine a world not bound by the constraints he encountered in his classroom and school. He imagined a school space that was not only physically different (i.e., a space where removing the poles was possible) but also different in terms of how individuals in power responded to students' concerns. Although Ms. Williams (the principal) had previously negated the possibility of transforming the gym space, in the imagined world of his video, Ms. Williams supported the boys' intentions, stating, "Yes, we should [remove the poles]. And we are going to try." As Joel imagined (authored) a world in which he critiqued and transformed the school space, and then proceeded to create that world, to act it out, and to make it consequential (Holland et al. 2001), he enacted a sense of *critical agency.*

However, at this point in the project, the role that math played in Joel and L. J.s' acts of agency is unclear. Given that both Ms. Font and I wanted the project to foster opportunities for students to learn and apply important mathematical ideas, I decided to probe Joel and L. J. on the role of math in their analysis. Initially, they suggested counting the poles ("You could be like, "Man, there's a lot of poles in there. Let's count them"), and upon further probing, volunteered to calculate the area of the gym. However, it was clear that finding the area was their way of appeasing a request to include more math; the area of the gym was irrelevant to their central argument that poles positioned in the middle of the court made it dangerous to play basketball.

L. J. and Joel's story is important because it illustrates the complexity of privileging students' intentions and sense of agency, while at the same time striving to keep math as a central part of their activity (e.g., Stevens 2000). While Angel's desire to prove that the girls' bathroom was too small led her to interesting math, for L. J. and Joel, the math *they* viewed as supporting their agency (i.e., counting the poles) was lacking in rigor. While both Ms. Font and I alluded to possible ways that math might have enhanced their analysis (i.e., using angles to calculate the reduced passing options and diminished visibility caused by the poles), both boys resisted these suggestions. In retrospect, our suggestions were not linked to their primary concern for player safety, and so their resistance is understandable, and suggests they were trying to subvert a teacher's attempts to transform their project into something it was not (which in itself is an act of agency). Instead, we might have suggested analyses that were more closely linked to their concerns, such as collecting data about injuries inflicted by the poles, or the number of times that players ran into poles during a game.

Ultimately, L. J. and Joel produced a short video that incorporated their initial ideas, and to meet Ms. Font's expectations, they included the area of the gym and calculated how that space might be shared among players during a game.

However, when they presented their video, they glossed over these calculations, indicating the minimal importance of these analyses to their central argument: "when we are playing, we can hit the poles going after the ball, since there is no space [without poles] to play." I see their continued commitment to ground their argument in students' safety as a way of maintaining their position as authors of a unique perspective on the school space. By conducting the mathematical analysis, and then deciding that the analysis did not contribute in meaningful ways to the story they wanted to tell, they evidenced a sense of agency—both agency over the narrative itself (i.e., the video) and agency over the use of math. The boys' actions suggested a critical orientation towards mathematical knowledge and a sensibility that, in some cases, math is not the best tool to understand and evaluate a situation. Perhaps a multimedia presentation that "showed" players in action running into poles would present a more convincing argument. I see this sensibility as an important component of critical mathematical agency.

Critical Mathematical Agency as Improvisation: Marlene and Jerica's Story

A third way that students enacted critical mathematical agency was through acts of improvisation. A number of researchers who place agency at the center of their work describe how agency is often facilitated by ambiguous, unlikely, or third spaces (Behar, 1995; K. Gutiérrez, Baquedano-López, and Tejeda 1999; Holland et al. 2001) that allow participants a range of possible actions—actions that might interrupt, contradict, improvise, and create—actions not as likely to emerge when situations are more scripted and predictable. Holland et al. (2001) describes the connection between these *improvisations* and agency as:

> Human agency comes through the art of improvisation. . . . Improvisations are the sort of impromptu actions that occur when our past . . . meets with a particular combination of circumstances and conditions for which we have no set response. Such improvisations are the openings by which change comes. (p. 18)

In the Overcrowding at Francis Middle School project, students improvised as they invented strategies for solving new problems, as they generated mathematical examples and models to justify their point of view, and as they posed particular scenarios to help them mathematically investigate different aspects of the overcrowding (e.g., "So let's say we did switch floors with Longmore, how much space would each Francis student have then? What about each Longmore student? Would it be fair?") Consider for example the story of Marlene and Jerica, two girls whose primary concern was the fire hazard created by the narrow hallway outside their classroom. In the following discussion, they improvise a mathematical way of evaluating this possible hazard.

JERICA: We are doing fire hazards. What we came up with was doing how many kids across, and how many kids could go up and down the hallway. And it came out to 96, but that's really really up against the wall, and we said that in a fire, no kids could be up against the wall, so we took away 3 [rows] and now it would be 87. That's how many kids. So now we are trying to find out how many kids is in each of these three classes for this hallway.

ERIN: I didn't quite get that, can you tell me again where you got the 87 from?

MARLENE: We went in the hallways, and we measured the width, and then we measured the length, and when we measured the width it was three people.

JERICA: And we measured it by kids because that's how many people is going to be in the hallway [if there's a fire] so we measured it in kids. Three kids can stand across, and then 32 people can stand this way (motions with hand to indicate the length). What we did was we lined up 1–2-3, and every time somebody moved, it would become—we would count one. [They stand up to demonstrate]. So it's 32 long by 3 wide.

ERIN: So you found the area in people?

JERICA: Yes, but then we are subtracting because if we did 32, that's this whole hallway, that would be up against the wall. You are not actually going to walk up against the wall, so we minused the three, which is the three rows

> up against the wall, and it became a 29, so then we timesed the 29 times 3. And now we are going to ask Ms. Font if we could see how many kids are in each of these three classrooms, so how many kids could fit in this hallway. 'Cause only 87 kids could fit in this hallway, if we are trying to get out of a fire. But maybe not even 87.

In this interaction, Jerica and Marlene improvised a model for measuring hallway space (i.e., an array of people) that differed from the method classmates were using (i.e., measuring dimensions and calculating areas). From the girls' perspective, calculating area in the traditional sense didn't seem useful, and so they improvised, basing their improvisation on their understanding and experience with the context. Their concern involved how many people could file out of classrooms into the hallway to exit the building, and so they measured the hallway space in terms of an array of people, and then adjusted that array on the basis of the context—"No kids could be up against the wall, so we took away 3 [rows]." Jerica and Marlene's improvised model became a tool they used to investigate and compare other hallway spaces, and to argue that their school's hallways did in fact present a greater fire hazard: "More kids could be killed in our school than in their school [Longmore], because more kids can fit [in the hallway] downstairs." In other words, their improvisation became a tool that supported acts of critical mathematical agency.[3]

It is important to note that Marlene and Jerica's improvised analysis was supported by various aspects of Ms. Font's classroom. First, Ms. Font encouraged students to evaluate the school space in ways that honored their specific questions (with the caveat that their investigations needed to include some form of math). She did not provide them with a list of options, but purposefully left the task as open as possible to facilitate student ownership and decision making, and as is typical in third-space learning environments, to encourage students to define themselves as capable, agentive learners (K. Gutiérrez 2008). Faced with the ambiguity of this task, lacking scripts for participating in particular ways—students were pushed to *improvise*. Second, while Marlene and Jerica were

3. It is important to note that investigating whether students could safely exit the school in case of a fire was a "real" and urgent problem for Jerica and Marlene. A building across the street had recently been damaged in a fire, and this project occurred just months after the September 11, 2001, World Trade Center disaster. Students were all too aware of the dangers of being trapped in a burning building.

the only students who used the concept of an array of people to evaluate area and crowding, Ms. Font facilitated frequent discussions about the meaning of area, the importance of standard units, ways to compare areas, etc., that were closely related to the girls' analysis. In this way, Marlene and Jerica were able to draw on the affordances of Ms. Font's math class, and then adjust those affordances to meet their needs and intentions (e.g., approximating a standard unit of measure through an array of people standing in lines). We see this as important because Ms. Font's classroom simultaneously encouraged invention and improvisation (that often led to acts of critical mathematical agency) and helped students develop the tools and understandings that supported those improvisations.

Critical Mathematical Agency as Critique: Lianna's Story

A final way that students enacted critical mathematical agency was through *acts of critique*. As students engaged in a project that focused on real situations in their lives, they began to think about how these situations, such as disparate conditions between neighboring middle schools, came to be. In other words, they began to interrogate and critique their reality, and to see larger social, economic, historical, and political forces reflected in their experiences (Gellert, Jablonka, and Keitel 2001; Peterson 1999). This critique began with critical reflection upon local circumstances, in this case overcrowding at their school, which can help students realize that "the injustices of our society are not isolated exceptions; they are logical consequences of the institutional structures of our society, and it does not have to be that way—there are other choices we can make to reorganize our institutions" (Frankenstein 1995, 180).

For example, in the vignette that opened this chapter, Naisha and Cristina argued that Longmore's "bigger space" was not random, but directly related to the race and socioeconomic status of students at the school. In fact, students repeatedly suggested that differences in the two schools' demographic characteristics were reflected by discrepancies in resources, and in the condition and size of school facilities. In this last vignette, Lianna's story, I highlight how students' mathematical investigations (specifically the comparison of space at Francis with space at Longmore) informed their critiques, and how they used math to defend their claims about the school's substandard condition, and in doing so, enacted a sense of critical mathematical agency.

Lianna's group decided to compare the total hallway area at Francis with the area of the hallways of Longmore. Lianna was particularly concerned about the narrow (1.25 meters wide) and highly trafficked hallway outside of Ms. Font's classroom. Not a student who was comfortable pushing her way through crowds of up to 80 children at a time, Lianna was often left standing just outside the door while other students passed in and out of adjacent classrooms. The measurements and area calculations that Lianna's group produced would qualify as rigorous math in any sixth-grade classroom. The students developed their own strategies for multiplying measurements, such as 18 3/4 meters by 1 1/4 meters (the dimensions of one hallway), and then totaled the areas of all hallways in the school.

But Lianna was not content with merely stating the total hallway area; she wanted to make her critique stronger or, as she stated, "use more specifics so people will listen." When she overheard that a classmate, Thomas, had calculated a hallway space per student ratio, she was intrigued.

LIANNA: How did you do that? We already found out the [hallway] area of Longmore, and I want to see how much [space] they will each get. You found out how much each person will get in Francis, and I want to do the same thing in Longmore. But I don't know how to do it.

THOMAS: You got to know how many students there are [at Longmore].

LIANNA: Sixty (number of student in entire school).

THOMAS: Sixty students, and how much is the area [of the hallways]?

LIANNA: It's 246 and 3/4 meters squared.

THOMAS: So I am going to divide 60 into 246, 'cause that way I can find out how much each person gets, 'cause it kind of divides it [the space] up.

With Thomas's help, Lianna figured out that if all Longmore students entered the hallways at the same time (which occurred between class periods), each student would have 4.1 square meters of space. She was quite shocked when she compared that figure to the less than 1 square meter of hallway space allotted to each student in her school.

LIANNA: I learned that Longmore's hallway space is bigger, cause that's what I studied. And they have less kids. And that our hallway space is a lot smaller than theirs and we have more students. And I learned that when you put all the kids in the hallways, in Francis, they don't even get a full meter. They get like about 9/10ths. And in Longmore they get like four meters of space.

Lianna proceeded to argue that the students in Ms. Font's class had a responsibility to inform the district about the results of their investigation, arguing, "We *have* to say something because we are the students and we are the ones that have to live in the school every day." By drawing on math to support her critique of the school space, and by advocating to share the discrepancies she discovered with others, Lianna enacted a sense of agency as critique.

Lianna's investigation of the discrepancies between Francis and Longmore invited her (and many other students) to reflect on the basis (arguably racist, classist, and otherwise unjustified) for this inequality. During a follow-up discussion, Lianna and two of her peers (Chris and Leo) debated whether the district would allow Francis to "switch floors" with Longmore, since Francis clearly had more students and, according to their investigation, Longmore had more space. While this "solution" to the overcrowding crisis seemed logical, Lianna and her peers expressed significant doubts about its viability. By the end of the conversation, they reached a consensus that *they* (referring to Longmore students, teachers, and district administrators) would be reluctant to move because the school catered to students that "had more money."

Significant here is the interplay between students' general critique of inequity in the world and their specific critique of unfairness at their school. On the one hand, the critical mind-set about the world that many students brought with them to this project helped them to critically interpret their particular experience of institutionalized racism/classism. On the other hand, the mathematical investigation of space that students conducted at the local level (comparing their school with a neighboring school) helped them to see how larger societal-level inequalities play out in their local circumstances. In a sense, their participation allowed them to write their own particular story into a larger critique about injustice and inequality.

Outcomes of Transformative, Hybrid, "Agency-Enhancing" Learning Spaces

I contend that the opportunity to develop and enact critical mathematical agency is a particularly important outcome of empowering math learning environments because it allows students to construct mathematical understandings as they investigate and act transformatively upon situations in their lives. In addition, the experiences of Ms. Font's students suggest that participating in a third-space, and I would argue agency-enhancing, learning environment, where "students begin to reconceive who they are and what they might be able to accomplish academically and beyond" (K. Gutiérrez 2008, 148), has the potential to impact students' perspectives on math, themselves as learners, and their capacity to work for change.

Perspectives on Math and Themselves as Math Learners

In Ms. Font's classroom, many students initially reported negative views of themselves as mathematical thinkers. For instance, Naisha noted that she "couldn't stand math" and that she felt good about her own math ability only when she "got the answers right." Naisha's comments reflect a common sentiment among students—"being good at math" meant being able to solve problems quickly and to recall memorized facts and procedures. In contrast, when students reflected on their experience in the Overcrowding at Francis project, they described themselves as problem solvers, people who "figure things out [with math]" and who "use math to prove a point." For example, Angel commented that she wanted to do the math in the project, because she felt "'quisitive." She explained, "[I was] like curious about different things, like [the project] makes you want to go deeper into it, and learn more stuff . . . like the legal width of the hallway and the dimensions of each room." Given that Angel had a history of disengaging during math class, her comments (like those of many of her peers) suggest that she was beginning to redefine her sense of herself as a math learner, as well as her stance towards the discipline. Attending to the mathematical identities afforded by particular learning settings is essential because the way that students see themselves as learners, and more specifically as mathematical thinkers, impacts how they engage with the discipline, and therefore, the nature of what they learn (Boaler and Greeno 2000; Cobb, Gresalfi, and Hodge 2009).

Additionally, students recognized that the knowledge they gained through this project was different, in important ways, from the knowledge gained in typical math classrooms. Naisha pointed out that whereas in previous math classes she studied the material but never had the opportunity to "do anything" with what she learned, in Ms. Font's class, "we did something with it." Angel echoed this sentiment, explaining that the Overcrowding Project allowed her to learn about situations that impacted her daily life.

> ANGEL: Look, it's like you are learning about things you be [sic] in every day, and it's a part of your life. Because you know something more, it's like adding to your knowledge. Because you can remember that. So when we did that project about the space [at our school], it was something you could keep with you, it is like information that could involve *you*.

Joel added that he enjoyed learning "useful information," such as how to find the area of different spaces, because "it's important, and I am not just doing it for an assignment. We are learning about things that are important. And we are not just learning it to learn it. It's important, and it's about our school."

Finally, students repeatedly commented on the importance of math in supporting and enhancing their arguments. Students felt that math helped them "to prove how most stuff is not shared evenly" and "to prove to the district that our school was smaller," and that math "gave more details" and "specifics" to their arguments, and afforded them "more defense" in the problems they were fighting against (see also Gutstein 2003 and 2006; Mellin-Olson, 1987; Peterson 1994 and 1999). Students also spoke eloquently about how they drew upon math to address "things in [the] community and school," and referred to this way of engaging with the discipline as "a life-long thing," that is not only about learning math but also about investigating and improving their lives. As Naisha noted, "I liked that project because they gave us answers that we was looking for, and it was good. . . . And without the math, we wouldn't have the area of the school, and we wouldn't really know. And the meeting [with the district] wouldn't have been as powerful."

Perspectives on Themselves as Agents of Change

As students considered how to respond to the "space crisis" at Francis, they grappled with questions such as: What can we really do about the overcrowding? Is it even possible to get a new school? Could we switch floors with Longmore? And what about the poles in the gym, can they be removed? An increasingly critical analysis of their school space (e.g., students' outrage when they learned that only one hallway and several classrooms were "legal" according to district building codes), coupled with a growing awareness about the limited possibilities for transforming that space (e.g., structural, financial, historical, political considerations), could have been disempowering to students, raising their consciousness about unjust conditions, but leaving them feeling powerless to affect change. An important part of critical mathematical agency is the opportunity to engage in some kind of responsive action, even if that action is as simple as sharing their findings with other students at the school. As Gutstein (2007) argues, these may be small steps, but they provide openings for students to develop a sense, and to imagine the potential, of their own actions in the world.

But how did students make sense of these "small steps"? In some cases, students concluded that change was unlikely, as in the following instance:

> L. J.: I learned that sometimes you can change stuff and sometimes you can't. Maybe we can change that this space is too small, but maybe we can't. Maybe this time, we just have to learn how to use it [the school gymnasium].

Many other students, despite their acute awareness of the constraints imposed by broader institutional structures (i.e., building a new school was not a possibility, nor was violating the structural integrity of the current building), valued the opportunity to inform others about the overcrowding, and retained a sense of hope that change was possible. They felt that their perspectives were important, and argued that by working collaboratively, they had the potential to impact change. As one student explained, "I think if there was only one or two of us they [the district] wouldn't really think about it, like no one really listens—but since there were so many of us, I think that they will actually think about it and might do something about it."

Students were also acutely aware that addressing the problem of overcrowding required convincing individuals in positions of power, such as school board members, that the school needed more space. Naisha believed it was important to keep pressuring district administration, because "if you keep talking to them, then they will probably listen, and you will get on their nerves, and maybe then they will want to give us more space, or let us be in a different building with more space, [a building] that is lawful." Yet aside from whether or not students believed that their efforts would result in any lasting change, as Lianna's earlier comment demonstrated, they experienced a sense of responsibility to speak out and take action against unjust conditions, particularly because their unique experience of those conditions was something that they alone could contribute.

Closing Reflections

What Happened at the School

As students became aware that the school space violated various district building codes, they argued that others—such as the Board of Education, the mayor, and even students at other overcrowded schools—needed to be informed about the situation at Francis. They ultimately decided to speak at a district meeting (i.e., Naisha's speech mentioned above), send letters to the district superintendent, and distribute fact sheets that delineated all the "illegal" aspects of school space to school board members. While the district was clear that they lacked both the funds to build a new school building and the space to move Francis students to another school, they did take students' investigations into consideration. As administrators made final determinations about student enrollment, they decided to reduce Francis' incoming sixth-grade class by approximately 25 students, so that the number of sixth-graders entering would be equivalent to the number of eighth-graders leaving the school, thereby allowing the school to retain its current size. While the result may seem inconsequential—the school was just as overcrowded the following year—for a school whose total enrollment was set to increase, a district decision to reverse that increase was welcomed.

Moreover, what seems most important is not whether this particular "battle," to use one student's words, was won or lost, but that students and teachers had the opportunity to conceptualize their struggle as one step in a larger process of conscientizacao, or developing critical consciousness (Freire 1970/1993). The history of social movements tells us that whether or not one wins a particular struggle, one has to accumulate the lessons that were learned, recognize what was gained that cannot be lost (e.g., critical consciousness, increased understanding), and develop a more protracted view. Teachers, researchers, and other adults can play pivotal roles in helping students to come to this understanding. Coming to "see themselves" as active agents of change means that students have not only opportunities to engage in transformative action, but also opportunities to develop an understanding of how their own actions fit into a larger story of social struggle, struggles that develop over time, and that consist of many gains and losses, including less visible but enduring gains such as shifts in understanding and increased critical awareness. These enduring gains, or to use Jhana's words, what students "learned" and "found out" and "proved" for themselves, are important because they can strengthen students' sense of themselves as knowledgeable, capable, political actors (e.g., their sense of critical mathematical agency), which in turn motivates them to continue to engage as critical agents.

Critical Mathematical Agency and Third Space Learning Environments

If we accept Gutstein's (2006 and 2007) argument that in math classrooms that provide opportunities for students to develop and enact agency, students' participation can become a means of fostering equity *in* and *through* math education, finding ways to facilitate and support the development of student agency becomes very important. Clearly, traditional educational environments fall short in this regard. In fact, research has noted numerous challenges to fostering agency, particularly critical agency, among students, namely (1) schools' role in socializing students as passive recipients of information, thereby minimizing their creative, critical power (Freire 1970/1993); (2) students' acquiescence to hegemonic instructional practices and their self-positioning as passive subjects, because "that's just the way school is" (Pruyn 1999; see also Martin 2000; Shor 1996); (3) increasingly restrictive high-stakes testing and standards regimens that limit teachers' use of liberatory pedagogies, and their ability to design and adapt curricula in ways that are responsive to the sociopolitical realities of students' lives (Valenzuela 2005), and that are silent about the economic and educational crises that plague many low-income urban schools (Gutstein 2010); (4) students' sense of powerlessness about the injustices in the world, feelings of "oh, well, what can I do about it?" (Gutstein 2003, 48).

These challenges are real, and deserve attention. And yet I argue that precisely because of these pressing challenges, because of the current educational and political situation that is particularly detrimental to students in poor, urban schools, there exists an even more urgent need to facilitate third-space transformative learning environments, like the one created by Ms. Font, that foster a sense of critical agency among students. As Bruner (1996) argued,

> Education is risky, for it fuels a sense of possibility. But a failure to equip minds with the skills for understanding and feeling and acting in the cultural world is not simply scoring a pedagogical zero. It risks creating alienation, defiance, and practical incompetence. . . . We must constantly reassess what school does to the young student's sense of his own powers (his sense of agency). (pp. 39 and 42)

The stories presented here suggest that various aspects of Ms. Font's math classroom (and of the school in which she taught) helped her to resist the challenges outlined above, and to engender a third-space, agency-enhancing learning environment. First, Ms. Font frequently positioned students as capable mathematical thinkers who had the capacity to understand concepts, improvise viable problem-solving strategies, pose questions, and claim mathematical authority. This positioning of students as competent established a sharing of authority among students and teachers, and may have helped students begin to see themselves as agentive—as people whose actions can and do make a difference. Moreover, *honest, critical* discussions were common in Ms. Font's classroom, and in other classrooms at Francis Middle School. Students were encouraged to express their opinions, even if they differed from those of their peers, to question one another, to challenge assumptions, and to raise critiques (Gutstein 2007). Many Francis students came to school with critical orientations to the world, and teachers, including Ms. Font, made it a priority to create spaces in school for students to openly dialog about their ideas and experiences. In fact, the school's mission was to create a diverse community of learners "who take seriously the politics of urban life, who study vigorously and inquire intensively, who co-construct knowledge, curriculum, and assessment" (Fine 1996, 13).

Additionally, by grounding her instruction in students' experiences, lives, needs, and concerns, and by providing students with a modicum of choice in all activities (the latitude of choice greatly expanded in projects like the one described in this chapter), Ms. Font's pedagogy helped to reconcile traditionally antagonistic teacher-student relationships, and therein support students' power and agency. That said, negotiating intersections between students' intentions and the disciplinary knowledge and practices that would support their endeavors is challenging, and understanding the various ways in which teachers negotiate this challenge warrants additional research. Moreover, it is important to remember that these negotiations occur in broader educational, economic, and sociopolitical contexts that necessarily shape and often constrain the curricular and pedagogical modifications that teachers are able to achieve. Teachers at Francis were bound by state standards, but had considerable curricular and pedagogical autonomy, which certainly facilitated the extended, project-based investigations described in this chapter. They also met frequently as a staff to discuss their practice and ways to best meet the needs of particular students, and to collaborate on curriculum design tasks. I suspect that these spaces to dialog with peers, and in particular to brainstorm ways to honor the vision of the school while at the same time addressing requirements related to standards and assessment, were critical to sustaining the empowering learning spaces that were characteristic of Ms. Font's instruction.

In closing, research has begun to document transformative math learning environments such as the one created by Ms. Font (Frankenstein 1995 and 1997; Gutstein 2006; Skovsmose 1994a and 1994b; Turner 2003; Varley Gutiérrez 2009), and in particular, to describe instructional practices and classroom norms that support this kind of teaching. Yet there is an ongoing need to interrogate *students'* experiences in such settings, and more specifically, the potential influences on their beliefs, dispositions, learning, agency, identities, and participation. The stories at this chapter were aimed at addressing this important need.

CHAPTER FOUR

A Narrative Pedagogy for Critical Science Literacy

One particular Thursday afternoon at lunchtime, Mrs. Davis and four of her seventh graders—Molly, Abi, Chris, and Mike—were having a conversation in her classroom with Edna about their experiences in seventh-grade science. The conversation began with the students talking about what they were currently learning and why it was "boring" to them. As Chris stated, "No offense to [Mrs. Davis], but 'atmosphere' is kind of boring." The four students began to contrast the weather unit in which they were studying the atmosphere with an earlier unit ('C3') focused on dynamic equilibrium (energy in and energy out) and the human body. As Abi stated, "I enjoyed C3. It was really fun. I enjoyed it a lot, compared to what we're learning now!" The other students concurred with Abi. They said that C3 was "fun because we get up close and personal" and that during the unit "we shared about our lifestyles and habits and stuff." What caught our attention was not that they liked the unit on dynamic equilibrium better than the one on weather, or even that it was more fun, but why they felt connected to the curriculum. As Mike stated, "I had stories for C3. I think I had *more* stories [in C3]."

In Mrs. Davis' seventh-grade science classroom, students can always count on Mrs. Davis to bring in her own personal stories during their classroom discussions. For example, while investigating how food choices affect one's health, Mrs. Davis regaled her students with stories such as her own struggles with her weight, how she has increased her daily steps taken by wearing a pedometer over a two-year period, how her doctor taught her how to eat around the outside of the supermarket to avoid the processed foods, and how she tries to buy fewer fast-food meals for her children. Indeed, stories were a purposeful part of Mrs. Davis' teaching of the unit on dynamic equilibrium. Not only did she personally connect to the science in the unit but also she believed that stories contextualized the challenges and the opportunities inherent in using scientific data to make healthy food (energy in) and activity (energy out) choices:

> I always try to pull my own personal stories in as much as I can. Last year [C3] was very new and relevant because of my own health problems. I had to drastically change my own diet. So as I was changing my diet, I was sharing the struggles I was going through with the kids, and how hard it is to change your diet and how beneficial it can be then in the end. And then, even after C3 ended last year, I was then able to carry that out throughout the year and the kids were able to see an improvement in my own health, um, versus, you know, how it was prior to that so that they were able to see the evolution. You know, hey, look at my teacher, she's getting healthier, so there was that. And then this year—because of the timing of C3, because it was at the one-year mark of me changing how I was eating—and so I was able to drastically go back and share with the kids how over the last year things have changed, like how much my cholesterol has dropped, from a 175 to a 123. I try to make them, try to bring that in as much as possible so that it is more meaningful to them.

As Mrs. Davis revealed, stories allowed her to connect her life to the content of the classroom. And yet stories, for Mrs. Davis, carried deeper meaning with respect to teaching science. Stories were also about how students, teachers, and science are positioned with respect to each other during the course of the school day and year. Mrs. Davis not only sought to humanize science, she sought to cultivate an ethos where the livelihood of students and teachers as capable and caring human beings mattered in the teaching and learning of science. As she explained:

> You know there are teachers that are like, it's their lives and there's school and this is their profession and it's separate. [For me,] I kind of try to merge those things together as much as I can. I think it just helps more, and they see me on a different level. I try to make it much more relevant to kids. I think anytime you can take them and you can say, 'This is the real life situation. This is what happened as a result of that'—like that kid who came in saying my grandfather had a heart attack this weekend—it's much more real than reading it in a textbook or, even though they, you know, they got grossed out

watching the video pulling the string of fat out, even much more relevant than a video, because it's much more real life.

In her explicit use of telling stories as a pedagogical practice, Mrs. Davis drew deeply from her personal experiences. She invited her students to do likewise, creating an environment in her science classroom where a hybrid science discourse was not only encouraged but also actively pursued.

This chapter reports on a case study of Mrs. Davis' teaching of a unit on dynamic equilibrium in the human body—energy in and energy out. We found this particular curricular unit compelling because, as we explain below, making food and activity choices is deeply rooted in culture and routine and shaped by larger societal and economic pressures, and yet the goals of the unit were for the students to bring scientific evidence and reasoning to bear on their food and activity choices. In particular, we wanted to understand how Mrs. Davis created a classroom community that functioned as a discourse community, sharing some of the characteristics of adult scientific communities while at the same time legitimizing the sociocultural worlds of youth as they navigated the complex system of food and activity choices.

Storytelling as Narrative Pedagogy

Storytelling as a pedagogical practice in families and communities has been in existence as long as the spoken word. Livo and Rietz (1986) assert that "the telling of stories is an old practice, so old, in fact, that it seems almost as natural as using oral languages" (pp. 7–8). In certain cultures and societies, such as the aboriginal and American Indian cultures, stories play prominent roles in education, especially in the teaching of values and customs (Little Bear 2000). Yet, stories have played only a peripheral role in the teaching of science or math in the prototypical Western school. When stories are valued in schools, it is generally for their verisimilitude rather than for any truth or proof they may establish about core content ideas (Bruner 1986; Kurth, Anderson, and Palincsar 2002). Indeed, stories or personal narrative have been described as the "precursor" to talking and doing "real" or "paradigmatic" science, providing both the space and the opportunity to try out science ideas in a more familiar way (Kurth, Anderson, and Palincsar 2002).

We use the term "narrative pedagogy" to more specifically refer to an approach to teaching that is built with and through the telling of stories.[1] As we describe below, we are particularly interested in how a narrative pedagogy frames intersubjective meaning making and embodied knowing as central features of coming to know and be in science and to build epistemological and ontological ties among teachers, students, and science. We also suggest how a narrative pedagogy allows the learning community to re-imagine the world (of science) and one's position in it, as one considers how to use both epistemological and ontological positionings to enact change.

Intersubjectivity, Embodied Knowing, and Stories

Stories, according to Miller, Cho, and Bracey (2005), are "cultural tools" imbued with "ways of seeing" and knowing that "privilege certain slants on experience" (p. 115). The telling of stories positions the story's author with the authority to make claims about what is real and true in the world and to background and foreground how those truth claims are situated culturally and historically. Egan (1988) posits that "the story then, is not just some casual entertainment; it reflects a basic and powerful form in which we make sense of the world and experience" (p. 2). Oral and narrative texts are often grounded in personal, experiential encounters and provide the storyteller and her audience opportunities to tell their stories, reflect on their stories, and learn from them (Coulter, Michael, and Poynor 2007). These ideas hark back to the feminist work on narrative, which calls our attention to how stories should "not be read one-dimensionally in the light of 'truth' or 'falsity' but rather should be seen as the moment of—and the space for—subject formation" (Kimura 2008, 19). Kimura's point here is that stories are always a "slant" but that the slant is educative, for it provides a specific take on experience meant to offer localized insight.

A narrative pedagogy potentially foregrounds how and why intersubjectivity matters in the production of knowledge. Intersubjectivity refers to how individuals come to agree upon a set of meanings, which in science classrooms is usually defined through the authority of the text

1. In this chapter, we use the term narrative pedagogy when we refer to the teaching approach that elicits and values storytelling as a central aspect of teaching and learning. When we discuss the actual narratives elicited by narrative pedagogy, we refer to them as "stories."

(Wertsch 1991). In a traditional science classroom where the official science text is the sanctioned authority/meaning, other texts (such as students' stories) are often silenced or, at best, weighted against the official narrative. We know, however, from decades of feminist and critically oriented work, that the process of agreeing upon meaning is always a struggle of position (Ellsworth 1997). How or whether one calls attention to or renders invisible one's own or another's text portends acts of privilege and oppression. Enacting a narrative pedagogy offers a platform for meaning to be negotiated as multiple texts are considered with and against each other, transforming the monolithic discourse of the classroom into a more heteroglossic discourse.

While we concur that stories are deeply powerful in how they provide potential entry points into more formal ways of talking or doing science, we also believe that a narrative pedagogy fosters the development of hybrid spaces that allow teachers and students to build powerful epistemological and ontological ties to each other and science that move beyond a master narrative. Third spaces have been discussed in the literature as important because they allow for the negotiation of meaning making, discourses, and identities to occur. However, little has been discussed with respect to how the emergent discourses and identities of third spaces can also transform the epistemological and ontological ties of those within the space. In classrooms where teachers have historically been positioned with "power over" students, both in terms of "what" they are to know and "who" they are to be at that moment, such potential outcomes of third spaces may help to advance our understandings of empowering teaching and learning

A narrative pedagogy widens what is considered as legitimate knowledge because "it encompasses not only what is explicitly learned but also what is learned practically, at a more tacit level, touching not only on the intellect, but the moral, practical, imaginative realm" (Conle 2003, 3). Therefore, the telling of stories made possible by a narrative pedagogy tangibly enriches a discourse when individual narratives are woven into the educational content of the curriculum. Educational storytelling is also regarded as a form of "narrative inquiry" (Barone 2000; Connolly and Clandinin 1994), where the telling and retelling of stories help one reflect and gradually impart meaning to one's own stories and those of others. As stories are often grounded in lived experiences, the embodiment of such knowledge becomes a key factor in both understanding the nature of knowledge and what it means to know.

Re/imagining the World and Stories

In addition to expanding and enriching what counts as legitimate knowledge, a narrative pedagogy of storytelling also offers a way to critique issues of social justice and enact social change. Delgado (1989) asserts that the dominant groups in society maintain their position of power through stock stories. Stories by people in the nondominant culture can therefore act as a countermeasure to resist and expose such oppression (e.g., Tate 1997). This is especially relevant in the discipline of science, which has a master narrative deeply ingrained with white, middle class, male characteristics. Counter stories reflect those stories of and by people whose experiences are not often told, such as low-income African American and Latino young people in urban schools (Delgado 1995). Counter stories challenge the perceived wisdom of those at society's center by providing a context to transform established belief systems, and can show new and different possibilities by combining elements of the story and the current reality (Solorzano and Yosso 2001, 475). While our focus on narrative pedagogy examines the broader role of story in the science classroom, attention to counter story is warranted. Counter stories, because they challenge the dominant narrative, can serve as a tool for exposing, analyzing, and challenging the stories of those in power, which are often a part of dominant discourse.

Telling stories in school or about school has also been advocated by many scholars as a way to empower at-risk students (Burk 2000) and to give them "voice" (Brunson and Vogt 1996), a way to "speak to the uniqueness of each student of creating ghettos of exclusion" (Kaswom 1993, 163), so as to create a "shared experience in the classroom" (Hogg 1995) where the value and significance of students' personal experiences can be legitimated. Elsewhere, we have reported on how storytelling, described as "science talk," allowed one marginalized student, Melanie, to gradually gain a foothold in her classroom science discourse, contributing to her eventual academic success at the end of sixth-grade science (Tan and Calabrese Barton 2008). Telling and sharing stories open up new spaces for engagement when new texts are legitimated in classroom discourse, allowing students to reimagine their inhabitation of the world of school science.

In the remainder of this chapter, we attempt to illustrate how Mrs. Davis' narrative pedagogy supports the ongoing re/construction of hybrid spaces that make these epistemological and ontological ties among teachers and students possible, redefining not only what counts as legitimate participation and expertise in science class but also what it means to develop critical science literacy. We begin by describing vignettes of narrative pedagogy in Mrs. Davis' science class, and discuss how the stories engendered by such a pedagogy opened up both curricular spaces for the pursuit of new knowledge as well as spaces of authoring for students and teacher to create identities that traverse both the world of science and their life-worlds.

Making Healthy Choices in a Struggling Urban Community

Adams County is known across the state for its high levels of unemployment (15.9%, according to the US Department of Labor) and its underfunded school system. Gardenside Middle School (GMS) is no exception. The school, which houses roughly one thousand seventh and eighth graders, is the only middle school in the district, serving all seventh and eighth grade students who do not opt for private or parochial options. The student population is largely white (52%) and African-American (41%), with 5% of Hispanic students and a very small minority of Asian and American Indian students. Sixty-seven percent of the student population is eligible for free or reduced-price lunch.

Despite the tough economic conditions, in many ways, Gardenside is thriving. While some school districts around the state have closed their doors and "hunkered down" in response to No Child Left Behind mandates regarding academic accountability, Gardenside's leadership has reached out to pull innovative programs into their school. Their hope is that these programs will not only provide needed resources for their students and teachers but also open the doors to the world for their students. Such programs, in the eyes of the principal, can only help test scores improve.

The leaders at Gardenside were excited to incorporate the C3 curriculum into their middle school science sequence. C3 teaches life science through investigating how the human body works; why a state of dynamic equilibrium—balancing energy in and energy out—is important in order for our bodies to function well; how conditions such as high blood cholesterol and high blood sugar develop and what we can do to prevent them; and how to make food and exercise choices that will promote health and decrease the risk of many lifestyle-related diseases, such as heart disease, type 2 diabetes, and some cancers. The curriculum provides teachers and students with rigorous yet relevant investigations into how an understanding of biology, the environment, and personal behaviors impacts weight and health. Classroom activities provide opportunities for students to explore their experiences and feelings, reflect on them through self-assessment of eating and activity patterns, as well as learn about consequences.

Furthermore, C3 focuses on supporting students in developing critical science literacy around an issue of high relevance to urban youth today. Focused on helping students use scientific evidence to make healthy food and activity choices, C3 is meant to scaffold youth in developing the knowledge and practices they need to push back against childhood obesity trends. Indeed, the issue of childhood obesity has become a national phenomenon (Action for Healthy Kids 2002; American Academy of Pediatrics 2003). The rates of childhood obesity have been increasing over the past two decades. Research on childhood obesity indicates that over 50% of the population in the United States is considered to be overweight or obese, with the number of overweight children doubling in the past two decades (Surgeon General 2001). Health workers, nutritionists, and social scientists have also shed new light on the long-term health implications of overweight children having increased risk for elevated blood lipids, increased cholesterol levels, type 2 diabetes, and social discrimination that could lead to obesity later in life (Goodman and Whitaker 2002; ADA 2000).

Yet, prevention of childhood obesity is a complex phenomenon, bringing together human biology, environmental factors, and personal choices. The amount of energy consumed from snacks with low nutrient density and from sweetened beverages has doubled, while screen-time watching TV and playing video games has increased, and physical activities have decreased about 40% (Surgeon General 2001). Clearly, youth have to make choices in an environment in which food is ubiquitous, tasty, cheap, and heavily advertised; being sedentary is easily setting them up for a lifetime of being in positive energy balance.

Our collaborating teacher, Mrs. Davis, headed the C3 program at Gardenside. A white woman in her 40s, Mrs. Davis has lived in Adams County her entire life, and expresses a deep commitment to the students and families there. She has personally witnessed the city take an economic nose-dive as the failing auto industry created a domino effect across the state, impacting the auto suppliers in her city. Energetic and caring, Mrs. Davis has been a science teacher for close to ten years and has just completed her master's degree in education while teaching full time. Widely regarded by the school principal and her colleagues as an exemplary science teacher, Mrs. Davis was nominated this year by her principal for the "Best Science Teacher in the Country" award, and recently won the Teacher of the Year Award for her school district. This is Mrs. Davis' second year of teaching the C3 curriculum.

From the initial class we observed, we were struck by how consistently Mrs. Davis told personal stories in her science class and invited students to do likewise. We started focusing in our field notes and in our classroom video analysis on when Mrs. Davis told stories, what those stories were, the response of the students, which students told stories, and the discussions that resulted. In analyzing the classroom video data, we approached it in two ways. First, we examined individual events to ascertain how Mrs. Davis elicited stories from her students and how these stories shaped the classroom discourse. Then, we examined these events collectively to elucidate the larger mechanisms that are set in motion when stories are consistently taken up by the learning community. Specifically, we looked at the epistemological gains and identity development of members of the community as a result of engaging in the telling of stories in science class.

As researchers, we observed Mrs. Davis' teaching during the C3 unit, from December 2008 to April 2009. Mrs. Davis and her sixth-hour class was one of two classrooms we were observing daily during that time period, and one of 15 involved in our larger study. Both teachers were using a new curriculum called *Choice, Control and Change* (C3) (Koch, Contento, and Calabrese Barton 2007), an inquiry-based science and nutrition program focused on helping students use scientific evidence to make healthful food and activity choices. We documented in detail the proceedings of the science lessons, what pedagogical strategies the teachers used to elicit student participation, what practices the students used to engage in science, and the learning outcomes in the key content area of nutrition and dynamic equilibrium. We collected multiple forms of qualitative data, such as videos of classroom proceedings and student work. We also interviewed students as well as Mrs. Davis herself.

Building Hybrid Spaces for Critical Science Literacy through Narrative Pedagogy

In what follows we tell two extended vignettes about Mrs. Davis' science class on January 26 and on January 28. While Mrs. Davis enacted a narrative pedagogy throughout the unit, we selected these two dates because the nature of the stories are quite different, and they were spurred on by fairly different curricular contexts within the same larger C3 unit, allowing us to see a broader range of the role of narrative pedagogy in science teaching and learning. We concentrate on only two classroom days, however, so that we can delve into a more nuanced discussion of the production of classroom narratives and their relationship to science learning. In order to demonstrate that these two lessons were indicative of a much broader pattern of narrative pedagogy, we summarize in Table 4.1 the presence of a narrative pedagogy throughout the unit and its implications for content development and student participation.

Sharing Salad Recipes: January 26

NARRATIVES ON HEALTHY EATING: ENGAGING AND EXPLORING SCIENCE IDEAS THROUGH FAMILY SALADS. In the first module of C3, the content focused on teaching students about the complex system that influences food and activity choices, including biological preferences, environmental factors, and intrapersonal factors. Mrs. Davis felt that while these three topics were well covered in the unit, the focus on family culture was excluded for broader cultural dimensions, such as the prevalence of fast food and sedentary life styles. She also wanted to posit familial culture in a fairly positive light. To that end, she assigned homework in which each student interviewed a family member for a favorite home salad recipe. Students were then invited to share their recipes with the class and to think about how to replace some of the ingredients with healthier alternatives. This was an extension activity Mrs. Davis designed that was not stipulated in the C3 curriculum. We note that the choice to use family salad stories is an interesting one. Family salad recipes—or salad stories—as they were affectionately called, reflect family culture (Kellas 2006). As Sanchez (2009) reports, "[a] family's collection of stories, including its themes, are instrumental in understanding who the family is in terms of its norms, values, and goals" (p. 161).

The excerpt below is a narrative account of the discussions that took place in class on the day the students brought in their "salad stories."

Mrs. Davis began the class by inviting students to share their home salad recipe. Dee is first up. Dee nervously read her recipe from her homework. Each time Dee seemed to be "finished" with her story, she was prodded to develop her story with questions from Mrs. Davis:

> DEE: You cut up onions, then you mix until, you mix the broccoli and the bacon and the onions, and some sunflower seeds. And then you mix the dressing and some spices together, and then you um, put it in the refrigerator for a little while.
>
> MRS. D: What kind of dressing did it have? Do you remember?
>
> DEE: It um, some vinegar and some um mayo.
>
> MRS. D: So vinegar and mayo?
>
> DEE: Mmhmm.

Mrs. Davis turned her attention back to the class and reminded them, "Now Dee mentioned in there bacon, didn't she? Could you come up with any idea? So cut down on the amount . . ." As if reading her mind, Dee cut in and finished Mrs. Davis' thought for her by saying "And not a lot of grease when you're cooking!" In an easy exchange Mrs. Davis again picked up on Dee's comments and expanded the thought:

> MRS. DAVIS: We're going to have to pat dry the bacon, don't we? One option is not to put a lot of bacon on it to begin with. Now for this particular salad we probably don't want to eliminate the bacon 'cause it would change the salad. Right?

This mini exchange repeats a pattern of student and teacher co-construction of story that we observed many times in Mrs. Davis' teaching. In this opening salad story, Mrs. Davis set the narrative stage for the class by asking probing questions to push Dee along in expanding her story. It ended with an exchange between Dee and Mrs. Davis that was so seamless that it was difficult to discern whether the narrative around grease and bacon was attributable to Dee or Mrs. Davis. Mrs. Davis also positions herself alongside Dee by suggesting that "we" are going to have to pat the bacon dry, indicating that this is something she has to worry about as well.

Mrs. Davis then punctuated the exchange by exclaiming to the class that not only would it change the salad, but also "It would change the taste!" and then stepping back to remind her students of the meat that they had discussed the previous week:

> MRS. D: Remember that little meat that we talked about last week that some of you were surprised that you could even make into . . . that you could get in like hot dogs and things like that. What was it?
>
> CHRIS: Tofu, was it?
>
> MRS. D: Well, I supposed you could. I don't know!
>
> CHRIS: Would turkey bacon?

The students are clearly enjoying the conversation. They are laughing at some of the remarks—It would change the taste!—and they are nodding in agreement with others. The story seems to reach its climax when Mrs. Davis wonders aloud whether it is possible that "they have some tofu version of bacon" and the class taking the question up as a serious consideration. Without much prodding, students offer suggestions—other than tofu bacon—for potential healthy salad adaptations, including not changing the salad at all but simply eating less of it as a "side dish."

While Mrs. Davis sought to use Dee's salad story as a context for investigating healthy eating choices, she also used the class' collective knowledge to begin a more critical discussion of what healthy eating choices might look like. Mrs. Davis clearly respected the story, and offered a range of possibilities for engaging it critically without diminishing its value or contribution. The salad could be changed with ingredient substitution, but did not have to be changed at all if portion size was considered.

After Dee's story, several students raised their hands to share their salad stories, in contrast to the opening of the lesson when Mrs. Davis needed to prod Dee to share hers. When Mrs. Davis called on Lionel next, he stood up from his seat. With his salad recipe written neatly down in his worksheet, Lionel described his mom's salad.

> LIONEL: I interviewed my mom. Her name is Susan Helen. That's why the salad that she got from the *Taste of Home* magazine is called Susie's Salad by my Grandma, who sucks to pick up names for stuff.

Chuckling, he continued,

but, um, first you cut the bite size flowerets of just the tops of the broccoli and cauliflower. Then you cut the peppers and the veggies and the other stuff into tiny pieces. Then you toss them all together. Then you add the dried cranberries, bacon, peanuts, etc., etc., etc. Then you toss again. Then you mix the Miracle Whip, sugar, and vinegar until creamy, and you add it to the veggies and stir well.

Mrs. Davis pointed out the similarities between Dee's salad dressing and Lionel's salad dressing. She then asked Lionel, "So what did you write for as far as what you could do to make it healthier?" Referring to his worksheet, Lionel suggested replacing the regular Miracle Whip with low-fat Miracle Whip. When asked whether he came up with "any ideas on the bacon," Lionel and the rest of the class laughed, and Mrs. Davis conceded, "Bacon can be a tough one."

After Lionel's story, many more students appeared eager to share, visibly waving their hands and pointing to their recipes. Chris, who had his hand way up and really straight as he stared earnestly at Mrs. Davis, was called on next. Chris promptly stood up and began:

CHRIS: All right, I made a taco salad. And . . . first you tear the lettuce, add the vegetables, kidney beans, and low-fat cheese. And then you sprinkle Boca beef on there 'cause we don't eat real beef. And um, then we add western dressing. Toss the salad, then add a half-cup of tortilla chips, then toss it again.

When Mrs. Davis wondered aloud if everyone knew what Boca was, Chris immediately answered, "It's soybean," to which Mrs. Davis further added, "Yep, it's a meat substitute so people who are vegetarians eat it. It looks just like hamburger." "And it tastes like it too!" chimed in Chris. Mrs. Davis built on Chris' story by adding one of her own regarding how her family "uses it a lot in our chili and you can't tell the difference." While the class learned about the soy meat substitute from Chris' recipe, Mrs. Davis validated his choice of this unfamiliar ingredient by adding a story of how she uses Boca as well.

Turning toward Chris, she continued, "So, soy is the actual 'meat,' so it's very low in fat, and you said you used low-fat cheese." Chris nodded. Turning back to the class again, Mrs. Davis asked why the beans in Chris' salad are good ingredients. Unlike some of the other class sessions where Mrs. Davis has to prod students to talk science, students in this lesson started calling out their opinions: "Because they're healthy!" and "Because they're green!" "But why are they healthy?" inquired Mrs. Davis. Jared explained that beans do not have a lot of fat and Mrs. Davis agreed. When Mrs. Davis then asked, "What else do beans have a lot of?" and a classmate loudly yelled "Calories!" Chris, the author of the recipe, chimed in "No!" and Mrs. Davis went on to explain that beans are high in protein and so are good for vegetarians who do not eat meat. Instead of just accepting that "beans are healthy," Mrs. Davis pushed the students for further explanation.

LEARNING TO NAVIGATE THE COMPLEX FOOD SYSTEM: REASONING AND PROBLEM-SOLVING WITH AND THROUGH STORIES. Mrs. Davis' comments on the salad stories pushed the class to consider what "scientific information" their recipes contained that offered insight into "tricks" for how to navigate the complex food environment. She initiated this new discussion by telling a story about one of her own salad recipe tricks at home:

> One of the tricks we learned at our house that I've taught my children to do, is when we get our salad dressing at home, I take the whole bottle and I pour it upside down in a spray bottle. You know, those spray bottles we keep clean just for that reason. And so that, when we put our salad dressing on, we spray it on our salad instead of pouring it on our salad. 'Cause really, the salad dressing is just there to give it flavor. It's just there, 'cause you don't need a lot. It's the same thing that you would spend a lot more money for in the store.

Her transition to talk about strategies turned the classroom discussion further toward the "content" of the lesson while allowing student narratives to drive its development. When she followed up her own story with "Who else wants to share one? Anyone?" the class began to build a collective repertoire of healthy salad tricks grounded in their own experiences cooking in the home, including ways to make spinach fun to eat, how to substitute for high-fat ranch dressing, and how to wash vegetables. She took the everyday concerns of her students rather seriously, and instead of using scientific evidence to push students to "give up their ways of eating" (thereby positioning students with less power), she used both the content learning goals in science and their family stories to help her students to construct new and reasonably do-able practices for navigating the system.

By using her students' stories as a legitimate dimension of science classroom discourse, Mrs. Davis positioned them as powerful stakeholders fully capable of understanding the science content and how the practices of science apply to their lives. Additionally, throughout the narrative, not only did Mrs. Davis use the student stories as data for examination in the construction of strategies for navigating the complex food system, but also she further unpacked the "challenge of taste," since part of the content involved is that humans have a biological propensity for fat and sweet foods. However, as is evident in her comments throughout the salad discussions, food industries have exploited the human desire for fat and sweet. When Melissa suggested that they could substitute fat-free ranch dressing for the standard dressing, Jamie piped in, "but that's one dressing I've never been able to do fat free. It's really grainy." The differences in opinion on food preferences became a space of scientific experimentation for Mrs. Davis.

SITUATING SCIENCE: SALAD'S OTHER SIDE. All throughout this lesson, Mrs. Davis sought to elicit and then draw upon students' salad stories to build a science narrative about how to navigate the complex food environment. During our conversations with her throughout the unit, Mrs. Davis often talked about how science in real life is more complicated than it appears in a textbook, especially when it comes to the human body. Learning to make sense of healthy food and activity choices—or energy in and energy out in the human body—is about more than just learning what dynamic equilibrium is. It is also about learning that achieving dynamic equilibrium is rooted in context. Toward the end of the salad stories, she used her own family story as evidence for the messiness or complexity of science. In a playful yet serious way, Mrs. Davis shared a story of how her husband claims to have eaten healthily because he ate from a salad bar, with no regard for the items in the salad bar he chose to eat. Mrs. Davis used this story to open up a discussion with the students on the ingredients to avoid at a salad bar, as shown in the narrative excerpt below.

> MRS. DAVIS: My husband does this, and I tease him about it. And that is, he'll say something to me about the fact that, oh, I ate healthy today. I ate off the salad bar. And then he tells me everything he put on that salad and he might as well have had a Big Mac!

The students laughed, and Mrs. Davis continued,

> So, although he's getting his fruits and vegetables in, as far as fat and that kind of stuff like calories, he wasn't really doing his body that much good. So think for a minute for me. When you go to a salad bar in a restaurant, what are some of the things that you might want to avoid in order to keep that salad healthy?

When Molly called out "Croutons!" Mrs. Davis built on Molly's point and, positioning herself again in solidarity with the students, exclaimed to the class: "*We*'re bread eaters. *We* eat a lot of bread and it's probably something we don't need any more of!" Mrs. Davis then used Molly's idea as another strategy for navigating the complex food system, that is, the typical American salad bar. Mrs. Davis continued to position herself and her students as active agents in the science narrative her class is developing, by telling Jared

> You walk up to the salad bar. . . . So it's one place we can eliminate, one easy place to eliminate bread. So croutons are an idea. What else? Jared? You're going to a place that has a salad bar tonight and you're going to make a side. When you walk up to the salad bar, tell something that you might want to avoid.

What followed was an intense exchange among her students about how to navigate the salad bar, including using less cheese and dressing and avoiding high-fat items, such as fried eggs, dark meats, and dressing. In this segment, students interacted more directly with each other to expand and challenge their stories. When one student suggested avoiding eggs, another responded by suggesting that only some eggs might be avoided while some egg preparations (hard-boiled) might be healthy choices, which Mrs. Davis qualified even further, for some eaters, such as vegetarians.

Again, Mrs. Davis used her own story about the salad bar to get her students talking science. The focus of the narrative pedagogy is on the content of the story "what would you do at the salad bar?" as well as the embedded science practice and the students' role as creators and enactors of those practices: You are at the salad bar, what do you do? What kinds of scientific reasoning and evidence will you use to make a good choice? This form of narrative pedagogy is highly engaging to her students. Not only do the typically quiet and "science shy" students participate in talking science, but also students appeared to become "more honest" about their everyday food navigation practices.

Salad stories and empowering science learning. Salads are typically regarded as healthy food choices. Vegetables and fruit, staple salad ingredients, are preferred food items for people who are nutritionally conscious. With this assignment, Mrs. Davis not only invited her students to showcase their home funds of knowledge by focusing on a home salad recipe, she and the students also critiqued the salad as a healthy alternative to regular meals by closely examining the ingredients in one another's salads and discussing ways to make the salad even healthier. The students engaged in scientific inquiry, learned from one another's recipes, and delved deeper into the content. They learned how to critically examine a generally accepted nutrition idea that salads are healthy to eat. By inviting students to think critically about a salad bar, something they encounter in their daily lives, Mrs. Davis positioned inquiry and curiosity as highly valued habits of mind in science class while positioning the funds of knowledge that students bring to doing science as essential elements in the inquiry process. At the same time, science is situated in context, and the notion that science is a monolithic narrative is challenged. When considering the choices available at a salad bar, extra virgin olive oil may be a healthy dressing if the only alternative is ranch dressing. If balsamic vinaigrette is present, it might be a better choice over extra virgin olive oil. These discussions help students experience scientific understandings in a way where no clear right or wrong answer is normative, and there is no one way of doing things. Negotiating multiple texts in this manner blunts the didactic edge that students often experience when engaging in canonical science, and makes the learning experience more authentic, not just to the complexities of their lives, but also to how scientific endeavors are undertaken by scientists. In so doing, Mrs. Davis' students developed critical science literacy, and were able to do so in a context where the science texts were drawn from their lives.

Calvin and Exercise, January 28

The second module of C3 focuses on "Bodies in Motion" or "How can we make sure that we get the right amount of energy to help our bodies do what we want them to do?" This module begins with a case study of a boy named Calvin who is "eating a lot of fast food, not being very active, and beginning to have health problems" (C3, 73). The story is used to help prompt students to think about the "three Cs": *Choice* (What choices did Calvin make? What choices do you have?), *Control* (What does Calvin need to understand that he can have more control over his eating and activity?), and *Change* (What changes can Calvin make in order to help his body do what he wants it to do?). Through the Calvin case study, students are challenged to help Calvin feel better as they learn about the principles of nutrition, digestion, metabolism, and dynamic equilibrium.

Similar to the lesson focused on salad stories, the use of stories in the Calvin lesson moves the students through three phases, which we refer to below as setting ground-rules, understanding over judgment, and situating science.

SETTING GROUND RULES FOR TALKING SCIENCE/TALKING HEALTH. This episode began with a story of Calvin presented in the C3 textbook that the students read as the introduction to the second module. Calvin's story describes how he enjoys a bit too much junk food, drinks sweetened beverages, and has no energy to play basketball or undertake any form of exercise. Facing her students in the front of the classroom, Mrs. Davis announced, "Today we are going to start looking at a young gentleman named Calvin. When we start talking about Calvin, he makes it a little more personal. Some of you might be able to relate to Calvin. Some of you know someone that might be able to relate to Calvin. But before we read Calvin, we need to establish some norms."

Mrs. Davis stressed that nobody should be made fun of as they explored Calvin's story, and that "weight is, and health is, a very sensitive issue to people." She reminded her students that the classroom should be a safe space for everyone and that nobody should make rude comments or pass judgments on other people on the basis of classroom discussion. She then stated rather forcefully but sincerely:

> So can we all make a promise that not in this room and not outside this classroom you're not to place judgments on other people based on what we learn in this room. 'Cause none of us are perfect. *None of us.* All right? Agreed?

Mrs. Davis waited until all of the students nodded in agreement. She then orchestrated the reading of the story by asking for student volunteers to take turns reading the story and passing out highlighters. At certain points in the story, she stopped and asked them to highlight segments of the text that related to Calvin's choices and their health impacts on Calvin.

Two important ground rules for talking science/talking health were introduced in how Mrs. Davis set up the Calvin story. First, her students had to commit to "not passing judgment" or "making rude comments." She wanted her students to know her classroom is a safe space to talk about health and to share personal experiences related to Calvin's story. Second, she used the highlighters to focus her students on the content of the story, so that they were paying attention to the nuances of Calvin's case study.

UNDERSTANDING OVER JUDGMENT: MRS. DAVIS' FAMILY FACES THE SAME PROBLEMS AS CALVIN! After students spent several minutes highlighting text, Mrs. Davis initiated a classroom discussion by asking, "So what do you think are some problems Calvin is having?" Destiny suggested that Calvin's habit of eating only at fast-food restaurants "is a bad one." Gloria pointed out that after Calvin's mother asked him to turn off the TV, he proceeded "upstairs to play video games."

Mrs. Davis then shared her own family's story, which, as she pointed out to her students, had many parallels to Calvin's.

> MRS. D: Probably that age, such behavior is typical. 11, 12, 10. I know my two children try to do that. It was homework time and he chose video time. But it's all the inactivity that he has in his life right now, right? He said he's tired all the time. Why do you think he's tired all the time?
>
> MIKE: Because he eats!
>
> MRS. D: And don't you eat?"

Mike paused, appearing to think through the question, then responded slowly, "He's eating very unhealthy food! He's putting on a lot of weight, so he has to carry that weight all day long."

Later, turning back to the class, Mrs. Davis asked, "How many of you think exercising makes you tired?" When several students raised their hands, Mrs. Davis responded by sharing with them her own exercise routine and how it made her feel:

> You know [exercising] can also make you feel better and give you more energy. I know if I get up in the morning, and I'm doing some activity level, then I set the tone for the day and I have a tendency to be more active. But if it's Saturday and I get up and the pajamas don't come off till later in the day and I'm sitting around watching cartoons with the kids or something like that, it kind of makes me feel that way the entire rest of the day, doesn't it? A lot of people, Mrs. W [the teacher next door] is one of them. She gets up very, very early in the morning and goes and works out at the Y before she ever comes to work!

Mrs. Davis was candid with her students. She admitted to her own children spending too much time playing sedentary video games and her personal tendency to lounge around on Saturdays in her pajamas. Yet her point was not to pass judgment on her family and, by extension, on Calvin. Her point was to focus on what patterns of activity she and her students likely engaged in, and how those patterns made them feel. This was a strategic move for two reasons. First, it shifted the focus from making good versus bad choices, or judging Calvin's choices, to understanding what the choices are, especially when his choices reflect a typical American teen lifestyle. Second, she called attention to a difficult science idea for students to comprehend. That is, if food gives you energy, then why does overeating make you feel tired or drained of energy? And, if exercises use up energy, how or why is it that exercising can make you feel more energetic? She repeated these points again after her story, making the connection between the content and her students' lives, using examples that the students will be familiar with:

> You know he has gotten out of that cycle of exercising and so therefore all these other things that you mention. Kind of like he's got caught in this loop and can't get out, right? And sometimes when we get caught in a loop, it's really hard to get out, isn't it? It's really, really hard to get yourself down to business then and go back and start at the beginning and make up all that work, isn't it? Well, the same thing has happened to Calvin. Calvin has gotten in this habit of eating junk and not exercising and eating junk and not exercising and now he's putting on weight and getting heavier. And so, he doesn't have the ambition to go out, and he's not been eating the foods that are good for his body, so they make him feel sluggish. His heart has to work harder. He's lying around the house a lot. And it's really hard once we develop those

> habits to get the ambition to change and to break that pattern. And that happens a lot of times throughout life. What else?

HUMANIZING SCIENTIFIC AUTHORITY. While story dominated this lesson thus far, unlike the salad stories, the stories in this class episode were primarily authored by the teacher and the text. Still, Mrs. Davis invited her students to co-construct their own narrative. When she asked, "What else?" (end of quote above), Dana responds by talking about how the cheeseburger and pop made Calvin feel good. When Mrs. Davis follows with her own story of overeating that is similar to Calvin's, the students prodded her along (as she prodded them in the salad stories), allowing Mrs. Davis to expand her story, which was a confession of sorts on overeating. This confessional caused much laughter on the part of the students and provided a rich context for Mrs. Davis and her students to elaborate on core content in the lesson, namely, what do we mean by "choice, control and change."

> MRS. DAVIS: Right, And TV is a really good time for that to happen. I told students in second hour what I did last night. I'd gone and gotten a container about this big and about this tall of dried vegetables, you know they dehydrate them? So they're not fried and they're not baked, they only thing is they've had all the moisture sucked out of them, so they're really crunchy. And there's like sweet potatoes and carrots and peas. And the thing about that is, you take those sweeter vegetables, you pull all that moisture out of them, it makes the sugar really concentrated, so they're really sweet so like the green beans are really good. But I had that container sitting on my table last night in class, and I intended on having just a few.
>
> STUDENT: [You] ate the whole thing!
>
> MRS. DAVIS. [I] ate the whoooole container! Because I was busy and preoccupied with something and you don't even notice you're doing it. So when you sit down at the TV or you're doing homework and if you're having a snack . . . you know, you need to pre-measure. You need to take a certain amount out, and eat just that. And someone in fourth hour today got into the discussion about the Super Bowl coming up this weekend, you know, and how much eating people do by watching the Super Bowl.

Throughout the story, many of the students laughed and nodded in agreement, calling out words like "yep" and "me too" and other words of encouragement. When one of the students even volunteered his own confessional story of overeating, nearly all of the students began talking at once to each other about their own experiences. This kind of overlapping talk focused on science suggests a high level of engagement among her students. Mrs. Davis allowed this moment to last longer than she normally does, presumably to allow her students to get their own stories out to each other. Stories of overeating and less than stellar eating habits are not always easy to share in public settings. This was a strategic move, we think, to subjectively position the youth as narrative experts without putting their own "confessional" under the microscope and she had done to herself.

Bringing the collective story of overeating back to the curricular content, Mrs. Davis pulled the class back by describing the potential health-related outcomes of overeating and a sedentary life style, namely, high blood pressure and elevated blood sugar.

The narrative pedagogy used in the Calvin lesson repositioned Mrs. Davis as more than the epistemic authority of the classroom. The stories "humanize" her as a person who struggles with a healthy lifestyle, just as the case study character Calvin did, and probably just as many of her students do. They also position Mrs. Davis as being centrally involved with the science content as she acknowledges to her students, through her sharing, how these concepts shown in the Calvin case study are playing out in her life, and that she is not exactly the "expert" in these issues. As she was invoking these stories, Mrs. Davis' relationship with her students transcended the teacher-learner dichotomy. These vignettes also illustrate the bidirectional flow between paradigmatic understanding and narrative understanding. We often talk about how narrative understandings open up space for paradigmatic understanding. We believe that for science to have "real" meaning in students' everyday lives outside of school, they must be able to move back and forth between formal scientific discourse and everyday talk. This movement cannot be in only one direction. We take up this point about movement between curricular spaces as an important "third space" in the discussion section that follows. In addition to the above vignettes, Table 4.1 shows a summary of the stories that were told in the rest of the observed lessons during the C3 unit, and the additional content threads that were explored as a direct result of these stories.

TABLE 4.1. **Narrative Pedagogy in Mrs. D's classroom**

Lesson & main objectives	Stories brought up by teacher & students	New content threads that resulted from stories
Sharing home salad recipes – lesson built on student stories • Is your salad healthy? • What can you do to make it healthier?	• Students' home salad recipe ingredients • Stevia plant/truvia • Washing salad/ E. coli poisoning • Hard cheeses healthier than soft • Dipping pizza crust in ranch dressing • How to make salad dressing healthier, use a spray bottle and 50/50 ranch dressing • Husband's eating habits from a salad bar	• What ingredients can be substituted in salads to make them healthier • Artificial and natural sweeteners • E. coli contamination of produce • Unhealthy eating habits • Ways to cut down on using salad dressing • What to avoid when eating from a salad bar
Our food environment – taste, food availability • Exploring the factors that affect our food choices	• Not eating meat during Lent • Indian cooking uses a lot of curry • Buying local, buying organic food • Always having a bowl of fruit sitting on the dinner table	• How religious practices influence food choices • How culture influences food choices • How personal food choices affect the environment • Easy access of food affects what we eat
Calvin case study • Calvin is constantly tired and hungry • How do these issues relate to his lifestyle?	• Teacher's children playing long hours of video games • Watching cartoons all day on Saturday • Exercising in the day or at night Eating out of boredom • Fainting and not making sense from hypoglycemia	• How personal lifestyles affect one's health • Does exercise make one tired or give one energy? • Eating habits and how to be mindful of them • Difference between hypoglycemia and diabetes, what happens when one has hypoglycemia, and the dietary requirements for the condition
Energy in, Energy out • Using a game called "energy cards" to simulate caloric density of different foods	• What happens to people's eating habits during the Super Bowl? • How people seem to love junk food	• How culture affects people's eating habits, what one can do to make healthier choices • Junk food can have addictive properties
Energy out • Using the pedometer	• How teacher increased her exercise in 3 years • Kids' current activities that are good exercise: Abi's dance, William's basketball, Chris's play rehearsals	• How to increase one's stamina for exercise incrementally • Good exercise activities for youth

(*continued*)

TABLE 4.1. ***(continued)***

Lesson & main objectives	Stories brought up by teacher & students	New content threads that resulted from stories
Indoor walking exercise in class using the pedometer	• What is an indoor walking exercise and how can it be done? • Intensity of exercise measured by perspiration • Certain illnesses can prevent people from doing exercises for a sustained amount of time	• Introduce students to exercises that can be done in-house when the weather is bad, relevant to the long winters students experience where they live • How to be careful when exercising if one has asthma or heart conditions
What is a healthy snack? • Students share their healthy snack choice under 2 dollars	• Discussion of the many snack choices students brought in • Closely examining nutritional labels of students' snacks • Where to buy these snacks	• What is considered a healthy snack? • How to read nutritional labels • Where can one find a healthy snack in the neighborhood?
Keep it Pumping • Measuring heart rate and breathing rate activity	• Teacher's father suffering a heart attack at age 42 • The choir teacher Mr. B had a heart attack and then lost a lot of weight • "30" rule from 15 years ago: 30% of males will have 30% of arteries blocked by age 30. • Consciously parking car at the back of the lot, taking the stairs instead of the elevator • College student who died after drinking a gallon of water in a minute • Water drinking contest that killed a woman	• How diet predisposes one to heart disease, which can strike at a young age • Guidelines such as the 30 rule change very quickly, numbers are probably worse now • Choices one can make in daily life to add more exercise • Too much water is unhealthy and potentially fatal, balance of water and body's electrolytes
Keeping the Flow • Simulating blood flow with clogged and unclogged arteries using materials	• "Don't be a patsy" public service announcement	

Narrative Pedagogy and Hybrid Spaces for Critical Science Literacy

Mrs. Davis' narrative approach to teaching elicited a range of stories that provided context, suspense, comedy, and passion to a subject often taken up as objective and clinical. They often positioned teachers and students in solidarity as they learned to navigate the complex food environment together. Mrs. Davis' narrative pedagogy drew upon story in different ways. In the lesson on healthy eating strategies, she set up an activity that enthusiastically elicited student story, and she played the crucial role of participatory audience member in the way that she asked questions and contributed to the stories to push them along. She drew from the content of her students' stories to craft a science narrative on healthy eating strategies, critically evaluating seemingly healthy food choices, and sugar and fat in the diet that linked their lives to the curriculum.

In the Calvin case study, however, Mrs. Davis' personal stories dominated the lesson in the larger whole-class public discussion. Her stories presented her as one who, just like Calvin and her students, struggled with healthy food and activity choices daily. Using her own stories as the primary narrative in the Calvin lesson seemed strategic because that lesson dug more deeply into some of the *negative* consequences of unhealthy eating and activity choices. Not asking students to position themselves as "failures" in the food and activity system (as Calvin was to an extent) by sharing her own stories, Mrs. Davis allowed the students to probe the content in a local and personal way, without the risk of having to "confess" to peers that their eating and activity are less than optimal.

Mrs. Davis' narrative pedagogy created hybrid spaces for learning that supported youth in developing critical science literacy. The stories elicited in Mrs. Davis' teaching served as moments of being "in-between" where the multiple and oftentimes competing knowledges and discourses of scientific understanding, the complex food environment, and students' lives came together, informed each other, and were themselves challenged and reshaped. While the student stories of the salad lessons were positioned to serve as the source of content for the lesson, Mrs. Davis' stories seemed better positioned to create a safe space to examine content ideas in more depth. Both episodes reveal that in spite of the constraints often felt by teachers and students to act and talk in more traditionally defined ways in the science classroom, telling stories became a powerful practice that allowed the students and their teacher to begin to collaboratively define meaningful frameworks for learning and doing science, to bridge their experiences and to strengthen their relationships and understandings of each other, as well as to take risks with and for each other as they worked together to author what it means to be scientifically literate.

Below we take up specifically how Mrs. Davis' narrative pedagogy enabled hybrid spaces for learning by expanding classroom resources for learning (stories as epistemic resources), by positioning students and teacher as creative agents in a complex science narrative (stories as subject and object), and by transforming the nature of science expertise/ science literacy (stories as transformative texts).

Stories as Epistemic Resources: Co-authoring and Complicating the Content Story Line

Stories in Mrs. Davis' classroom were valued as epistemic resources that enriched the science discussions and complemented the official C3 curriculum. As Mrs. Davis' students explained, having relevant stories to bring to class very much enhanced their motivation to understand the science content being taught *and to appropriate* the science content to relevant areas of their lives. According to Molly, combining home stories with school science helps because "you can relate it to your life . . . and you can see how it relates to other people's lives." Mike explained how stories allowed students a friendlier route to access the classroom discourse: "More people wanna talk about their experiences than they do about science."

The stories that the students and Mrs. Davis brought into the classroom were important not simply because they legitimized the resources that students bring to the classroom as worthwhile epistemic resources, but also because as epistemic resources, as seen from the vignettes and from table 4.1, they transformed the content narrative itself. For example, by assigning the favorite family salad homework assignment and devoting an entire lesson to having students present their recipes in class, Mrs. Davis' students had the opportunity to engage in a discussion about a food choice that is widely accepted as healthy, and to analyze and critique one another's salads as to whether they were really healthy, and what ingredients they could substitute. Investigating salads was not a lesson from the C3 curriculum, but rather a lesson that Mrs. Davis added to the curriculum. The sharing of salad stories provided a context to develop practical strategies for making healthy food choices at home and at restaurants, including portion size, fat content, and food substitutions, without trading off enjoyment. Each one of these strategies was discussed and weighed against the scientific evidence accumulated through the curriculum and their experiences and was linked to earlier content ideas in the unit. When students and teacher alike were unwilling to give up bacon because of its taste and texture, they collectively decided that "taste matters" and that they needed to locate other possible strategies to keep the bacon. The official lessons on food choices were concerned with investigating fast-food options and school food options, focusing on processed and fried foods. By having students interview a family member and then share their stories on home salads, Mrs. Davis and her students expanded the C3 curriculum, and the students gained knowledge that they would not have otherwise.

Later in the same module focused on the food environment, stories brought in questions and comments about how religious practices and culture influence food choices, how personal food choices affect the environment, and the control of food choices by the local economy. Each one of these dimensions is relevant to how students figure out how to draw upon their scientific understandings to navigate the food system. These new content threads advanced student understanding, because students were presented with more perspectives and could therefore better appreciate the complexities inherent in making health and nutrition decisions. The teacher and the students were equal stakeholders in contributing stories; thus, the learning community collaboratively defined meaningful frameworks for engaging with science.

Similarly with the "snack under two dollars" activity (see Table 4.1), Mrs. Davis and her students extended their knowledge in reading nutrition labels and discussing the criteria of a healthy snack, which was not part of the official C3 curriculum. Although Mrs. Davis decided on these extension activities, they were entirely scripted by the students because the content of the task was dependent on students collecting data from their out-of-school lives. Through such stories, however, more than just the science content was enriched. Other communities germane to the students' lives had a key presence in the science classroom as stories of family eating habits, choir instructors, playing volleyball, and attending dance classes were discussed.

As the students explained, stories allow them to insert their voices into the science discourse in a less threatening way, and more students are able to do so because they are experts of their own experiences. As Molly explained, there is a much lower risk of getting things "wrong" when one is sharing about one's personal experiences. Positioning students with such narrative authority is empowering because students identify personal areas of expertise they can offer that will further the school science discourse and will challenge the tight boundaries between home and school science discourse.

Stories as Subject and Object

Mrs. Davis' narrative pedagogy positioned both the students and herself as creative agents or actors in the science narrative. Instead of engaging science content as an acquisition of facts or big ideas, engaging science content meant figuring out how one is a part of the science narrative. Students talked about their "tricks" and "strategies," which became the substance for scientific descriptions of healthy eating, by making evidence-based claims such as "I made this choice, and this is why it's healthy" rather than "A healthy choice based on reducing fat content is this." We noted that many of these "shifting events" involved not only shifts in discourse and positioning, but also exchanges of "hidden" resources and identities among Mrs. Davis and her students.

Because stories elicit the magnification of the personal and the particular, they enabled students and teacher alike to share aspects of themselves and their families that enriched the science narrative, even though these aspects are atypical in science classrooms. Being the "overeater," the "vegetarian," the "gas station store food expert" all were critical expert roles played by students because of their out-of-school experiences. Each role brought with it resources that were necessary to the development of the content in the classroom. In some cases, these roles and their attendant resources were used to "messy" the content narratives in ways that reflected the students' realities poignantly.

When Mrs. Davis introduced her husband's eating practices at the salad bar, she introduced a complex problem, including a number of food choices to make sense of, taste preferences, contextual features (is the salad the actual meal or a starter?), and decision making. By using her husband as the individual navigating this complex problem, and then inviting her students to navigate it alongside her husband, the students were positioned as both the subject and the object of consideration.

Their stories on how to make healthy choices defined the boundaries of the investigation in the moment, but also positioned their experiences and their histories as relevant to solving the problem.

Yet, we also note with caution that the act of building hybrid spaces through story is risky for both teachers and students, because of how the discourses position teachers and students as particular kinds of players in the school setting and how stories disrupt these hierarchies. For example, when the class was discussing what kinds of cheese (hard or soft) were healthier, Mrs. Davis admitted to "not knowing." While this might seem somewhat trivial, normative practices in school are for teachers to "have the knowledge." Further, by "confessing" her sometimes-unhealthy food and activity choices, Mrs. Davis further positioned herself as just like Calvin.

Stories, because they are discursively generative, expanded how the students' and teacher's own subject positioning was just as important to learning to use science as the content itself. For example, as shown in vignette 1 with the salad recipes, Dee's sharing motivated other students to want to share their recipes as well, even when those recipes carried with them obviously nonhealthy choices, as did Dee's with the bacon and mayonnaise. As students listened to their peers' sharing, they recognized that they themselves have "data" relevant to the science discussion, even as they were learning new knowledge from their peers.

As Mrs. Davis and her students negotiated the multiple and competing texts presented by the stories—I don't like the grainy taste of fat-free dressing and choosing lower-fat options is a healthy choice—even audience members who did not share stories potentially gained from the juxtaposition of the multiple texts. Even if they are not forthcoming in adding to the conversations, hearing others share their life experiences elicits "me too" reactions and triggers memories from one's own experience. As suggested by some scholars (Gerrig 1993; Conle 2003), such narrative encounters that foster many such connections are "productive curricular events because they facilitate a reshaping of one's prior experiences in light of the current encounter" (Conle 2003, 11). This was evident in the abundant student stories shared more privately amongst each other after the two narratives on overeating. Therefore, storytelling offers both the narrator and the audience opportunities to engage in narrative inquiry, reflect on their experiences, and learn from the stories being shared. As Abi concluded to the class after sharing her healthy salad recipe, the act of narrating "helped us realize what we put in our salad," knowledge that previously may have been taken for granted and not critiqued with perspectives collectively informed by science and the act of storytelling.

Stories as Transformative Texts

Stories brought new and fairly nontraditional characters and identities into the science classroom, transforming the monolithic discourse of the classroom into one that was heteroglossic. In addition to what is described in the official science curriculum, students and teacher's families, friends, and other characters in their stories became legitimate members of the school science discourse. Beyond building bridges from science to the students' life-worlds and collapsing the boundaries between them, widening the community related to science also positioned students and teacher in the science researcher roles—collecting valid data from their lives outside of science class that will enrich the discussions they have in science. Therefore, story afforded more science-related roles to teacher and students, further strengthening opportunities to engage with science.

Apart from content-based learning outcomes, stories also created a space of authoring empowering identities in science (Holland et al. 2001). Telling stories allowed students' lives to be woven into the discourse of school science in a way that enriched the school science experience for them, because the relevance of what they are learning and their lives outside of school is foregrounded. The discussions in the classroom were dependent on the students' stories. The classroom dynamic is reshaped in the process and becomes less hierarchical, in the sense that the teacher is no longer the sole expert of the subject. As Mrs. Davis led by her example and actively solicited students to share their stories, the classroom discourse transformed to be hybrid in nature. The official school science text (i.e., the C3 curriculum) ceased to be the sole reference point and standard measure, and life stories—texts from outside of school science—were actively pursued. The two discourses were deftly woven by Mrs. Davis and her students into a hybrid discourse that reflected both official science content and the community's personal expertise related to the science content.

As the science teacher, Mrs. Davis led by example, explicitly and consistently presenting her identities as a mother, a wife, a woman in her 40s concerned about her health, to her students as she invoked personal stories. These identities, in addition to her identity as a science teacher, were all relevant in her classroom and to the science she was teaching. She humanized herself as well as the science content as more than just academic. Mrs. Davis was passionate about nutrition and health because of her own personal journey, changing her eating habits and lifestyle to improve her well-being. Mrs. Davis herself exhibited critical science agency as she drew from her own experiences to frame the discussions during C3 so that students learned to be analytical and critical in their approach to the subject. From having personal experiences with nutrition and health issues, Mrs. Davis recognized these experiences as valid data and legitimate knowledge that can complement the official C3 curriculum. By participating in telling stories, Mrs. Davis and her students were "co-inquirers and co-learners" about nutrition and health, and the community benefited in learning outcomes in both science content rigor and a developing sense of critical science agency.

Conclusion

Mrs. Davis and her students have shown us that a narrative pedagogy is powerful. It levels the playing field for more students in science class and thus makes access to science discourse both more equitable (most students have science data in the form of stories versus relying only on epistemic knowledge) as well as more empowering (students have voice in the science classroom and can help shape the science discourse) for students, because they have more opportunities to be positioned as experts rather than as only novices.

A narrative pedagogy sets in motion "a process propelled by the imperatives of individual self-development" (Hopkins 1994, 146) when students consistently ask, "What does this subject mean to my life? How does it help me make sense of my life or give it direction?" (Conle 2003, 13). More than inserting their voices into the existing school science discourse, teacher and student stories help to transform the school science discourse in ways that allow more students to take ownership over the discourse, as well as to stretch the content to include what would be left out if the official school science discourse was strictly adhered to. At the same time, students are authoring positive identities related to science. As Lindsay (2001) posits, one's identity and knowledge are partially constructed by the stories we tell and hear; therefore, it is crucial to author the stories in addition to living them. Through stories, students reimagine the world, in terms of both how a science class discourse should be, and how they can make better food and lifestyle decisions leading to future positive changes in their lives and in their community.

While the stories themselves were expertly taken up by Mrs. Davis in her science teaching, a narrative pedagogy is not without risks. Mrs. Davis was willing to share epistemic authority with her students. She was willing to listen to their narratives whether or not they aligned with the grain of normative science. Indeed, she leveraged those stories that ran counter to the traditional science narrative—because they made the learning more complex, more culturally grounded, or more critical of the role of science in society—as moments of learning for her students. But stories can just as easily shut out students, if the risk is not mediated by a teacher who is willing to be changed by her students. In addition, Mrs. Davis had to decide to carve out time for storytelling, which lengthened the overall time spent on the unit. Given the syllabus that she had to cover for seventh-grade science, she could not afford to engage in narrative pedagogy in this manner for every unit. However, consistent engagement in narrative pedagogy has enabled Mrs. Davis to identify and capitalize on fruitful opportunities to invite student voice through stories in her teaching. Her increasing expertise in narrative pedagogy, together with a supportive school administration, allowed Mrs. Davis and her students to have the space and time to build stronger personal connections with science while delving deeper into science content.

CHAPTER FIVE

Becoming an Expert: Critical Engagement with Science and the Community

In the summer of 2007, Ron, X'Ander, and Kaden, along with 17 other youth, spent five weeks investigating whether their city, River City, exhibited the urban heat island (UHI) effect. One particularly hot afternoon, with laser measuring tapes, digital thermometers, notebooks, digital cameras, and video cameras in hand, they had spent hours generating data that would help them to discern whether and how the downtown neighborhood exhibited the UHI effect. At the end of the afternoon, Kaden held the video camera up to Ron to capture one last scene. Ron made the following remarks, in dramatic tenor:

> This is ace reporter Ron Brown. Boys and Girls Club News. I am surprised that people don't think this is an urban heat island. Right now you can actually see the beads of heat-induced sweat. Do you see it? [Ron points to his forehead where he is visibly sweating.] They are beads. Not little droplets. Beads! I cannot believe this! . . . The people around here are so unknowledged [drawn out]. We should really do something about this. Have a heat island awareness day. Yah. This is Ron Brown, from Boys and Girls Club News, signing off. Catch you on the flip side.

Originally published in a slightly different form in Angela Calabrese Barton and Edna Tan, "We Be Burnin'! Agency, Identity, and Science Learning," *Journal of Learning Sciences* 19, no. 2 (2010):187–229. Copyright. Reprinted by permission of Taylor & Francis, http://www.tandfonline.com.

This quote, featured in the boys' video documentary, *We're Hot! What about You?* [6:46–7:04], captures one of the threads of their seven-minute video created from their data set on whether downtown River City is a UHI. The boys were alarmed that nearly everyone they interviewed was unaware of the UHI effect and its implications for River City. Yet, they also espoused a confidence in their knowledge of UHIs and in their abilities to act on that knowledge to make a difference. To situate themselves as individuals who can create "awareness" and educate the "unknowledged" brings into focus the intersecting roles of knowledge and action critical to these boys' developing knowledge base and a sense of self in science.

The purpose of this chapter is to delve into how youth practice their content knowledge expertise and their agency in a community setting. We use this exploration to rethink the connections between learning, critical engagement with math and science, and agency.

The Role of Agency in Empowering Science Education

In the second chapter of the book, we described how empowering science education transforms the context, content, and outcomes of learning. In this chapter, we delve into the construct of agency as one way to link the three ideas.

Although it is fairly common in its application, some have cautioned against a more generic assessment of agency as "free will" because such a stance neglects the social nature of agency and the "pervasive influence of culture on human intentions, beliefs, and action" (Ahearn 2001, 114). Generally speaking, those in informal and science learning have heeded such cautions and have turned in the other direction, drawing upon Bourdieu's (1977) structure – agency dialectic that, embedded in a practice theory framework, emphasizes the recursive loop involving actions and social structures. Such a stance holds that one's actions within a given field are enabled or constrained by the social structures available there, and which then themselves are recreated (or reinforced) by the actions one has taken. For example, in a study of an eighth-grade science community, Olitsky (2006) shows how the discourse of school science offers limited subject positions for youth to take up, thereby removing from view the varied options that students can create for themselves with/in science. Yet, students can and do creatively take up resources within these highly constrained settings to expose tensions that may exist between dominant expectations and youth's efforts to re/create themselves in science (Elmesky 2005).

Cultural Anthropology and the Figured Worlds of Doing Science for Change

The structure-agency dialectic resituates agency from the personal to the social realm, calling attention to how agency cannot be ascribed to any given individual, but rather is field dependent (Sewell 1992). While we concur with the socially mediated nature of agency, we also take a more critical approach to understanding agency to call attention both to the socially transformative nature of agency and to the intersecting roles of context, position, knowledge, and identity with agency. Ahearn argues that the structure–agency dialectic "leaves little room for resistance or social change" (2001, 118). We amplify Ahearn's concerns with our own struggle with what the agency-structure dialectic does not actively account for, which is the way that position, prestige, and power play out locally in how individuals seek to access and activate resources and in the meanings they ascribe symbolically and otherwise. These power dynamics are certainly field dependent but they are also deeply entrenched culturally and historically, and socially in time and place. This is why we turn to cultural anthropology's orientation to practice theory to help us better understand these dynamics in the construction of agency.

Holland, a cultural anthropologist, offers a framework for moving beyond the abstract divisions of labor to consider how agency is locally instanced with her work on figured worlds. Figured worlds are stable and shared "realm[s] of interpretation in which a particular set of characters and actors are recognized, significance is assigned to certain acts, and particular outcomes are valued over others" (Holland et al. 2001, 52). As historical phenomena, figured worlds act as "traditions" offering form and meaning to our lives. But as socially organized and reproduced phenomena, they are also "webs of meaning" where activities, discourses, performances, and artifacts are coproduced, over time, and where our senses of self are often "divided" and "distributed" across many different fields of activity (p. 51).

The value of figured worlds in understanding agency emerges in how they set up identity and positionality as situationally contingent and under constant transformation. As Urrieta (2007) describes, "Through

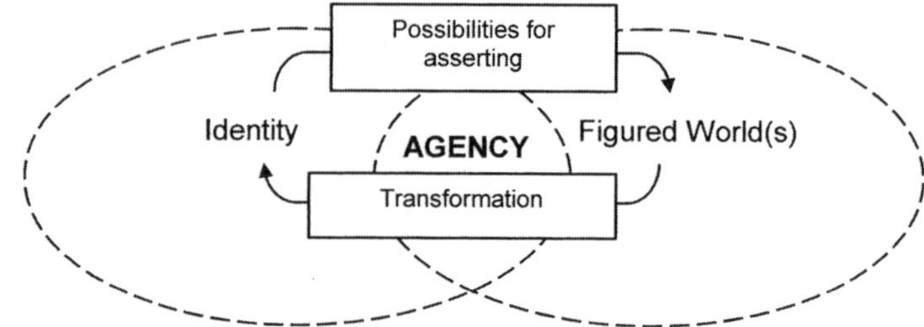

FIGURE 5.1. The relationship between student agency, identity, and figured worlds

participation in figured worlds people can reconceptualize who they are, or shift who they understand themselves to be, as individuals or members of collectives. Through this figuring, individuals also come to understand their ability to craft their future participation, or agency, in and across figured worlds" (p. 120). These "as if" worlds are created and sustained by how people figure themselves within them. These worlds offer new and different possibilities for how people work to figure themselves (i.e., trying out new identities that can help transform contexts) and be figured (i.e., how contexts themselves transform identities). Agency is at once the possibility of imagining and asserting a new self in a figured world at the same time it is about using one's identity to imagine a new and different world. This stance differs from the structure-agency dialectic, which asserts a persistence of deeply embedded relations of inequalities (Ahearn 2001). What makes this a more compelling alternative to the structure-agency dialectic presented in sociological terms is in how figured worlds call attention to the real and imagined nature of these worlds, directly implicating the locally instanced nature of identity work in the construction of agency (see Figure 5.1).

Holland offers the example of participation in Alcoholics Anonymous to make her case for the dialectical relationship between agency, identity, and figured worlds. She states that, "In AA meetings participants tell stories about their lives before they joined the organization. . . . They come to name themselves, and often to see themselves, as 'alcoholics' and not just drinkers. All these elements of AA are meaningful in, relevant to, and valued (or not) in relation to a frame of meaning, a virtual world, a world that has been figured" (p. 51). It is this very juxtaposition of what is real and what is imagined that offers a tool not only for unpacking the instanced work of agency but also for realizing the problematic nature of that work in how power and position facilitate and constrain such possibilities.

On initial entry into a figured world, novices gain social positions that are accorded by the established members of that world. Such "positional identities" (Holland et al. 2001, 125) are inextricably entangled with power, status, and rank. In addition, there is a set of appropriate dispositions tagged alongside positional identities. How novices choose to accept, engage, resist, or ignore such cues will shape their developing identity-in-practice and will determine the boundaries of their authoring space, which is driven by a sense of agency. In the struggle to establish an identity in a new figured world, it is important to consider the influence of the other worlds that one simultaneously inhabits.

In the learning sciences, a growing number of researchers believe that, in order to shed light on how students actually engage in learning, it is imperative to look at opportunities to author and enact identities to understand the interactions and potential tensions between student and school and/or disciplinary identities (Brickhouse, Lowery, and Schultz 2000; Carlone 2004) as well as between learning and engagement in both informal (Nasir and Hand 2008) and formal (Brown, Reveles, and Kelly 2005) ways. Take, for example, the recent work of Nasir and Hand (2008). In this study, the authors argue for the importance of practice-related identities in when and how youth engage in basketball and math. They make the point that classroom math, compared with the basketball team, yields lower levels of engagement and thus less meaningful learning because youth have limited access to the domain, constrained opportunities to take up integral roles, and fewer legitimate modes of self-expression. Who one is and who one has the opportunity to become—as made possible or not through access, role-playing, and expression—fundamentally shape the process of learning. Yet opportunities to develop and draw upon practice-related identities for meaningful learning can be constrained by the very figured worlds in which they operate. Take, for example, Brickhouse and Potter's (2001) case studies of urban girls that reveal how girls access rich networks of science/technology resources including, as Nasir and Hand might say, access to the domain, role-playing, and self-expression. Yet, such domain-specific practice-related identities for some girls carry little authority when those enacted identities do not reflect the values of school-mediated engagement. Successful participation in school science or technology, despite a lack of resources in the home environment, can be better facilitated when students have a science-related identity they can fall back on. One of the primary claims made in this study is that students who aspire to scientific competence while not desiring to take on aspects of the identities associated with membership in school science communities often face difficulties and even school failure.

Thus the idea that identity work involves the participation of others and the social worlds they inhabit signals how youth may grapple with the sociohistorical and cultural politics that motivate identity work and frame participation within and across figured worlds.

The Figured Worlds of School Subjects

This culturally situated approach to agency suggests that how individuals value activity depends, in part, upon the purposes and goals of that activity, its relationship to local knowledge and resources, and the relative positions of power of the agents within that setting. Sharma's (2008) work with students in India highlights how youth draw upon their experiences with household electrical circuits to selectively negotiate new positions in school science discourse. However, the youth also purposefully positioned themselves as conforming to the norm of passive learners when classroom activity marginalized resources from the figured worlds of home and community.

Issues of power and position matter in how youth leverage resources towards making change, as we see with Sharma's students. Indeed, we desire to struggle more to foreground the role that a critical awareness of the world and the social, cultural, and political power dynamic therein play in how youth construct themselves as agents. Yet, also cutting across Sharma's thesis is the idea that knowledge of the material world matters and is selectively used by agents to assert differential positions in a science classroom.

To write about "science agency" demands that we layer onto our understandings of how identity and figured worlds dialectically interact, the role of science as a range of contexts and tools for enacting agency. As a context, science serves as its own "as if" world, allowing students the space to take up new identities and practices for tackling questions normally constitutive of others. Yet, with science as a tool, by engaging in the knowledge, practices, and identities in science in embodied ways,

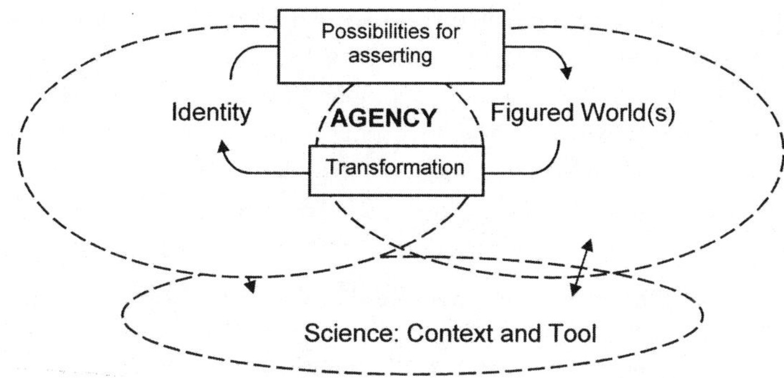

FIGURE 5.2. Agency with and in science

youth can also transform the worlds they traverse, which includes the "as if" world of science. Thus, agency with and in science implies that students use the knowledge, practice, and context of science to develop their identities, to advance their positions in the world, and/or to alter the world towards what they envision as more just (see figure 5.2).

The Figured Worlds of GET City

GET City (Green Energy Technology in the City) is a "voluntary" science/technology/social club for youth aged 10 to 14. The program began in summer 2007 with 20 students and currently enrolls 40 youth. GET City is funded by the National Science Foundation and holds dual goals: the fostering of deep and meaningful learning among urban youth in the areas of advanced information technologies (including data acquisition, management and analysis tools, and communication tools) and the science and engineering of green energy issues. As a weekly after-school program at the Boys and Girls Club, it is also a social space for youth to congregate and talk about friends, music, school, and other social experiences that matter to them. The club largely serves youth from minority and low-income backgrounds. Because GET City also revolves around the use of an advanced wireless laptop cart, the youth who participate use their access to the computers to gain status among Club youth as well as to foster the social nature of the program by using the program space to afford access to email, YouTube, and other youth-oriented e-spaces.

We use the term "voluntary" in quotes rather purposefully. While we openly recruited youth between the ages of 10 and 14 to voluntarily participate, adult staff at the club, including the President, also informed other youth that they "had to participate." For example, a sixth-grade boy who was doing very poorly in school and facing difficult circumstances at home was told by the club president to join GET City in the hope of giving him a positive experience in an academic and social environment. In terms of the number of students, we were limited by the number of laptops available. We wanted every student to be able to work on her/his personal laptop. We ended up with a diverse group of GET City youth with differing levels of academic success in school and interest in science and GET City.

GET City is housed in the "club room," which is a multipurpose room serving as cafeteria, auditorium, and classroom space. With movable walls, it can be split into 3 smaller rooms, though GET City regularly uses two-thirds of the space for meetings. The room is spartan, but displays foldable tables and chairs, a white board, three flags (US, state, and club) and a piano. The room is located off the main social area where kids of all ages (5–18 years) hang out or line up to the canteen to buy candy or hotdogs. This social space opens up to the game room, the bathrooms, the computer room, the canteen, and the hallway that leads to the gym, the teen room, and the children's room. To state that it is always bustling with activity would be an understatement. The result is that GET City is positioned in the center of activity. Noise from the social space leaks into the room, and there is constant movement between these spaces, as youth excuse themselves momentarily to get food from the canteen, use the bathroom, and leave for a few moments to see friends not in GET City. At the same time, the location also gives GET City status, with youth knocking on the door asking when they can join GET City.

Another important dimension to the location of GET City is that by virtue of being housed at the Boys and Girls Club and not in a school building, the program operates on the students' turf. The Boys and Girls Club is where they rule—socially—and arguably may be the most important figured world of their lives apart from school. A recent survey we conducted with the youth shows that 92% of the youth in GET City have participated in the Boys and Girls Club since they were in the sixth grade, with most of the youth having participated in the club since third or fourth grade. Nearly all of the students, on average, attend the club 4 days a week for three to four hours a day (4 pm–7 pm), although many stay until closing time (9 pm). The main reasons youth state for joining the club are summed up by Camden, age 13—"[I] have been coming here since I was six years old. What I like about the club is that it keeps you from getting into trouble"—and Le'Don, age 14—"I have been coming here for 3 years and I enjoy being around kids where I can be myself."

Youth who do not necessarily have a lot of power or position in school do have that at the Club, and they can use that position to barter for how they participate in GET City, something that they may not be able to do in their classroom. For example, a group of girls made a case for why they should be able to write their PowerPoint presentations in "youth speak" and "hip hop language," forms of discourse that include new words, or old words with new meanings, abbreviations, combinations of numbers and letters, and symbols, often all in lowercase letters (e.g., u r gr8). For example, D'Amani's PowerPoint is peppered with statements such as "Im goin to da 7th grade and I go 2 valley magnet skool" and "Ma fave subject iz lang. artz!!! I like cuz I can be creative!!!" Yet discursive patterns are related not just to forms of talk, but also to how the youth blend their talk about science and their lives in ways that frame their roles in GET City, as was evident in the titles that youth gave to their UHI videos: *We Be Burnin'* and *Where Da Heat Go?*

While GET City is a formal after-school program, where attendance is structured and there are rules for conduct and participation, it is a hybrid space that skews more towards the youth's worlds with different stakes. GET City takes place at the Boys and Girls Club, the social domain of the youth. Youth do not receive grades as they do in school. They are not ranked and their success is not metered by high stakes exams, as is common in their schooling experience. As teachers, we work to forge a more collaborative relationship with youth than is often found in schools. Youth call us by our first names, and we actively solicit their help in negotiating and co-planning activities. We also have the freedom from standards and district curricular requirements such that if student interests dictate that we spend more time than intended on a particular area, we have the freedom to do so without worry of penalty.

GET City also brings youth into close contact—through science—with members of the public. In their investigations into the energy crisis, they interviewed the mayor's deputy, presented their public service announcement to the local state representative, and premiered their documentaries to scientists and engineers at the local university. In the unit that followed the UHI, the youth investigated the issue around the "energy

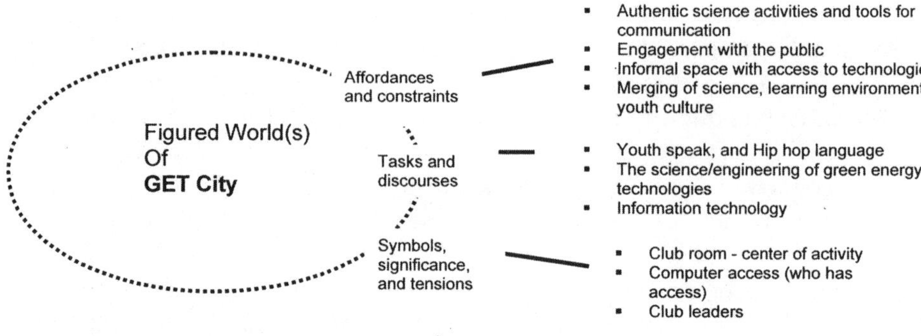

FIGURE 5.3. Figured world of GET City

crisis" and what it would mean, two generations down the road, should energy consumption continue to escalate. They created 30-second and 60-second public service announcements using iMovie, and their public service announcements have been televised on their local CBS affiliate station. Some of the youth also proposed that we conduct another UHI investigation in a bigger, more built-up city four hours away, as a comparison to what they found in River City. In this sense, doing science in GET City is framed around how and why one might want to engage in discourse with a broader range of people about why green energy technologies matter. This last point serves as both a tension and an affordance in that the youth have a chance to engage science in ways that are authentic, but at the same time, they experience real pressures to accomplish meaningful tasks that can often take on a school feel (i.e., editing text, making sense of scientific ideas, figuring out how to represent data) (see Figure 5.3).

A Glance at the Content Story Line: Is River City a UHI?

The UHI phenomenon was explored with the GET City youth during the five-week unit during June and July 2007. The youth met three times a week (Monday, Wednesday, and Friday), for 2.5 hours a day (1 pm–3:30 pm). First, we asked them to consider whether River City is a UHI and how we might find out. Because none of the youth had ever heard of this concept before (as we anticipated), we asked them to consider the question: Where would you rather be on a hot summer day, standing in the middle of a mall parking lot or under a shady tree? An animated debate followed, raising a set of relevant issues: A mall parking lot would be hot and uncomfortable but a desired location because it meant you were heading to an air-conditioned mall to shop. A shady tree would be cooler and relaxing but possibly boring with no proximity to air conditioning, shopping, and cold drinks. Immediately, the youth pushed beyond the intended science question of which decontextualized space would be cooler and thus more comfortable, to the more complex consideration of how these spaces are situated physically and socially with everyday desires and practices.

In the next three sessions, the youth investigated the idea of UHI through a series of controlled experiments that uncovered the relationship between surfaces, temperature, and building design. Our purpose was to engage the youth in using the scientific process to learn that when various surfaces are exposed to similar environmental conditions, surface temperatures may vary because of differences in thermal properties among the surface types. We also wanted them to consider how the use of light-colored roofs and ground surfaces may help reduce UHI effects. The youth were then charged with building model homes out of dark- and light-colored poster board, and systemically and repeatedly recording indoor and outdoor air temperatures in a variety of youth-determined locations around the club property using digital thermometers. They then constructed bar graphs representing their average results and built theories about the relationship between surface types and temperature. For example, Jeremy offered this explanation: "In this experiment a black house in the shade outside was 77 degrees Fahrenheit but in the sun it was 105.4 Fahrenheit. The outdoor temperature was 77.6 Fahrenheit in the shade and 98.9 Fahrenheit in the sun. This is important because if we had lighter colored houses it would not be as hot. If we had a rooftop garden it may not be as hot and it would help absorb carbon dioxide."

Next, we engaged the youth in exploring the relationship between land cover and surface temperature. Our original lesson design was to have the students build model landscapes, such as a simulated city with a high percentage of land space covered with building and streets or a simulated park with high percentages of green space, and then to repeat the experiments conducted with their homes. Our intended goals with this lesson were to help the youth distinguish the three main types of "urban" environments–urban, suburban, and rural–by learning characteristic land-cover types, and then investigating the effects of different land covers on local air temperatures. We wanted this to build up to the youth predicting surface and air temperatures from aerial photos showing various land-cover types found in River City.

However, when we initiated the conversation around land cover, the youth were, on the one hand, intensely interested and somewhat knowledgeable about the differences in land-cover and surface temperature—indeed their talk about the heat in parking lots, playgrounds, and asphalt basketball courts framed our talk. On the other hand, they were disdainful of the idea of building more models. They became quite keen on really "seeing" the difference for "real." Using their suggestions, we replanned the curriculum to explore the land-cover of the River City community using geographic information systems (GIS) and to predict which areas of River City may exhibit the UHI effect due to the built environment (Field notes, June 2007). This approach allowed us to introduce youth to spatial thinking through GIS (Google Earth), and to give them voice in how we constructed our investigation. Youth were to select a geographic area in Google Earth, document its location, print the map, and provide an explanation for why their site might exhibit the UHI effect. Through voting, we selected two locations to conduct our work: downtown River City and Eagle Island, a local park with a lake and wooded trails. Through their selection of these two locations that would most likely present a big contrast in temperature measurements, geographical features, and population density, the youth demonstrated their understanding of the relationship between land cover and the UHI effect.

As a group, we designed a set of data generation strategies to help prove or disprove their hypothesis. The youth generated the following ideas, which were directly modeled on their in-class experiments: (1) temperature recording in multiple sites, in both sun and shade; (2) measurements to determine square footage of built areas versus green areas; and (3) documentation of the nature of the built and green spaces (i.e., kinds of buildings, colors of roofs, vegetation). However, a small number of students lobbied to "talk to" people who worked or lived in these buildings to see if they could "feel the heat" radiated by the human-built structures. Thus we also added to the design: (4) interviews with residents and workers in these spaces about their "heat island" experiences; and (5) photographs of critical design factors in their environment.

Because of time constraints, we visited just one of these sites, which was downtown River City. The youth worked in three groups. Each group was assigned an adult leader, a youth group leader, a recorder/interviewer, a measurement keeper (temperature and space, using digital thermometer and laser measuring tape), a camera crew, and a photographer. The youth had prepared for the investigation by listing questions they wanted to ask community members. Some of these questions were "Do you like it at downtown River City in the summer?," "Do you know what an urban heat island is?," "Where in River City do you think will be an urban heat island?," and "How do you stay cool in the summer?" (Field notes, student handouts, 2007). While we encouraged them to think about how they might "talk science" with the residents and workers they interviewed, the youth themselves were concerned with how the UHI phenomenon might position them through issues of comfort and accessibility to both the science ideas and their bodies, as is evidenced by the questions they generated.

During the two hours, the youth conducted their experiments, interviewed individuals, and took pictures. Each group followed a different route or pattern. Some interviewed individuals who worked in the state legislature, while others interviewed workers in the state capital building and police officers.

Our original plan was to have students write up their results in a format that could be presented to the mayor's office. However, the students became very excited about their video footage and they expressed an interest in being able to do something with their video. We have had success in the past in working with youth in creating video documentaries, so we offered that as an option to the students with the requirements that the documentary (1) present their data findings, (2) educate others about the UHI effect, and (3) be 10 minutes or less.

Using an iterative process of storyboarding, video editing, and concept-mapping, the youth produced three video documentaries: (1) *Where Da Heat Go?*, (2) *We Be Burnin'*, and (3) *We're Hot! What about You?* (http://www.getcity.org/UHI.html). The minidocumentaries featured the students investigating the UHI phenomenon in the downtown area of their city with temperature sensors, laser tape measuring devices, observations, and interviews they conducted with members of the commu-

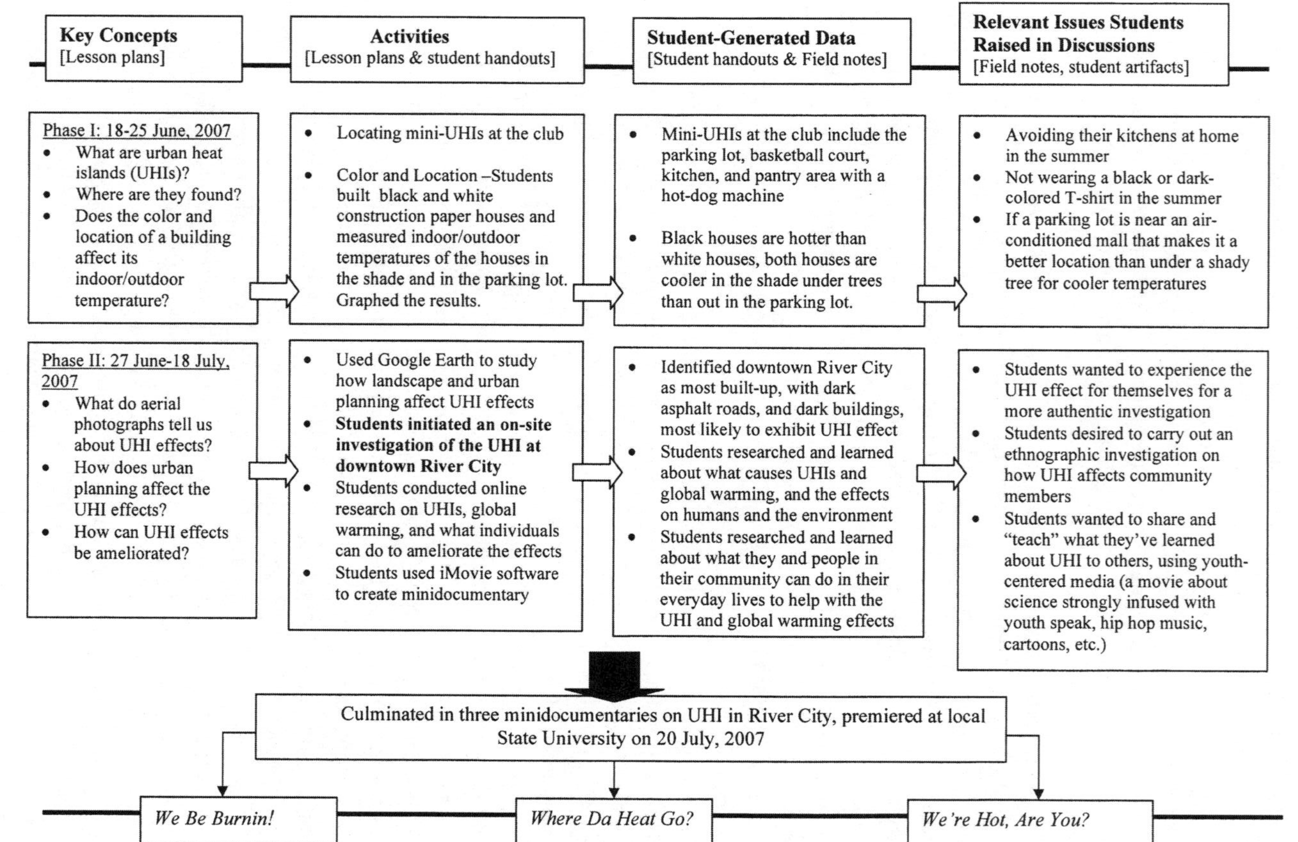

FIGURE 5.4. Data flowchart of UHI investigation process at the Boys and Girls Club

nity. The documentaries were the final, culminating product from the students' investigation and are representative of the youth's issues and concerns about UHI that spanned their investigation (see Figure 5.4). They incorporated the data students generated during the five-week unit (i.e., images, figures, and graphs produced from experiments conducted) as well as youth culture (i.e., music selections, discourse, etc.).

Critical Science Agency: Becoming Community Science Experts

We stated earlier that agency with and in science involves a critical awareness of the role science plays in the world and a critical awareness of the world itself, alongside understandings of scientific ideas and ways of thinking that can be used toward making a difference in the world. Yet we also stated that how these actions are taken and the meanings they carry are situated in the contexts that generate them. As we sought to operationalize agency as the dialectic relationship between the expression of identity and the figured worlds in which one moves, we began to see the importance of how youth represented themselves in GET City, and in particular within the context of the video documentaries, one of the most public displays of their efforts. It is from this perspective that we argue that the youth assert themselves as becoming Community Science Experts. We use the phrase Community Science Expert (CSE) to impart the idea that the youth actively position themselves as individuals who are knowledgeable in science, and in particular about the UHI phenomenon—in what it is, in how to generate and interpret evidence about the phenomenon at the local level, and in why this is important for their community to understand. To make sense of how the youth did so, we first share an extended vignette, *Where Da Heat Go?*

Where Da Heat Go? is a scientific documentary (8 minutes 41 seconds long) produced by four students: Jeremy, Shernice, Naomi, and Kathy, all of whom were rising sixth graders. Two of the students (Jeremy and Naomi) had an interest in science and were set to start at the science and engineering–focused middle school in the fall, and the other two (Kathy and Shernice) spoke passionately about how science is for nerds, except in GET City, and were set to attend a middle school for the arts and a zoned non-themed middle school respectively:

SHERNICE: Sometimes I like to be scientific, but sometimes I don't. I don't like to be scientific. Most of my friends are cool and you be scientific and they think you are a geek.

KAY (interrupting): We don't think that.

SHERNICE (forcefully): At my school. OK!? I kind of do like to be scientific here because it makes me look like I know it all and that is kind of fun.

KATHY: Well, at my school? No! Well, because just like Shernice I am not scientific around my friends because at my school it doesn't matter. (Interview, October 2007)

While Jeremy and Naomi wanted to be in GET City, Kathy was told by the club president she needed to join, and Shernice then joined to share more social space with Kathy. Table 5. 1 shows the breakdown of the main sections of *Where Da Heat Go?*

This vignette reveals how youth take seriously their commitment to developing and sharing an understanding of the UHI effect and its impact on human and environmental health and global sustainability. If we unpack the vignette, we begin to see that there are several mechanisms the youth leveraged to assert themselves with and in science. While we use the video as the focal point in this analysis, it is important to remember that the video represents a culmination of several weeks of work and decision making. They pointed out common misconceptions about UHIs with the opening interviews—that UHIs are real islands and that UHIs cannot exist where it rains. They offered scientific explanations tailored to their context and drawing upon a range of scientific evidence, including primary evidence they generated and data available from the Environmental Protection Agency. They juxtaposed select musical lyrics with scientific discourse to hone in on what they considered to be the critical ideas and the timely imperative such ideas raise, such as in their penultimate scene with the Black Eyed Peas, "Where Is the Love?" (2003) featuring the lyrics "We've only got one world."

An analysis of our data reveals that while youth used a variety of means to assert their knowledge in science, we can find at least two patterns that reflect powerful mechanisms by which students assert themselves as Community Science Experts (CSEs) through appropriating the ideas, discourses, and practices of science: (1) authoring an investigation and (2) taking an expert stance. These mechanisms are powerful because they show that, as CSEs, the youth are knowledgeable about science, and that they consistently blend what they know

TABLE 5.1. **Main Sections from the Minidocumentary *Where Da Heat Go?***

Section Focus	Screen Shot	Text/Subtitle	Narration/Music
Part 1: Setting up the movie, youth present themselves and ask questions about UHI	Black screen	Blue text, GET City: Where Da Heat Go	Chris Brown's "Run It" (2005)
	Group's photo	Text "The Heat" layered on top of photo	
	Black screen	Look at what people think . . . . . . Do they really know????? Is downtown River City an Urban Heat Island?	
Part 2: Youth interview adult community members in downtown River City about UHI, highlight adults not knowing about UHI	Shots of youth interviewing community members at the Capitol	Exemplar interview transcript: Youth: Is River City an urban heat island? Tour Guide: No. I wouldn't consider that, no. Youth: Why not? Tour Guide: Why? Umm, just because we're in the city, we have more businesses down here, which would mean, yes, we would have more heat, but we get a lot of rain in Michigan and we're right in the middle of two huge lakes. . . . No, I don't think we are heated.	Brief musical interludes with snippets from Mims' "This Is Why I'm Hot" and Buster Poindexter's "Hot Hot Hot"
	Black screen	"I don't know!" caption that follows each interview vignette	
Part 3: Presenting scientific evidence about the UHI effect	Downtown area data: temperatures recorded in the sun and shade at various "green" and "built" points around the Capitol property	Jeremy offers an explanation of the experiments and how they provide evidence for the UHI effect.	Musical interlude between data presentations with Buster Poindexter's "Hot Hot Hot"
	A series of pictures of the model houses the students built earlier in the summer		
	Image of Jeremy punching himself in the face while making a funny face is shown with the subtitle "Expert Reporter."		

(continued)

TABLE 5.1. ***(continued)***

Section Focus	Screen Shot	Text/Subtitle	Narration/Music
Part 4: Youth explain UHI phenomenon	Pictures of major urban centers in the United States where the UHI effect has been documented by the EPA (i.e., Atlanta and Los Angeles), and other cities that matter to the youth (i.e., Detroit and River City)	Shernice: An urban heat island is where urban heat air and surfaces have temperatures that are up to 10 degrees F higher than the surrounding natural land covers. Downtown River City is an example of an urban heat island. Kathy: Consequences of an urban heat island. Cities experiences higher relates of illnesses and death due to dehydration. Approximately 7,421 deaths occurred between 1979 through 1998 due to urban heat islands. Shernice: Consequences of heat islands to the environment. Heat islands produce ozone pollution, which provides great damage to vegetation and local ecosystems. Together: HEAT ISLANDS ARE A BIG NO NO! WHAT CAN YOU DO ABOUT IT?	Rihanna's "Umbrella" (2007), a current hit hip hop favorite, is playing. Youth selected this song because some UHIs have been documented to create their own weather patterns causing more rain to fall on the eastern edges of these cities, as the youth learned by exploring data offered by the EPA (http://www.epa.gov/hiri)
Part 5: Youth present reasons why we should care about UHI and what action we can take	Pictures of polar bear families and their voice-over focus on the relationship between UHIs and global warming and its impact on biodiversity	Text: "Polar bears are drowning because the arctic ice is melting."	"Where Is the Love" (Black Eyed Peas 2003), where the lyrics describe that "something is wrong with the world" and how we need to act to turn it around
	Pictures showing planting trees, riding a bicycle	Explanations on "what can we do about it"	R. Kelly's "World's Greatest" (2002), suggesting that kids can and will make this needed difference

and can do with who they are and desire to be, tenets central to developing agency.

Authoring an Investigation

The youth authored the UHI investigation in three ways: (1) insisting on a real-life, community-centered investigation; (2) framing the UHI challenge by highlighting personal accounts; and (3) positioning oneself as an agent.

INSISTING ON A REAL-LIFE, COMMUNITY-CENTERED INVESTIGATION. As teachers, we had initially authored a summer program on UHIs. The participating students performed the requisite activities and experiments we had designed. They reflected and blogged on questions such as "What color T-shirt would you wear on a hot day to keep cool?" They made predictions about what building material properties might have an impact on ambient indoor and outdoor air temperature. They discussed images of the main types of environments–urban, suburban, and rural–and made conjectures about characteristics of land-cover types. They built model cardboard houses out of different-colored poster board and recorded temperatures in sunny and shady locations, graphed and compared results, and built theories. After building cardboard houses, several of the youth indicated a desire to not build more models, but to investigate whether this phenomenon was actually real in their city. They wanted to do an on-site investigation of their community.

Doing an on-site investigation grew out of one boy's fascination with "thermal images." The group had taken what they thought were "thermal images" of their houses in the sun and shade (using the "thermal camera" effect in their iSight camera[1]). They had recalled similar thermal images of cities we had shared previously to engage the youth in conversation around thermal stratification in the built environment. They shared their pictures as part of their data set, setting off a conversation about whether any images of River City existed that revealed its thermal stratification, but no one could find any on the Internet.

Documenting the UHI effect in River City had been part of our summer plan, and the youth were aware that toward the end of week three we would make field trips to various locations in the city to col-

1. iSight's thermal effect works off brightness, not heat, so this really is not accurate.

lect a set of data parallel to our initial experiments. Yet the talk that initially emerged from the group of boys around their "thermal image" set off a cascade of requests to do the field trips now! We decided to listen to their pleas and engaged them in dialog around "what would they do" to figure out whether River City exhibited the UHI effect. While it may very well be that the real impetus for getting on to the trips was to get out of the classroom, embedded within their negotiation were indicators that they understood the content well enough to drive the investigation—but equally as important, they were the ones uniquely positioned to know how and why this content mattered to them and to the residents of their city.

As discussed earlier, after selecting a portion of downtown that contained to them the most densely built spaces, they produced a viable scheme for gathering useful evidence. This included taking multiple temperature readings at various locations, measuring the square footage of the built versus natural land cover, and documenting the nature of the built and natural land cover (i.e., white concrete versus black asphalt). We encouraged them to add another element: interviewing local residents and workers, in ethnographic fashion, to gather ethnographic evidence for human impact. The youth took up this suggestion enthusiastically and spent time writing potential interview questions and practicing on one another. Before embarking on the field trip, the youth also practiced their interview skills with the adults at the club.

FRAMING THE UHI PHENOMENON THROUGH PERSONAL ACCOUNTS. As discussed in the section on the content storyline, the youth lobbied to include interviews and photographs as part of their data-gathering strategies of the UHI phenomenon in the downtown area. Their prepared questions included a focus on how the UHI phenomenon might frame residents and workers' experiences. In the actual data-gathering process, the youth expanded upon these questions such that, when residents or workers did not know about the UHI phenomenon but could explain how or why they might feel hot in the downtown area on a sunny day, the youth would integrate a discussion of what they knew about the UHI phenomenon with such feelings, in what seemed to be an effort both to personally connect with residents and workers' stories and to engage them in thinking about UHIs.

In the quote below, Ron and Kaden are talking with the Parking Enforcement Officer (PEO) whom they encountered while gathering data downtown. While neither boy explicitly shares his knowledge of UHIs at this point in the interview, they seem to be using what they know about UHIs to direct the conversation to focus on how the UHI effect can have a significant impact on one's occupation. When Kaden asks about the cars, he pushes the Parking Enforcement Officer to reflect on how the car's air-conditioning system may contribute to the UHI effect. Given that the youth had learned about how the use of cars, factories, and air conditioning add more heat to the dome of elevated temperatures over a city, we see this question loaded with implication. Knowing about UHIs matters not only in being able to describe what a UHI is, but also in understanding the relationship between the causes and effects of UHIs and everyday living and work life.

PEO: It was pretty hot about three weeks ago. It was already 94 degrees with a heat index of 100. And I was working the [community college] area and it was really hot. I can see it got hot.

RON: What do you think is the impact?

PEO: Well, I guess it would impact as far as me walking the streets and the sidewalks radiating the heat. People leaving on vacation for the summer, to get out of the heat from their jobs, so I don't have that many areas to patrol. So I think those are two ways.

KADEN: Do you have a car, like those little cars that you drive around?

PEO: Yes, I do.

KADEN: And, do they absorb more heat when you have your air on or off?

PEO: We don't have air conditioning on our scooters. They are three wheel scooters and they don't have a/c. We could have a/c on them, but the city does not supply that. Right now we are parking them for most of the day. We only drive to our destination and back to our check point.

That youth turned the added-on component of interviewing community members into the centerpiece of their argument provides further evidence of how they value these personal accounts. In each of the documentaries, an average of 2:08 minutes was used in presenting community member interviews (of an average total of 8:23 minutes). In each documentary, the interviews were presented primarily in the first half and used to set the case for the UHIs, by presenting common misconceptions, showing how UHIs affected people differently because of occupation, and showing a lack of awareness on the issue (see Table 5.2).

Take, for example, the opening scenes of *We Be Burnin'*. Similar to

TABLE 5.2. **Summary of Minidocumentary Content**

	Da Heat (8:41)	Burnin' (8:44)	We're Hot! (7:44)
Community Dialogs	Female tour guide (0:38-1:00) Man visting Capitol (1:10-1:44) Man walking to work (1:51- 2:04) Woman and friend walking downtown (2:11-2:23) Two women walking downtown (6:15-6:45)	Male Capitol building worker (1:54-3:02) Two guys standing under a tree during lunch hour (3:34-4:43)	Female parking enforcer (1:51-2:20) Female tour guide (2:22-2:38) Male police officer (2:50-3:35) Visiting family from Texas (4:12-4:27) Female Capitol staffer (4:27-5:18)
Supporting comments and ideas to directly educate community members	Cierra pointing to trees (1:20) Cierra referring to downtown River City (2:00)	Explanations of UHI effect, as it relates to particular people's occupation (3:11-3:31)	Probing about vehicular use and heat emission (2:10-2:20) Impact on police officers' jobs (2:50-3:35) Offers definition of UHI (4:34-4:41)
Types and kinds of misconceptions noted in community member knowledge	Islands (bodies of land surrounded by water) are urban heat islands (2:11) Urban heat islands cannot exist where it rains (38:14) Urban heat islands cannot exist where there are lakes (1:00) A highly populated area in a city does not contribute to the UHI effect (1:10) General lack of knowledge (1:51)	General lack of knowledge (1:54-3:02; 3:34-4:43)	UHI effect must be present 100% of the time to be a serious consideration Urban heat islands cannot exist where it rains (2:22) Urban heat islands cannot exist where there are lakes (2:26) A highly populated area in a city does not contribute to the UHI effect General lack of knowledge (3:40)
Foci of specific UHI claims	UHI definition (3:37-3:42; 3:44-3:49) Human consequences (3:54-4:00) Environmental consequences (4:00-4:09) Cities where UHI effect is known (4:15-4:35) Recommendations for UHI effect reduction (4:49-5:32)	UHI definitions (2:10-2:17; 4:04-4:12; 5:02-5:20) Global warming explanation (5:54-6:04) Human consequences (5:21-5:47) Environmental consequences (6:05-6:22) Recommendations for UHI effect reduction (7:10-7:32)	UHI definition (4:34-4:41; 5:38-5:59) Human consequences (5:59-6:07) Causes of UHIs (6:08-6:29) Explanation of investigation (1:37-1:49) How to mitigate the UHI effect (6:29-6:35)

Forms of evidence used to support claims (including types and quantities of representations)	Temperatures in downtown locations taken in sun and shade, in various stages of "built" spaces (2:57-3:06; 6:58-7:35) Explanation of experiments conducted with graphical representations of findings (3:06-3:18, 3:18-3:27) Graphical representations of temperature stratification (3:22-3:27) Figure demonstrating UHI effect (3:42-3:44) Infrared images of five major cities (3:44-3:49) Images of the built environment (4:15-4:35) References to EPA findings on UHIs (3:44-3:49)	Map of River City (0:05-0:09) Explanations of research roles: temperature taker, photographer, etc. (0:27-0:57) Temperature readings in various locations (1:13-1:29) Images of UHI effects Cartoon images of a hot earth (5:48-5:53) "Expert" scientist opinions on UHI and global warming (5:02-5:47; 5:54-6:22)	Temperature recordings (0:33-0:52) Observations (0:59-1:24) Images of the sun (0:52) Cartoon images of a hot and polluted earth (6:36) Images of selves collecting data (digital thermometers, charts, etc.) (0:33-0:52) Google Earth Fly into River City (highlighting built environment) (0:00-0:26)
Localized explanations	Why you should care (3:54-4:00; 4:35-4:49) How it affects River City in particular (0:00-2:23; 3:42) What kids have to do with it (4:49-5:32)	Explanations of UHI effect, as it relates to particular people's occupation (3:11-3:31)	How UHIs impact workers in a variety of occupations
Affective triggers	Photos of people and animals, and music to evoke emotional responses (polar bears, children, polluted environment) (4:35-4:49) Behind the wacky scenes (5:32-8:41) Music— Run It! (Chris Brown) Irreplacable (Beyonce) This Is Why I'm Hot (Mims) Hot Hot Hot (Buster Poindexter) Umbrella (Rihanna) Where Is the Love? (Black Eyed Peas) World's Greatest (R. Kelly)	Photos of people and animals, and music to evoke emotional responses (polar bear with cubs, polluted environment) (1:48-1:50; 6:23-7:09) Music— Mercy Mercy Me (Marvin Gaye) Umbrella (Rihanna) The Power (Snap) Stop! In the Name of Love! (Supremes) Please Remember (LeAnn Rimes)	Beads of sweat (3:40) Animals (2:50; 4:03) Music— The Heat Is On (Glenn Frey) Wish It Would Rain (Temptations) Peanut Butter Jelly Time (Buckwheat Boyz)

Da Heat, the movie starts off with the title "WE BE BURNIN'!!!" in yellow block text against a black background, followed by the question, "What's wrong with this planet?" Marvin Gaye's (1971) song "Mercy Mercy Me" plays loudly in the background. A map of Michigan showing River City and Detroit is then shown, with the text "River City . . . That's where we live!" Another question pops up, "Why is it so hot???" against a background of a photograph showing an adult staff member at the Boys and Girls Club, Anna, looking down at Kay, outside the club on a very bright sunny afternoon, positioned to suggest that she is asking Kay the question. Another scene is a screen shot that reads "BURNin', BURNin', BURNin'" against a background photograph of a brilliant sun. Two more questions then are presented, "Do you wonder why we be burnin' in the summer???" followed by "What are people sayin'??" This leads to a series of interviews conducted by Kay. Kay first interviews a worker in the state capitol building. The worker appears hot and sweaty and is sitting in a chair looking a bit tired. When she asks the man to name a UHI and he cannot, she tells him that downtown River City is one. When he laughs with surprise, she asks him whether he knows why it would get so hot in the summer in downtown River City, and the man shakes his head, looking somewhat baffled:

WORKER: [shakes head] Umm, uhh . . . I think, scientifically I don't . . .

KAY: There are trees and there are grass and it helps the heat island effect because, it makes it more shady . . . and instead of everybody being hot and instead of people being, people not like, being, not to like being downtown, they can kind of enjoy it if they just go in the shade.

As we can see in the transcript, how Kay talks about her understandings of UHIs and with whom this expertise is shared differs from school science talk. Kay focuses her talk on how the design of the urban environment can help to mitigate the UHI effect, and how one can find relief from the heat. Given that the man she is interviewing is clearly tired and hot, this explanation positions her as the expert who is trying to help. Kay admittedly has one of the weaker understandings of UHIs of all of the students in the summer program, but she is also the youngest member of the group, being the only ten-year-old in the program.

In each of these examples, we see how the youth use their mini-ethnographies to give perspective to the UHI experience by situating the phenomenon personally. We also see how the youth use the interviews to offer a range of informal insights into the phenomenon. However, if one follows the dialog the youth have with the informants, one can also see a hybrid account of the UHI phenomenon emerging—that is, an account that is scientific in that it presents the viewer with scientific terminology, reasoning, and representations, but also in that it is only made possible by how it is situated by the varied personal accounts.

POSITIONING ONESELF AS AN AGENT. In addition to the mini-ethnographic accounts, both the planning for the downtown experiment and the resultant text in the movies were presented in an active voice with an explicit agent. This is in contrast to traditional science discourse, which favors a passive and more impersonal voice. Schleppegrell (2001) demonstrated that such a discourse imbues scientific language with a sense of technicality and therefore authoritativeness. However, by explicitly situating their text and emphasizing an agent, the youth took a stance and created a sense of urgency and immediacy that demanded a response from the audience. With the montage of polar bear photographs in the last segment of the *We Be Burnin'* movie, the following text accompanied the pictures together with LeAnn Rimes' (2000) song, "Please Remember":

Text	Song Lyrics
POLAR BEARS . . . THEY ARE OUR FRIENDS . . . Please don't kill us.. . . . It's not our fault.. . . . We want to grow up and live.. . . . What can we do to help our friends the polar bears? What can you do to reduce the heat island effect? Everyone can do something!	Goodbye, there's just no sadder word to say And it's sad to walk away with just the memories Who's to know what might have been We'll leave behind a life and time We'll never know again

How the youth highlighted the plight of the polar bears exerts more authority in possibly evoking a response from the audience than would a passive, impersonal presentation of the same information. However, what we think is important is the blending of these personal and emotion-invoking accounts that deeply situate the experience with more formal presentations of what UHIs are—presentations that include the use of real-world data, scientific representations, and scientific terminology—which position the youth as authentic Community Science Experts.

In each of the cases presented and throughout the documentaries, what makes the representation of scientific expertise different from school is the focus on tailoring the knowledge to the perceived needs of the receiver as well as on situating these understandings within the subjective and the everyday. Even in the latter part of the videos, where explanations are meant to be deeply scientific, these explanations are rooted in the personal and meant to connect to the viewer at a visceral level.

As expert reporter Jeremy does in *Da Heat*, as described in the opening vignette, the funky scientists in *We Be Burnin'* offer explanations of the UHI effect, drawing upon scientific discourse combined with emotion-evoking images, scientific representations, and youth imagery. After viewing the scientific speak about health and environmental implications of UHIs, which includes statistics taken from the EPA, five still photographs of polar bears are presented as the spokes-animals of global warming prevention. Subtitles added to the pictures are: "Polar bears . . . They are our friends . . . Please don't kill us . . . It's not our fault . . . We want to grow up and live . . ." The pictures are shown in succession: a pair of bears, a pair of cubs, one lone bear lying on his back, one bear lying on his belly, a mother bear with her cubs. With the pictures, the following scrolling text is added and the whole sequence is coupled with the stanza from LeAnn Rime's song "Please Remember," as shown above.

These juxtapositions of scientific thinking with emotion also draw on the use of music and cadence. The subtitles the girls wrote for the polar bear montage were personal and entreating. The polar bear is presented more as kin (rather than a separate species on a lower hierarchy than humans) with the same needs and rights as human beings—the right to grow up, to live, to not have their habitats destroyed, and to not be driven to extinction. The girls coupled these subtitles and pictures with specifically chosen song lyrics to hint at the possibility of the tragic consequences should the polar bears exist only as a distant memory.

Taking an Expert Stance—Engaging in the Practices of an Expert

Evident in our description, authoring an investigation is the idea that the youth had developed understandings of the UHI phenomenon such that they could share these understandings with others in ways that were accurate, supported with evidence, locally and personally relevant, and demanding of attention and action. In this section, we examine more closely the ways in which youth took an expert stance in asserting themselves as CSEs. In particular, the youth engaged in practices of an expert by:

- Providing a detailed, scientific explanation of UHIs using hybrid discourse
- Supporting their stance on UHI with multiple forms of data, some analyzed by themselves using technology
- Displaying the attitudes of an expert with their work ethic
- Presenting their documentaries to an authentic audience with a Q&A session

In each of the documentaries, the youth offered explanations of the UHI effect and modeled how it impacts human and environmental health. However, while each video asserts an authoritative stance on the topic, each video also waits until approximately halfway through the documentary to provide a concrete explanation. For example, in *We Be Burnin'*, it is at 5:02 (in an 8:44 video) that two of the youth, Michelle and D'Amani, enter the documentary as experts. In response to interviewees who "did not know," the following comment flashes across the screen: "Hmm . . . they're not sure either. . . . Time to talk to some experts!!" Then, the song "The Power" (Muenzing and Anziotti 1990, performed by Snap!) comes on, followed by the titles "Introducing . . . The funky funky fresh scientists—Dr. Michelle & Dr. D'Amani." The two girls, while sitting under a shady tree, state:

MICHELLE: Heat islands are caused when trees and vegetation are displaced by tall buildings and roads. Heat and air are trapped and waste from vehicles, factories, and air conditioning. Heat islands are bad for human health. Between 1979 and 1998, more than 7,421—whew!—deaths result from heat islands. What can we do to help out? Cut down the bad effects of heat islands? How are heat islands related to global warming?

D'AMANI: Global warming is the warming up of the earth's air and surface, with increased temperatures caused by greenhouse gases like carbon dioxide. Climate change can affect human health. Habitats can also change so drastically that animals can become extinct. For example, the polar bears are dying because it is getting too hot at the North Pole. Weather patterns can also change, like the damage Hurricane Katrina caused.

The formal presentation of the UHI concept in the latter part of the documentaries set up an interesting dynamic with respect to knowing science and communicating ideas meaningfully. It seems that on the one hand, youth wanted to foreground the local residents and workers' experiences with "heat" in the urban environment alongside a general lack of knowledge in this area. On the other hand, such a move positioned them as the experts who provided explanations but situated them in locally relevant ways because of their insider status as community members.

As experts, the youth also use a variety of representations to educate the viewer after the stage has been set in the local context. Representations, which serve as symbols, take several forms: scientific representations, such as graphs and figures, that provide a generalized explanation of the phenomenon under investigation; cartoon images that caricature the problem posed by UHIs; pictures of cities that show in real terms how the built environment that supports the UHI phenomenon looks; and images of people and animals meant to evoke feelings and to remind the viewer that understanding and taking action upon UHIs is a matter of life and death.

In both *We Be Burnin'* and *We're Hot*, the youth offered multiple explanations of UHIs in their interview clips that were presented before their more in-depth science explanations, such as Ron did in the example about the staffer. This is more evident in the documentary *We Be Burnin'*, where Kay, the primary interviewer, uses the opportunity of interviewing others to also educate them about UHIs and their relationship to global warming. Each time the interviewee states that they don't know or are somehow baffled by her questions, she offers an explanation in what appears to be an attempt to educate and to allow the conversation to advance their experiences and opinions. In fact, Kay uses this maneuver in each of the three interviews presented in the documentary (see Table 5.1). Thus, being a CSE not only requires the youth to have the scientific knowledge base of the UHI phenomenon but also calls for the students to leverage their identities as community insiders. As insiders, the youth had the skills to engage in and facilitate the conversations with their community interviewees; they strategically drew out from their interviewees the information that was salient to their documentaries.

Being a CSE also cuts against mainstream media's stereotype of low-income urban youth as lazy and disinterested in science. The documentaries show an active curiosity about the UHI phenomenon and a desire to help others learn about its causes and effects. Powerfully, when the youth discussed their products in an interview five months after the experience, the very first words they use to describe them is how the movie made them feel important and powerful, and not lazy, in direct contrast to the memes that frame urban youth in popular culture. By authoring the identity of a CSE, the youth displayed the attitudes and work ethic of experts in being strategic, persistent, and meticulous over the production of their minidocumentaries.

EDNA: Mhmm . . . Naomi, how did making the documentary make you feel?

NAOMI: Oh, it made me feel proud 'cause I know I had put a lot of stuff into movie, in that I actually made a movie, I'm going to be a star . . . and like, it's just a great experience.

EDNA: Shernice, how did making the movie make you feel?

SHERNICE: Um, making the movie made me feel . . . it made me feel good to know that I am a super starrer! And I am a movie starrer! And it made me feel really good that I could do a lot of work, and that I'm really not lazy!

EDNA: Jeremy?

JEREMY: Well, being the director and the founder of the movie . . . it makes me feel very proud that I produced the movie with me FELLOW teammates 'cause they were very good too. . . . But, you know . . . I did A LOT of the work. . . . I'm so proud . . . that the movie can be shown at [the local university].

SHERNICE: Okay, I like the people to think of me as a smart intelligent person, that knows what she's talking about. And, and to think that she's very smart and intelligent.

In an interview conducted five months after the completion of the summer investigation into UHIs, youth could still articulate clearly what a UHI is:

RE: The movie was about UHIs. What do you know or what can you tell me about what a UHI is? We still start with Jeremy.

JEREMY: An urban heat island is when it's 2 to 6 degrees more the surrounding areas because of buildings, black cement areas, and not enough green area.

KAY: [Interrupting Jeremy] Wait, my turn. An urban island is an island, well, not really an island, but it's a place where there is a lot of people so it makes it really hot.

It is worth noting that Kay uses her turn in the group interview to stress that UHIs are an island-like phenomenon in that it's an effect felt in a concentrated area, but that they are not really islands. This was a misconception that she, along with many of the youth, held for quite some time during the summer program.

Additionally, after the youth premiered their documentaries to the engineers, scientists, and science educators, they were asked some rather easy questions, such as "How did you feel making these movies?" When thrown tough, content-oriented questions such as "Why does restoring buildings help to mitigate the UHI effect?," the youth stood their ground and offered science-based reasons, as Shernice did when she answered, "If you restore old buildings, you don't have to cut down more trees to build new buildings. . . . You could just restore the old ones."

In short, youth asserted their community science expertise in ways that made science talk accessible to others by situating scientific talk and

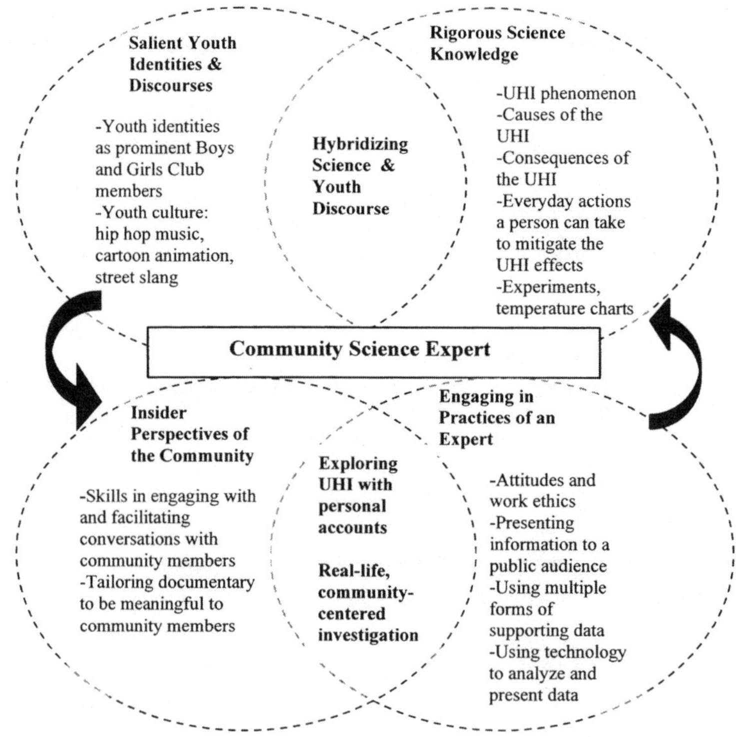

FIGURE 5.5. What it means to be a Community Science Expert

thinking within the workday lives of ordinary people; within the hip hop genre of being cool, stylistic, and fashionable; by being playful yet serious; and by linking their ideas and their thinking with serious life and death concerns. Furthermore, their talk seem oriented toward taking a stance in terms of taking personal responsibility and action. Figure 5.5 shows what is encompassed in being a CSE.

Discussion

We have argued that the youth asserted themselves as CSEs in the figured worlds of GET City by positioning themselves as individuals who are knowledgeable about UHIs and capable of taking action on the basis of this knowledge. Asserting a CSE identity allowed the students a platform in which to engage in scientific ideas and discourses while also offering students the freedom to work and be in their community in ways that mattered to them. Being a CSE was fashioned out of a hybrid discourse that did more than blend the first space of "science" with the second space of the "personal/cultural." It also collapsed the core tensions between being scientific and being agentic that seems to be so prevalent in science learning settings by allowing students to merge the seemingly contradictory roles of producer/critic. Central to the youth's embodied activities, and indeed their performances, as CSEs are the dual and often contradictory roles of being a producer and a critic of science. Often being a producer and being a critic happen together by ascribing new meanings to artifacts and symbols.

With their science documentaries, the youth problematized common symbols in science (or things that carry symbolic meaning) and in so doing, turned their meanings around toward their own purposes. One of the symbols is that of a science expert. The master narrative of science as a discipline typically emphasizes the exclusivity and elitism of scientists. Scientists typically belong to an insular community where specialized knowledge is shared through professional channels, such as scientific journals, and conferences sequestered from the general public. The notion of a CSE is novel and also antithetical to that of traditional (or at least stereotypical) scientists. The distinctly circumscribed way of investigating the physical world in science has resulted in the abstraction of science, making it more alienating to some students (e.g., Lemke 1990; Halliday 1993).

In contrast to this established symbol, the youth authored their role as CSEs dialectically with the community members. By socially situating themselves within the community, the youth were able to co-construct such an identity as the CSE. By engaging in conversation with community members, the youth shared ideas about UHIs with community members, which helped to shape both subsequent interviews the youth conducted, as well as their own understanding of the UHI phenomenon. In somewhat similar ways to the youth in Jurow, Rogers, and Ma's (2008) study on recontextualization models in conversation, by creating opportunities to engage in authentic dialog with community members, youth were able to further advance and situate their explanations of UHIs.

Another symbol the youth critiqued and transformed involved the ways scientific ideas were communicated and represented. Scientific language is often rendered as dense, technical, and abstract. The abstraction of science works especially to obscure concrete life experiences into conceptual entities and generalizations. In all three documentaries, we see that the youth instead chose to specifically place their scientific ideas in context and to situate the meaning of their knowledge claims, rather than to represent ideas removed from context. *Da Heat* presented specific cities with a pronounced UHI effect, such as Atlanta and New York City; *Da Heat* and *We Be Burnin'* focused on a specific animal victim of global warming—the polar bear, using pictures that evoke visceral responses removed from the objectivity of science. *Da Heat* also featured photographs of a man riding his bike as opposed to driving, and children planting trees to ameliorate the UHI effect. All three documentaries offered specific suggestions for individuals to take steps toward mitigating the UHI effect. With these forms of representation, the youth succeeded in localizing a seemingly remote concept of the UHI.

Specific contextualization and situations positioned the youth as both producers and critics of science rather than as mere recipients of scientific ideas. This is further emphasized by the language in their movies, which is heavily grounded in youth genre that stresses the dramatic. We see this operating on two different levels. First, the youth inflected the text they used in their documentaries with that of youth linguistic practices, such as slanging. While B. Brown's (2006) minority students concluded that "it isn't no slang that can be said about [science]" (p. 119) in expressing the discursive conflict they experience with science, the GET City youth succeeded in negotiating for expressing their science ideas in their own ways. This can be seen from the movies, especially with the titles *Where Da Heat Go?* and *We Be Burnin'*. The youth were also very particular with how they wanted the phrases spelled and structured. When first creating the title *Where Da Heat Go?* we had been working with the group to show them how to insert titles into iMovies. When they said their title should be "Where Da Heat Go?" we misinterpreted them and then by way of demonstrating titles typed in "Where Did the Heat Go?" We were immediately corrected that it is not "the" but "da." So we retyped, "Where Did Da Heat Go?" After much laughter we were corrected again, this time with Shernice doing the typing: "Where Da Heat Go?" She told us it has to be that way because whenever it's hot out and she is in the car with her auntie, she would always say "where da air go?" in reference to her nonfunctioning air-conditioning system. In critiquing both symbols, the youth were emphatic in bringing in identities and relationships salient to them—being popular and sociable young adults who speak their own youth-centered language.

These forms of youth speak were evident in their formal scientific explanations as well. When serving as the UHI expert, Ron breaks his cadence of science talk to interject comments regarding how the heat makes you crazy: "An urban heat island is where the air temperature in the urban areas is higher than the rural areas." Ron then looked at Kaden, who was off camera, smiled, and said, "People are makin' faces! I'm gonna getcha." Then Kaden, who is still off camera, can be heard saying, "I recorded that!" Without hesitation and with two fingers pointing at the camera, Ron then says, "See, this is the effect that you get [from a UHI] 'cause people act crazy and insane! The four causes of heat islands are greenhouse gases, displacing trees and vegetation, tall buildings and narrow streets, and waste heat from cars and businesses."

This break in cadence shifts the mood and location of science expertise to be both playful and everyday. This disruption in the traditional science discourse was evident in the other two video documentaries as well. As discussed earlier, both *We Be Burnin'* and *Da Heat* used playful, funky science characters to introduce scientific explanations. Thus, through discourse and discourse disruptions, the youth transcended the technical cadence and register of canonical science and in the process claimed a sense of ownership over the science content.

In producing and critiquing science through the process of making a science documentary, the youth were able to negotiate, within the affordances and constraints of the GET City figured world, to momentarily transform their engagement with science. They problematized established symbols of science, authored alternative identities, and displayed agency in their transforming acts that challenged how science should be presented, contemplated, and understood, not just to their peers, but also to the general public, since they were clear in their intentions that their movies were "not just for kids, but for everybody."

Moving Forward with Agency

The youth in GET City expressed agency with and in science in how they worked to identify and position themselves vis-à-vis the figured worlds of science, their community, and GET City. We have argued that to enact agency with and in science, youth have drawn upon a knowledge of UHIs alongside culturally and socially situated explanations for why UHIs matter and how such concerns might be communicated to others. We have also argued that these understandings are grounded in a critical appreciation of their communities, of their world, and of the role that science can play in them.

Youth engagement with both the vertical and horizontal dimensions of learning was iterative and generative. Developing understandings of UHIs positioned youth to engage a broader audience through emotion and a sense of responsibility in their desire and ability to meaningfully pair content ideas with specific pictures and music selections. Likewise, the youth strategically engaged area workers and residents in personal accounts that valued their experiences while simultaneously reframing them in light of the scientific accounts of the UHI effect. Learning is not just about developing the practices of experts, it is also about re-creating those practices in locally meaningful ways. This stance on learning demands that we consider the role of agency in youth development.

We see that youth's efforts in enacting agency with and in science worked not only to transform their participation in the figured worlds of science, community, and GET City but also to enlarge/transform their identities and spheres of activity and influence within these figured worlds. To enact agency with and in science, youth drew upon resources and relationships available to them across their figured worlds in order to expand what they can do within any of these worlds. They used these resources and relationships to reposition themselves within these communities. At the same time they worked to transform the communities themselves.

Their ideas about studying "real" UHIs rather than only models of them positioned them to engage real community members in actual dialog about UHIs. They talked with legislators, police officers, capitol workers, and residents. They were surprised that, with few exceptions, almost no one in their city knew much about UHIs. In fact, they pointed out when these individuals had incorrect assumptions about UHIs.

By producing high-quality science documentaries intended for audiences broader than themselves, the youth positioned themselves to speak to a wide range of communities that have influence over scientific, political, and educational work. Through a sequence of events with somewhat of a snowballing effect, the youth eventually presented their work to engineers, scientists, science teachers, state representatives, and community foundation officers and rubbed elbows with people who are generally outside their worlds. Their work even provided the evidence needed to win a local foundation award to support doubling the size of the club's mobile learning lab. These activities further worked to increase their visibility and status in the club. By presenting their work to a group of local scientists, engineers, and educators, the youth also expanded their access to the science community. Several of the scientists and engineers were so moved by the documentaries that they have donated time at the club to talk to the youth about professions or to help out with activities.

We also believe that the stories presented in this book suggest that the process of enacting agency also involves a process of co-opting activities to allow youth to express who they are and who they want to be in ways that meaningfully blend their social worlds with the world of science. This advances us beyond the structure-agency dialectic, for it shows how youth engaged science both as a context and as a tool for change. Yet, we also believe that their performances in GET City worked toward a complex set of goals that were much more complicated than we had initially conceived, or that we could even discern from our locations as relative insiders/outsiders. Our program was designed to offer youth opportunities to engage in advanced information technology and the science of green energy technology in ways that built upon their social worlds. We began the project with the hope that we might, somehow, craft with youth such blended or third spaces, allowing them the space and maneuverability to be both scientific and youthful and to feel empowered to take some action beyond themselves. Yet, unpacking youth's enactments of community science expertise and their negotiations of the tension inherent therein, we believe that their participation was more complex in the sense that many of the participating youth strove to make their knowledge claims—about UHIs and the nature of science—accessible to a wide range of community members, something we underestimated their desire to do. Further, we observed an intensity around their desire to be the community science experts on UHIs, with an ownership and a curiosity about the phenomenon. We had hoped they would engage this topic, but did not anticipate them staking an identity within it with the intensity and influence that they did. Finally, we noted that the youth often struggled to balance their newly asserted identities with their new visibility in the club. From actions like Jeremy strategizing how to carry his computer from the conference room to the club room (open with the song "Peanut Butter Jelly Time" [Buckwheat Boyz 2000], playing loudly), we learned how they sought to make this delicate balance advantageous to them. And yet, we were surprised by how some of these balancing acts challenged our own assumptions of youth participation, such as the time that D'Amani wanted to be sure that her cameo as the "funky funky fresh scientist" was shown in the early fall recruiting meeting to nearly 100 youth.

The GET City youth have shown themselves to be purposeful and strategic learners in science. By actively negotiating for the form and function of their participation in GET City, the youth show us the complexity inherent in enacting critical science agency and the disservice that is done to them by restricting the range of their expression of and engagement with ideas—a restriction that occurs, more often than not, within the strictures of the traditional classroom. Genuine engagement in science learning demands that science educators attune themselves to the multifaceted learning possibilities that are created when we frame learning as agency. We do note that with GET City, such engagement was strongly facilitated by our freedom from pacing guides and school policy demands, elements that would no doubt be challenges to science teachers in the classroom embarking on third-space science teaching and learning.

CHAPTER SIX

Community Spaces as a Part of Hybrid Math Learning Spaces: Integrating Multiple Funds of Knowledge

Maura Varley Gutiérrez

The fifth-grade girls who were part of an elementary math club looked nervously at me and then approached the microphone stand placed between the aisles of folding chairs set up in the overflowing cafeteria. The girls eyed the panel of adults sitting at a long table at the front of the room facing the microphone. Zara[1] took a folded piece of paper and began to speak to the crowd of around 600 community members in a low yet forceful voice. She introduced the Girls' Math Club and the digital story that they were about to present. In turn, each girl spoke her name into the microphone, and then the digital story began to play on a large screen set up behind the panel of adults. The digital story outlined a series of arguments, weaving together mathematical analysis and social concerns through the use of narration by the girls, photos, and mathematical representations, such as graphs. The arguments were specifically crafted to counter arguments given by the district superintendent, who sat in front of the girls, watching the video. The superintendent initiated the school closure process as a solution to an unbalanced budget in a district with a history of financial mismanagement. The three primary criteria used by the district to decide which schools to close were (1) low

1. All student and school names are pseudonyms.

enrollment trends, (2) a low performance label based on standardized tests, and (3) sufficient capacity of and close proximity to potential receiving schools. The video aimed to convince the board members who were also present to vote against closing their school, Agave. For example, the video included an analysis of test score data showing improvement trends to counter the district argument that the school is considered underperforming according to district criteria.

Following the video, a series of community members (including teachers, parents, and elected state government officials) took turns at the microphone to address the panel of voting school board members. The girls listened intently as a mother described how, unable to formally read or write beyond a primary grade level, she encourages her young children to pursue an education. Through tears, she described her own schooling experiences as being rife with feelings of exclusion, while in contrast, she described her children's schooling as centered in a relationship of caring that exists at Agave. Other adults who spoke drew upon the girls' digital story to bolster their own arguments against the closure, often weaving in the mathematical investigations outlined by the girls.

This scene took place after several months of work that occurred both inside and outside of our math club, after the announcement that the school board would vote on the closure of four district schools, including the one where the math club took place. I had been working as a facilitator (and graduate student researcher) of the all-girls math club since the start of the school year. At the time, the seven girls and I had decided to focus on school safety in our mathematical investigations in the club. However, when the potential closure was announced, as Margarita said, "What point is there to do school safety when there's gonna be no school?" We then embarked upon a series of investigations involving math, yet grounded in the very real concerns of the community over the closure of the then 86-year-old neighborhood elementary school (Agave).

The above vignette illustrates an alternative kind of math learning space, one in which mathematical investigations are intimately tied to the community in which they take place. In this case, it was the community context that drove the investigations. Challenging the district arguments in an effort to save their school drove the girls not only to engage in the math, but also to integrate their intimate knowledge of the needs of their community, knowledge overlooked by the superintendent.

This unique hybrid learning space (K. Gutiérrez, Baquedano-López, and Tejeda 1999), namely a space where the learning was centered in the genuine interests and concerns of the students, allowed for the fluid interaction of multiple knowledge bases of the girls. Given the consistent exclusion of the funds of knowledge of students of color and their communities in schools, this is significant in that it allowed the girls to see their community knowledge as a necessary component of their mathematical investigations (which served to open up the discipline of math). Further, the knowledge they generated was then validated within a larger community movement for change. For example, as reflected in the description of the community forum above, arguments from the girls' digital story were taken up by adults addressing the school board.

In this chapter, we outline the evolution of one of the counterarguments generated by the girls in order to illustrate how multiple knowledge bases (knowledge about the needs of the community, knowledge about math, and knowledge about ways to critique the district) interacted within this hybrid math learning space. A distinguishing characteristic of this particular space was the fluid movement between our space in the math club and the community context of the investigations. This movement between spaces supported the interaction amongst knowledge bases, as knowledge bases are often tied to particular spaces. Ultimately, this hybrid learning space fostered an alternative kind of mathematical activity that challenged the often exclusionary, yet dangerously portrayed as neutral, role of the discipline of math, and opened up entry points for the collective development of mathematical and critical knowledge for the students.

Funds of Knowledge and Critical Math Education

Despite the potential for math education as described in the opening vignette, one that fosters students' sense of themselves and their communities as valued aspects of their educational experiences, and that helps students recognize the power of math to act upon their world, the reality is that for many students, the reverse is often true. Nondominant students in particular experience school as disconnected from their homes and communities (Moll and Ruiz 2002; Tate 1994; Valenzuela 1999). This is especially the case with a subject like math that is often presented in a decontextualized manner, providing students little indication of how they will benefit from the content they learn (Chazan 2000; Martin 2000;

Noddings 1993). Moreover, the proceduralistic nature of most math classrooms runs counter to the kind of people many students want to be and want to become—reflective and agentive participants in their lives (Boaler and Greeno 2000, 171). These issues are particularly salient for low-income students of color, who are overrepresented in basic skills–oriented classrooms (Oakes 1990 and 2005), and whose perspectives and experiences are often disregarded by mainstream curricula (G. Anderson 1989; Ladson-Billings 1997; Nieto 1999).

Statistics on educational attainment and achievement suggest that the disconnect between students' school experiences and their lives outside of school can have devastating consequences (NAEP 2005; NCES 2006; Pew Hispanic Center 2006). In a recent study conducted with youth who dropped out of school, students noted disinterest and a lack of rigor in their classes as primary reasons for leaving school (Bridgeland, DiIulio, and Burke Morrison 2006). Students' refusal to engage may be their way of resisting an educational system that fails to take their capacities, perspectives, and experiences into account (Chazan 2000; Shor 1992 and 1996).

Consistent with a broader critical educational paradigm that seeks to disrupt the societal and educational structures that marginalize nondominant youth (Apple 1992; Giroux 1983; Giroux et al. 1996), we argue that math education should not only empower students with the skills and understandings to succeed academically, but also prepare them to critically investigate, challenge, and act upon issues in their lives and communities (Frankenstein 1990; Gutstein 2003 and 2007; Gutstein, Middleton, and Fey 2005; Skovsmose 1994a; Tate 1995). We contend that one way to work toward this goal is through *empowering, hybrid learning spaces* that engage students in learning and using math as a tool for change. In the case of this chapter, a key component of these hybrid learning spaces is the fluid movement across multiple learning spaces, spaces that offer the possibility of the integration of multiple knowledge bases.

Integrating Multiple Funds of Knowledge

COMMUNITY FUNDS OF KNOWLEDGE. A large body of research that addresses equity in math education centers on how learning environments form the basis for student empowerment by viewing their background, funds of knowledge, and linguistic skills as assets in learning (e.g., Civil 2007; González et al. 2001; Licón Khisty 1997; Moschkovich 2005). Research on funds of knowledge seeks to counter deficit perspectives of students by seeing the historically accumulated knowledge bases of their families or communities and the home language as the basis for education, rather than as a barrier (González, Moll, and Amanti 2005). This research is important because it explicitly attempts to counter deficit perspectives of students of color in relation to math education, an essential component of reconceptualizing math education and the discipline of math. González et al. (2001) reveal that one of the most important ideas that emerged from their research with *mathematical* funds of knowledge is that students must be engaged in becoming "producers of mathematical practices" (p. 130), which counters the traditional notion that the center of power in math classrooms lies with the teacher or within the domain of math. Rather, knowledge is generated in a hybrid learning space, where power is distributed as students and teachers take on roles as knowledge producers.

One approach to integrating multiple funds of knowledge in math learning spaces would be to ground the mathematical activity in authentic situations in students' lives and communities. In this sense, you are neither trying to find the math within a community nor bringing the community into the math classroom, but are working within a hybrid space where they are not necessarily separate.

CRITICAL FUNDS OF KNOWLEDGE. A funds of knowledge framework has the potential to be an important element in social justice pedagogy in which the goal is for students to see themselves as social actors. Incorporating the *critical* funds of knowledge of students, in terms of the families' or communities' own knowledge about confronting inequity (Vélez-Ibáñez and Greenberg 2005), could further connect this work to critical pedagogy. For example, in work with Latina/o immigrants in Arizona who participated in an afterschool math club in the years prior to this study, students discussed family involvement in the immigration protests that took place across the country in the spring of 2006 (Turner et al. 2009). The familial and community funds of knowledge related to community-based activism served as a necessary catalyst to understanding the importance of subsequent mathematical investigations related to immigration. An important component of critical pedagogy is to recognize familial and community funds of knowledge related to families' strategies for survival in an oppressive society (Vélez-Ibáñez and Greenberg 2005). These funds of knowledge are essential to understanding specifically how the marginalized cope with, transcend, and transform oppression and the role this knowledge plays in a critical math education environment.

Framework for Integrating Multiple Knowledge Bases in Math Education

Building on the tradition of centering education in students' experiences, Gutstein (2003, 2006, and 2007) offers a particular framework, "teaching mathematics for social justice," that argues for integrating students' community *and* critical knowledge in the teaching of math. This framework outlines the multiple knowledge bases that must be integrated in order to implement critical math education. This integration not only ensures the validation of the knowledge students bring to the classroom and the emphasis on rigorous mathematical knowledge (as argued in work on equity in math education focused on access and achievement), but also fosters an explicitly critical stance toward math and society. Gutstein (2006a) terms these three knowledge bases the three Cs: Community, Critical, and Classical knowledge, each of which is essential to a potentially empowering and transformative math education.

Building on work on funds of knowledge, Gutstein (2006a) defines community knowledge as involving "how people understand their lives, their communities, power, relationships, and their society" (p. 110). Gutstein (2006a) describes critical knowledge as "knowledge about why things are the way they are and about the historical, economical, political, and cultural roots of various social phenomena" (p. 110). Critical knowledge is fundamental to a potentially empowering math education because it supports students' capacity to understand (and potentially act upon) the sociopolitical contexts of their lives. Classical knowledge refers not only to the specific skills and competencies typically seen in math classrooms, but also to the ability to understand that this equates to mathematical power. Therefore, as argued by Apple (1992), classical knowledge in itself is not enough and can serve to reproduce the status quo, while an understanding of the power structures in relation to math allows for this knowledge to be employed in transformative ways.

The above frameworks influenced the creation of the context of this research (the Girls' Math Club), which I will outline in the following section. These frameworks also guide the subsequent section of the chapter, where I present analysis of how multiple knowledge bases were central to this hybrid learning space. Finally, I describe outcomes of this sort of hybrid math learning space (i.e., *humanizing math*, *mathematizing the world*, and *public valuing of multiple funds of knowledge*) and conclude the chapter with participants' reflections on the experience.

The Context: The Girls' Math Club

The vignette that opened this chapter describes an investigation conducted by a group of seven fifth-grade Latinas who attended a voluntary all-girls afterschool math club at a small neighborhood elementary school in the US Southwest. All of the girls identified as Mexican or Mexican American, and although all were born in the United States, several of their parents emigrated from Mexico. While several of the girls were bilingual, those who were not claimed affiliation with the Spanish language (e.g., "It is what my *nana* [grandmother] speaks") and at least understood some words and phrases. They represented a wide range of mathematical abilities, confidence levels, and orientations toward math as a discipline. I (Maura) had been a cofacilitator of a similar afterschool program (although coeducational) for the previous two years at the school. Because this was an afterschool setting and because I had a relationship with the school, I was given complete curricular freedom and support from the staff and teachers. The group met once or twice a week for two hours and engaged in extended problem-solving and community-based projects that reflected the interests and experiences of the girls.

The school where the math club took place, Agave, is located in a large, urban school district spread across neighborhoods of contrasting income levels. Because of years of financial difficulties leading to budget deficits, the district began taking measures to save costs, including, as mentioned above, proposing to the school board to close several elementary schools at the end of the school year. The district superintendent urged the board members to "decide [whether to close the schools] on facts and figures, not emotion." The district presented their process for determining which schools to close as a neutral and fair "mathematical" procedure. According to their analysis, Agave was chosen because it was underenrolled and low-performing and all of the students could be accommodated at the proposed receiving school, Samota Elementary, "conveniently" located 1.3 miles away. One by one, the girls began to discuss, dissect, and counter each of these mathematical arguments, primarily by drawing on their knowledge and experiences in

TABLE 6.1. **District Arguments and Girls' Counterarguments**

District Arguments	Girls' Counterarguments
• Closures are the only option to saving money to overcome deficit.	• Savings of 1% of total district budget is "not worth it."
• Low-performing label of school (based on standardized tests) justifies closure.	• Test scores could be interpreted in different ways, indicating improvement in scores, AND the school's worth is measured in many ways other than test scores.
• Enrollment trends indicate decrease in student population, below capacity.	• District is not accounting for the school's preschool program, which, when included, indicates the school is at capacity.
• "Seamless move": All Agave student will fit into a school down the road; no need to split students among several schools.	• Needs of the community indicate the move would cause additional problems. District is overlooking other costs, such as busing to the new school some students who currently walk.

the community to further our understanding of the impact of the closures. Table 6.1 provides an overview of the district arguments and our "counterarguments."

I used the development of each counterargument for the digital story to frame my analysis of the interaction of knowledge bases. Triangulating across interviews, videotaped girls' math club sessions, related mathematical or other written work, along with the actual text and images of the digital story, I coded for how girls drew upon various knowledge bases to craft the arguments that were presented in the digital story.

For the purposes of this chapter, I focus on one particular investigation, centered on the district's argument that all Agave students could easily transfer to the same school (Samota), resulting in what the superintendent called a "seamless move." The voices of community members and conversations in the math club revealed that the move would be anything but seamless for Agave families. The integration of the social realities and concerns of the community illustrated the important role of integrating multiple knowledge bases, for re-envisioning both the discipline of math *and* math education within hybrid learning spaces. I illustrate these themes through the telling of additional pieces of the narrative about how arguments in the digital story emerged and evolved in our hybrid learning space. My discussion involves highlighting the multiple knowledge bases as they emerged in each phase of the investigation in order to better understand their role in hybrid learning environments.

Multiple Knowledge Bases in Hybrid Learning Spaces

"I Actually Feel Bad for the Kids That Do Have to Walk"

Early in the closure process, the district held community forums in which they first presented their arguments and then allowed time for community member comments (with no response from the district officials). Several of the girls and I attended the first forum, and the following day in the math club we discussed community members' arguments regarding the closures, one of which was opposition to sending students to Samota. Zara brought up the following argument to persuade the board members to vote not to close Agave: "Because if [the board members] don't want little kids to go walking to Samota. Even when it's raining, cars go fast by like that (*indicates quick movement with hand*) and it can get them soaking wet and they can get sick and all that." Zara was imagining issues that would complicate the notion of a "seamless move" to the new school for the families that attend Agave, considering younger students (like her brother and sister) and their safety.

Zara and Margarita went on to describe the walk to the new school as "a really long way" and "it's all the way to downtown." Although at this point their general sense that the new school would be "a long way" away from Agave guided their critique of the district argument, we later engaged in further investigating of the walk in order to craft a more convincing argument to include in the digital story (discussed further below). However, at the time, the conversation continued around issues related to how students would get to the new school. Zara reasoned, "You can go in [a] car but if you don't have one, then . . ." Zara brought up the fact that some families could drive to the new school, yet drew upon her knowledge that other families may not have that as an option. Catalina then connected to her own experience, saying, "That's why if I go there, my parents will always drive me so I don't have to worry." Zara responded, "They [other kids] go by themselves. You go with your dad." Zara went on to bring up other options, such as the city bus, yet reasoned, "But you have to pay [for the city bus] so they [some families] wouldn't have much money like that."[2] She then thought of yet another option, "You can go on taxi, too. No, that would waste money, too." This

2. In this city, public buses are not free to students, although there are discounts for low-income individuals and schools can provide bus passes for some students.

exchange illustrates how Zara's knowledge of her community and their needs entered this hybrid learning space. In this case, the integration of Zara's knowledge about the needs of the community (knowledge about socioeconomic status, for example) created a learning experience for Catalina, who, unlike Zara, initially spoke only of her own needs. Later in the conversation, Catalina evidenced a shift in her thinking, expressing her concern for others, "Even though if I go there [and] I am sure I'm not gonna have to walk, but I actually feel bad for the kids that do have to walk." Catalina shifted from her earlier stance of not needing to worry about the walk because she would always be driven, to claiming that despite being driven, she felt "bad" for those who did not have that option. The discussion presumably convinced her to think of others in such a situation, a key component of developing critical consciousness. The inclusion of the experiences and perspectives of the other girls in the conversation allowed this shift to happen.

During this conversation, several patterns arose with respect to critique of the district's proposal to close the schools and send Agave students to Samota. Through conversation, the girls showed concern for others, convinced each other to show concern for others, and complicated the notion of a "seamless move," all grounded in their knowledge of the circumstances of their own families and the school community. From the start of this project, they interrogated the district's mathematical arguments for closing the school by bringing in knowledge about their own lives and their own community. Although the conversation was not explicitly about math at this point, it formed the basis of a subsequent mathematical investigation of the walk to Samota.

". . . And It Might Not Be a Pretty Picture"

During a discussion of the potential move to Samota, the girls decided we should investigate the walk ourselves, compelling us to leave the physical space of the math club and go out into the community. We took the walk between the two schools and documented it with video and photos, and by timing the walk. During the walk, the girls observed broken glass, dangerous intersections, construction sites, and other hazards and identified them as potential safety concerns for walking students. The girls then used this information to develop an informed critique of the "ease" of closing Agave to include in the digital story. The girls included the following passage in the digital story, highlighting both the safety concerns related to the walk as well as the results of their mathematical analysis:

MICHELLE: What I'm going to talk about is the walk that I took with the girls' math club and how dangerous it is.

MICHELLE: When we went to go take the walk, it seemed pretty dangerous because of all of the construction sites. [video footage of construction worker helping us to cross the street at the construction site]
And some kids might go there, well, through there, and it might not be a pretty picture.

The photos, the video, and their first-hand description of the walk proved to be a powerful experience that the girls could draw upon to support the subsequent mathematical investigation (see Figures 6.1 and 6.2). Upon returning to the school, the girls began the analysis of the walk by counting the number of blocks from Agave to Samota on an enlarged neighborhood map to determine our average walking rate. They negotiated how to interpret the map, in terms of what to count as blocks and where to begin and end the counting. It took us around 40 minutes to walk the 13 blocks, including stopping at intersections and construction areas. Using a variety of strategies, the girls determined their average walking rate per block. For example, Margarita started by stating that it was a division problem. Zara began to draw a long rectangle divided into smaller rectangles to represent the thirteen blocks (see Figure 6.3).

Zara then predicted it would take two minutes to walk each block and wrote a two under each of the thirteen blocks to test this prediction. Presumably, she was able to come up with a reasonable estimate and accurate model to determine the solution by drawing on her experience of the walk and her number sense. Zara then determined that at that rate (2 minutes per block) our walk should have taken 26 minutes, which was less than the actual time. Therefore, she adjusted her prediction, reasoning that their walking rate was approximately three minutes per block, which she then modeled and confirmed. Although the total was 39 minutes at this rate (instead of 40), she reasoned that some of the extra minute could have been used to take photographs and videotape, and so three minutes per block was a reasonable estimate of the actual

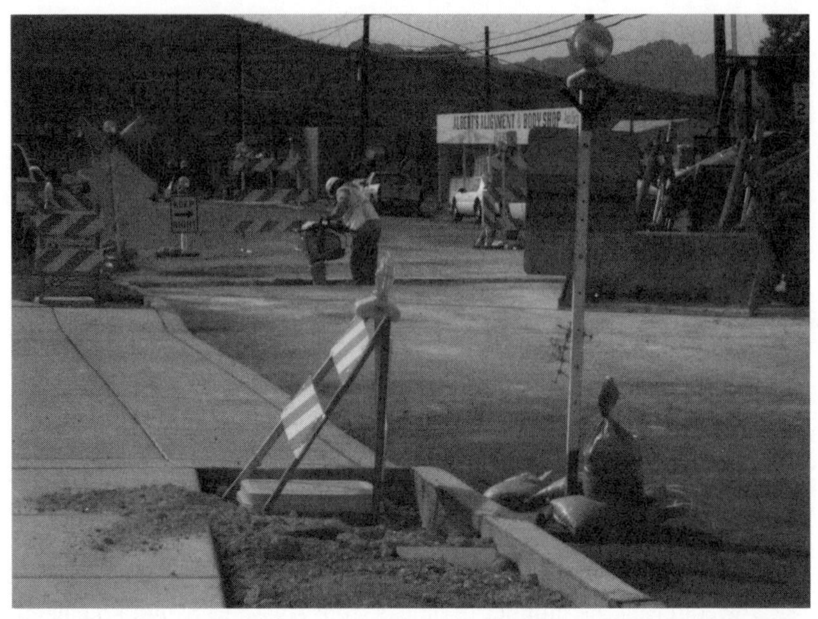

FIGURE 6.1. and FIGURE 6.2. Hazards along the walk from Agave to Samota

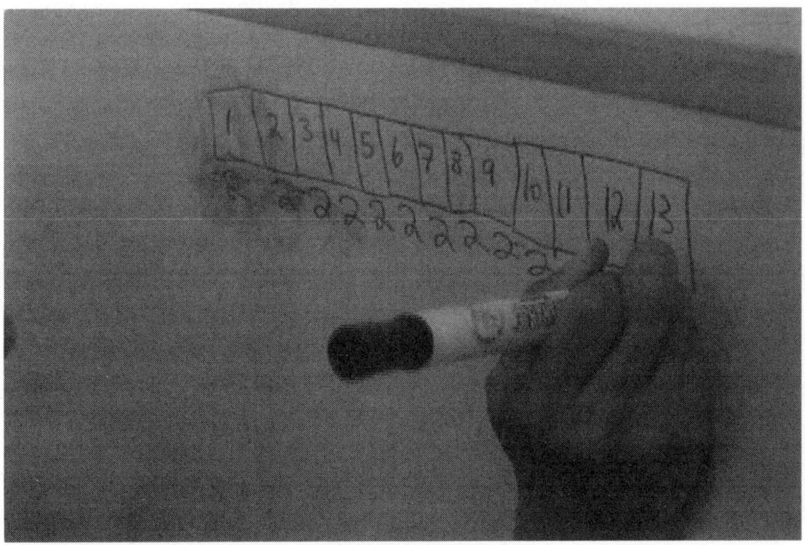

FIGURE 6.3. Zara's representation of the walk to Samota

rate. The experience of going out into the community to collect this data became a source of knowledge to draw upon when calculating the walking rate back in the math club.

Once they had determined an average walking rate, the girls used data collected from students at the school to calculate distances students lived from Samota and walking times for these distances. Following my (Maura's) suggestion, they then used a line plot to represent the range of walking times (see Figure 6.4).

The collaborative process that ensued to organize and represent the large amounts of data illustrates the nature of the mathematical activity in this learning space, partially prompted by the complex nature of dealing with real data. For example, Michelle created a list of all of the intersections reported by students indicating the locations of their homes, Margarita and Vanesa located these intersections on our neighborhood map, and the girls worked together to determine distances and calculate potential walking times. Knowledge of the community coupled with the mathematical practices of organizing and representing data shaped this learning activity.

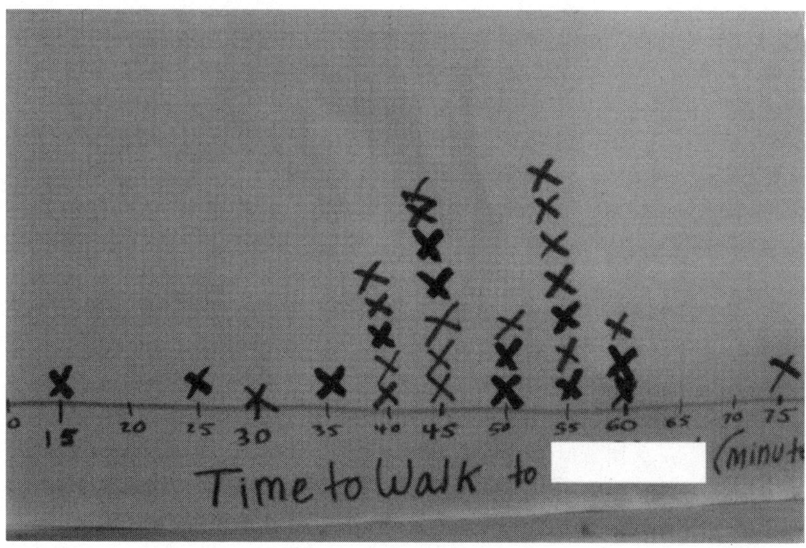

FIGURE 6.4. Line plot of time to walk to Samota (in minutes)

In the digital story, we presented these findings in the following way:

MARGARITA: Well, we are going to talk about the line plot we made that represents how long a person needs to walk from their residence to Samota. We did the math and we came up with 13 blocks to Samota from Agave. We made a map as well. Each block was average three minutes so, for example, a person who lives on 33rd Street would have to walk an hour. That's a lot of time, so we are very concerned about that.

In the digital story, Margarita clearly used the mathematical investigation of the walking rate coupled with her knowledge of the reality of the walking time to the new school to critique the district's argument. The mathematical knowledge evidenced in this portion of the digital story arose from their experience taking the walk, coupled with time in the math club to determine the rate in a way that made sense to them. In addition, the experience of taking the walk also generated knowledge of the dangers of walk, a form of community knowledge, which bolstered their critique.

In the subsequent portion of the digital story, Catalina reasoned about the line plot data, "Lots of students would have to walk a lot. Students usually last about five to ten minutes to get to Agave. Now if they would have to go to Samota, most would have to walk 40 minutes to one hour." This hybrid learning space encouraged students to draw on their knowledge of what would be reasonable or difficult for the community, which helped them to interpret the mathematical results. The 40-minute walk, for example, did not have meaning until they also connected it to the context of their knowledge of the community and what that walk would mean for families at the school. The interaction of multiple knowledge bases (their own and their community's experiences, data they collected, and their mathematical analysis) positioned them to critique the district's argument that the move to Samota would be "seamless."

"Wait, I Got a Great Idea!"

Around the same time, the girls conducted a survey of selected students at Agave. They intended to use the information to strengthen their argument to keep the school open. The idea for the survey was brought up at the start of the investigation, when Margarita shared her knowledge of a tool that can be used to make change. Convinced that a survey would generate a compelling argument to not close the school, Margarita said, "If you just ask a whole bunch of people [what they think about the school closing], then we can say how much people agreed that it shouldn't close." Vanesa contended that this would be powerful because, she predicted, "I bet you it's gonna be a little bit of people that disagree [with the idea that the school should be closed]." We returned to the idea of a survey later in the investigation, and began the process of deciding on questions, then crafting, conducting, and analyzing the survey. The first question on the survey related to how students traveled to Agave, on the basis of Alma saying: "Wait, I got a great idea. How about we put up the number of kids who walk to school, take the bus, and who have their parents drive them to school?" On the basis of their knowledge of students in their own classrooms, the girls predicted that the majority of students walked to Agave and could imagine that this could then be a powerful tool to convince the board members. In this case, the integration of critical and mathematical knowledge about the power of surveys to convince, combined with their knowledge that the majority of the Agave community walked to school, led to the collective creation of a survey.

In the subsequent section of the digital story, Margarita reported her prediction of how many students would be walking to Samota based on the results of the survey given to students at Agave. Because half of the surveyed students reported that they walk to Agave, she predicted that half of the entire Agave population, or about 130 students, would also walk to Samota. This particular portion of the digital story highlights engagement in the mathematical practices of collecting and analyzing survey data, interpreting results, and predicting based on these results. Finally, she leveraged this information to consider unforeseen costs of moving students to Samota, in that busing would need to be provided for some students. On several occasions, the girls similarly indicated a critical stance toward the closings by foreseeing costs or additional issues that the closings would cause, such as overcrowding and the subsequent adverse learning conditions at the receiving school. By leveraging the mathematical results (drawing on the mathematical knowledge generated with the survey) and predicting the impact of certain decisions (drawing on their knowledge of the community), they presented an in-depth critique of the notion that moving students from Agave to Samota would be "seamless."

Just as their community knowledge informed their interpretation of the math in relation to the walk to the new school, their mathematical knowledge informed their understanding of the impact of the district proposal on the school. Vanesa remarked that she would use math to convince the board, saying:

> It [mathematical arguments] would give them an idea that we don't want to close our school and that we're doing so much math. If we show them our math, they will know that we are doing so much for the school [like] figuring out the surveys.

In reflecting on what she was learning during this project she shared, "I've actually learned a lot of math—I'm getting a little better. I don't know how we would figure out things like the percent [of the budget] they are saving if we didn't do any math." Vanesa's comments highlight an understanding that the girls' mathematical analysis was an essential component of their argument against the district's proposal to close the school. Such realizations, facilitated by the hybrid nature of the learning space, are an essential goal of empowering math education, in that students realize the power of the discipline to support change.

Outcomes of Integrating Multiple Knowledge Bases in Hybrid Learning Spaces

The community and mathematical investigations that we engaged in within and beyond our critical math learning space allowed for the integration of the multiple knowledge bases of the girls. As the girls critiqued the district's arguments for closing Agave, they naturally brought up concerns that the district had overlooked. Because the district was talking about their own school and their own families, the girls could imagine how a move to a new school would impact their community. They could imagine younger siblings and other young students having to take the long walk to the new school. They were then able to further develop these ideas and build their own knowledge about the walk by taking it themselves. They gained firsthand experience of the dangers along the way and could then further articulate the issues with the move, deepening their critique. This experience then influenced the mathematical activity they engaged in upon returning to the school. They could visualize the problem of determining a walking rate, which helped Zara draw a representation to solve the problem, for example. The experience of taking the walk aided in making sense of the mathematical investigation. Their mathematical investigation then furthered their critique of the district arguments as evidenced in the digital story. In the end, their digital story proved to be a valued and unique contribution to the larger community movement to make change. Given the fluid movement between the mathematical investigations and community investigations, each phase of the project created further spaces for critical or mathematical learning and often generated the need for further investigation. The fluid movement between physical spaces inside and outside of the club, and in and out of the community movement, is what created a hybrid learning space that fostered the integration of knowledge bases.

The analysis of the creation of the girls' counterarguments offers several potential insights into the power of hybrid learning spaces where multiple knowledge bases are integrated. First, connecting math learning to students' communities allowed the girls the opportunity to interpret their world through a mathematical lens (*mathematizing the world*). Second, and perhaps more importantly, it allowed them to bring their world into the math that they did (*humanizing math*), thus challenging and even transforming the math. Finally, because the work that the girls did was made public, in this case through the showing of their digital story at a community forum, the girls were able to experience the knowledge they generated being regarded as legitimate and valued within a larger community movement (*public valuing of multiple funds of knowledge*).

Mathematizing the World

In attempting to find a way to counter the arguments outlined by the district, it became necessary to begin to find ways to use math to analyze situations in their lives. Thus, the participants engaged in *mathematizing* their world (Gutstein 2006). Math is often used to describe and to abstract from reality. Mathematical models are used to determine a plethora of systems in our daily lives, such as mortgage rates and the location of community resources. Unfortunately, math is often a tool used to oppress (Skovsmose 1994a), highlighting the need for the subsequent theme that emerged from this analysis, which I will discuss below. However, if a goal of critical math education is to develop critical consciousness within students, it is necessary that they have opportunities to understand how math operates within society—what structures it underlies and what systems it contributes to. The girls in the club were given access to the mathematical arguments the district used to justify school closures, and in turn came to understand *and* critique this use of math in their lives.

Humanizing Math

R. Gutiérrez (2007) advocates for the notion that we must open up the discipline of math through the integration of the multiple knowledge bases of marginalized students. Because the discipline traditionally excludes these students, she argues that their knowledge is essential to its transformation, namely to transform the discipline from being a tool for oppression to being a tool for making change. In the case of the girls' involvement in the movement to save their school, the first thing they did when they heard the district's mathematical arguments to close the school was to bring a humanistic element into the discussion. The district's mathematical justification lacked attention to the context of the school, the students, their families, and the community. The girls challenged this nonhumanized mathematical interpretation of the closings by integrating their intimate knowledge of the situation at the school, the community needs, and the factors related to the closings. This situation repositioned the knowledge and experiences of low-income communities of color as essential to transforming the oppressive use of the domain of math.

Public Valuing of Multiple Funds of Knowledge

In this particular case, the multiple knowledge bases of the girls proved essential to their counterarguments, which then became public through the digital story. This public valuing of their knowledge, through the taking up of their arguments by adults who spoke after their story was shown, and through providing the space for their work to be shared, proved essential to the experience of an empowering learning space. Because the hybrid learning space spanned the math club and community settings, they were given a chance to bring their investigations back to the community and contribute to the community movement in a legitimate way. In this way, the idea of education moves beyond schooling. "Education" involved participating in a community movement, rather than containing their learning within the walls of a classroom, as in traditional notions of education as "schooling." The purpose of education moves beyond these traditional notions of learning a body of knowledge to later participate legitimately in society, but rather, becomes the development of critical consciousness (Freire 1970/1993). The public valuing of the knowledge of students of color could then also contribute to their feeling of having a sense of voice within a movement to make change.

Conclusion

Throughout the project, students had opportunities to reflect on their experiences and on the mathematical investigations they conducted. The girls indicated that the experience impacted them in several ways, primarily related to being a part of a collective (important component of critical knowledge) and to learning the power of leveraging math to make change. This was most likely solidified by the fact that the board ultimately voted not to close their school. For example, Margarita described what she learned from the project in the following way: "I learned that if you work together you can do something—you can make a difference. . . . I would say teamwork is important because people together make such a big difference, not just one person."

The girls spoke of the difficulty of the math and the extent of their hard work as contributing to this collective movement. Michelle said, "The Girls' Math Club is doing a lot of hard work and they are convincing you to keep the school open." Her comment reflected a sense of confidence in the power of their collective work to make a difference. Margarita also described what she learned through the project, saying, "I also learned that it takes a lot of hard work to try and keep your school open. Trying to keep your school open takes a lot of perseverance and patience and hope." At one point or another, all of the girls shared a belief that their work made a difference and that if the board knew everything they knew or had learned about Agave, they would not vote to close the school.

The integration of the multiple knowledge bases of the girls allowed for the valuing of their multiple identities—in terms of who they are, where they come from, and who they want to become. They were seen and recognized themselves as contributing the math to the community movement, an important role for Latina women to play in the domain of math, a domain from which they are traditionally excluded. In essence, this hybrid learning space—hybrid not only in the sense of being co-constructed through the integration of the multiple knowledge bases of the participants, but also in terms of physical space inside and outside of the math club—served as an empowering space for the girls to develop both their mathematical and sociopolitical identities.

Despite the potential that such a hybrid learning space holds for marginalized students, the project also brings forth various tensions related to this kind of work, particularly given our current political landscape. First, this work took place in an afterschool setting, where there was complete curricular freedom. The reality of schools today is that classrooms are becoming more and more restricted in terms of what is taught and how. This project points to ways in which we must reframe math as reflected in curricula from being a set of concepts to cover, to being a set of practices in which students can engage. Second, in a related matter, this case highlights alternative ways to look at outcomes of such hybrid learning spaces. With the current focus on accountability in education (often based solely on test scores), for this work to be valued on a larger scale, these alternative ways of assessing outcomes must be considered. Finally, in the case of this project, parents were willing and, in fact, essential participants in the same community movement to save the school. If we are to bring community and critical issues into the classroom on a larger scale, we must be careful to involve the parents and community members of our students, in order to have support as well as in order to genuinely connect to larger movements.

CHAPTER SEVEN

Hybrid Spaces for Empowering Learning in Math and Science

We started this book by examining critically what science and math "for all" might mean and entail. In chapters 1 and 2, we discussed the importance of equitable and empowering learning environments. Science and math learning environments ought to support students in developing and using their math and science knowledge and practices in authentic contexts in addition to providing equitable access to resources, so that all students (especially underrepresented minority students) can be bona fide beneficiaries of science and math education policy initiatives, such as "Science for All" and "Everybody Counts." The stories in chapters 3 through 6 have shown what such empowering science and math learning can look like, in both classrooms and afterschool programs.

A common thread runs through all the stories in these chapters: In creating these equitable and empowering environments, hybrid spaces were brokered for and sustained by the learning community, inclusive of both teachers and students. It is through the collective creation of hybrid spaces that students were able to engage in critical math and science literacies and to translate such critical knowledge into authentic, real-world action, thereby exhibiting their critical math and science agencies. In this last chapter, we look across these hybrid spaces and discuss how they are crucial to breaking down the inequitable opportunities that exist and to furthering the cause of science and math for all. We look at cross-cutting themes that reverberate through these hybrid spaces and consider their implications for science and math education.

The following research questions guided our interest and inquiry into empowering math and science classrooms. They were introduced in Chapter 1 and bear repeating now:

- What do empowering learning environments in urban math and science look like, and what meaning do they carry for urban youth and their teachers?
- How are such environments constructed inside and outside of formal learning environments?
- In what ways are empowering learning environments made possible through the hybridization of youth's Discourses and funds of knowledge alongside the Discourse and culture of schooling as well as the disciplines of math and science?
- How do these empowering learning environments help students cultivate a sense of critical math and science agency?

Expansive Hybridity

Chapters 3 through 6 provide a set of images and conceptual frames for making sense of and exploring different aspects of empowering learning in science and math. What we learn across these chapters is that when math and science Discourses, perspectives, and resources are hybridized and made richer by the purposeful inclusion of youth texts drawn from youth genre and lives and concerns outside of the classroom, science and mathematical content gets reframed in new ways that position teachers and youth with more resources and agency. Such hybrid spaces transform mathematical and science learning by creating new modes of engagement and broadening the boundaries of the learning community by intentionally recruiting varied perspectives and voices to enrich the science and mathematical hybrid Discourses.

We refer to the vision of hybrid spaces presented in this text as expansive because such spaces are rich and open to and informed by a plurality of Discourses, perspectives, and resources. We appropriate the term expansive from K. Gutiérrez (2008) and Engeström's (2001) use of it to describe learning. An expansive view of learning, as we discussed in chapter 2, considers both the horizontal and vertical dimensions of learning. How developing the expertise of a discipline (vertical learning) intersects with the cultural practices individuals carry with them and strategically adapt as they navigate across the communities in which they live and learn (horizontal learning) is critical to understanding hybridity.

However, we like this term also because of its use in science and math. In science, we can think about thermal expansivity, for example. Thermal expansivity or thermal expansion refers to how matter changes in volume as a response to temperature change. Most of us have driven over bridges composed of thermal expansion joints. We can see them as metal gaps in between concrete slaps or we can feel their rhythmic thud against the wheels of the car as we cross over them. These gaps are important because they prevent cracking as the bridge materials expand and contract with shifting seasonal temperatures and other sources of heat. The idea that hybridity is always taking shape in the moment in ways that are responsive to the conditions of the moment in ways that make the future possible captures great power for us as well.

In math also, we think of expansive functions, such as the Taylor Series. These are functions that are infinitely differentiable, allowing an ever more closely determined approximation of a phenomenon. We also believe that hybrid spaces that are expansive support the kind of hard work that makes possible ever more authentic, meaningful, socially just, and empowering learning environments.

As these points intimate, cutting across these chapters are several themes that describe the ways in which expansive hybrid spaces take shape over time and how such spaces frame the process and outcomes of learning. At the same time, these themes shed light on the tensions emergent in working toward empowering math and science education and the implications this has for how and why teachers and students take up and resist such efforts. These themes include Multiple Discourses, Multivocality and Identities for Practice, and New Learning Outcomes. We take up each theme in turn in this section.

Multiple Discourses, Perspectives, and Resources

Hybrid spaces allowed the coalescence of multiple Discourses, perspectives, and resources, leading to a transformation of the learning environment that is at once equitable and empowering. In all the classrooms and afterschool programs described, rigorous mathematical and science content grounded the learning experiences of the students. There were no instances where the science and mathematical content was "watered down" in order to allow for easier access by more students. On the contrary, in-depth content knowledge was demanded of the students if they were to participate meaningfully. For example, the fifth graders in the afterschool Girls' Math Club had to demonstrate competence in mathematical knowledge and skills such as measurement, estimation, scale, and mathematical operations (including multiplication, division, and averaging) so as to investigate and report on their findings of the distance and time required to walk to the new school. Mrs. Davis' seventh graders had to learn how to read nutritional labels and how to apply the information according to portion sizes; they had to keep a careful log of their food and beverage intake, including number of calories (calculated from nutritional labels); and they had to log their exercise routines and daily activities to estimate how many calories they used. Similarly, the youth at GET City had to grasp the scientific principles on the causes and consequences of urban heat islands (UHIs)—including greenhouse gases, urban development, heat absorption of specific materials, and waste heat generated from electrical appliances—before they could create a movie to educate their community about how the UHI phenomenon is affecting their lives.

Furthermore, in each of these instances, students played an active role in negotiating for in-depth coverage of science and math that was not a required part of their curriculum. One could argue that, in an afterschool setting such as GET City, students have the freedom to deviate from the normative content path to cover topics of greater interest, such as the impact of UHIs on the human experience. However, as evident in Mrs. Davis' classroom, students pushed for further investigation into health consequences of dynamic *dis*equilibrium in the human body, and actively took up the homework and lesson extensions that Mrs. Davis brought to the required unit. Thus, the disciplinary Discourses of math and science were strong and fundamental components of the hybrid Discourses in these learning environments. Such activity on the part of students unravels the assumptions that students do not want to engage science and math deeply, that a more multicultural and social justice–oriented approach to teaching neglects meaningful content engagement, or that the world of youth and that of science and math are discontinuous.

The continuity between youth's worlds and that of science and math is a central tenet that cuts across the stories in this book and that contribute the power of hybrid spaces for learning. By continuity we suggest "that students' ways of conceptualizing, representing and evaluating their lived experiences should be viewed and treated . . . as generative resources in learning new ideas and traditions of inquiry" (Warren, Ogonowski, and Pothier 2005, 121). As Warren et al. further state:

> Children's inventive use of narrative, animated modes of argumentation, dynamic ways of imaging themselves into the phenomena, among other sense-making resources, have repeatedly challenged teachers and researchers to examine their own, often limited and limiting, assumptions about what constitutes productive reasoning and deep understanding in the sciences. (p. 122)

Thus, equally important and not secondary to the discipline Discourse was the strong presence of cultural and local Discourses. The fifth graders who worked to save their school focused their mathematical investigations around a very real and pressing problem the community faced—being evicted from their own school and sent to another. In each of these stories, multiple communities and Discourses were interwoven to produce a rich, hybrid Discourse that promoted a deeper engagement with the content and practices of science and math. The resultant hybrid Discourses were heteroglossic in nature—students needed to be adept at expressing themselves in both math and scientific terms so as to have useful tools and knowledges that equip them to critically examine local issues relevant to math and science. At the same time, they also needed to be able to articulate the concerns of their communities drawn from pertinent local issues in order to leverage their acquired science and math content skills and knowledges. The different Discourses and perspectives act on one another to further encourage students' deeper engagement in each of these Discourses. With such a positive feedback mechanism, the resultant hybrid Discourse is ever transformative, responsive to new areas of expertise acquired by the learning community in both discipline-based and community-focused domains, gaining complexity and saliency to students as more connections between the disciplines of math and science and their lives are surfaced and strengthened (see Figure 7.1).

Multivocality and Identities for Practice

The heteroglossic nature of hybrid spaces supports a multivocal ensemble of participants, which allows students to draw from identities and resources outside of math and science as they engage in and give meaning to mathematical and scientific practices. Multivocality has been em-

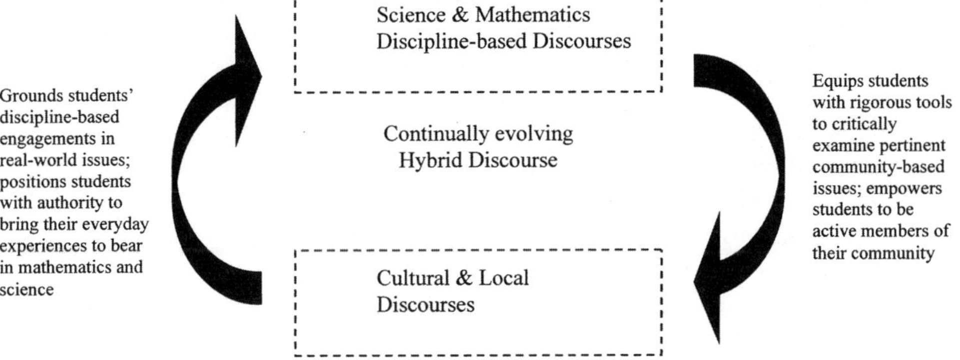

FIGURE 7.1. Positive feedback loop of discourses building on and reinforcing one another

ployed as a practice, primarily in archeology, in order to encourage the interplay of multiple and divergent narratives situated within "different histories" and "belonging to people who have engaged with the site and landscape in quite different ways" (Rountree 2007, 7).

In the stories told in this book, we observe the importance of multivocality in promoting meaningful learning. In these cases, multivocality means more than encouraging multiple narratives, although this point is important. The practice of multivocality also involved creating metalevel awarenesses of one's own place of engagement in science and math, giving both meaning and perspective to the questions at hand. The students in Francis Middle School ultimately were somewhat successful in bringing real change to the overcrowding situation in that status quo was maintained by keeping the number of incoming students the same as the number of graduating students. The overcrowding issue still exists, but the students also learned about the complexities involved in the issue. The students communicated their findings backed by robust math, and had to reconcile their opposing positions: students advocating for more space for their school versus students who still need to be in this particular middle school where it is currently situated. Multivocality allows for questions at hand to be examined from varied perspectives, not all of which are in alignment with each other or with the normative practice of schooling. In the case of Mrs. Davis, we see a teacher who gives voice to the science standards that are demanded of her students. At the same time, we see a teacher who deviates from the script in order to tell her own stories about her struggle with making healthy food choices. We see a classroom environment that relies on student and teacher stories to craft an in-between space that accepts the limitations and challenges of eating healthy in the technological food system, where access to healthy food is limited among some demographic groups and where cultural practices are shaped by difficult economic times. That the dollar menu at McDonald's is a more affordable option than a home-cooked meal for some families is a reality that Mrs. Davis is willing to acknowledge *as part of* learning to scientifically navigate the complex food environment.

Multivocality also allows students and teachers to author novel identities as modes *for participating more meaningfully, authentically, and expansively in the science and math hybrid spaces.* We use the preposition "for" quite purposefully. Practice theory has invoked the idea of identities-in-practice, suggesting that identities are formed dialogically with/in the communities of practice in which the individual participates. For example, on initial entry into a new community of practice, novices gain social positions that are accorded by the established members of that community. Such "positional identities" (Holland et al. 2001, 125) are inextricably entangled with power, status, and rank. Tagged alongside positional identities is a set of appropriate dispositions. How novices choose to accept, engage, resist, or ignore such cues shapes their developing identity-in-practice and determines the boundaries of their authoring space, which is driven by a sense of agency.

We advance the idea of identities "in" practice with the term "for" to suggest both a generative and a transformative element in this dialogic relationship, especially with respect to the kinds of hybrid spaces presented in this text. As youth (and teachers) invoke new Discourses, perspectives, and resources for participation, they often enact or try out novel identities that are a part of the hybridized practices being created. While these novel identities certainly do exist in practice, they are also crafted for a kind of practice meant to expand a kind of reflexive and critical dialog between science, math, and everyday life. For instance, the youth at GET City authored identities as community science experts (CSEs) during their investigation of the UHI phenomenon. The CSE identity is authentically authored and grounded in students' identities as both learners of science in an afterschool program and active community insiders. The students' dual expertise in science (UHI phenomenon) and their community (understanding peer concerns and "hooks"; understanding jobs in the community, such as traffic police officers) was what made it possible for them to author the identity of community science experts. Likewise, the girls in the afterschool math club who were facing school closure used their mathematical expertise to conduct research in the community to make a case against closing their school. For the school board, the girls were community representatives who were directly affected by the school closure with a mathematically sound case to present; for the community, the girls were math experts and community spokespersons who had the skills to use math to make an informed and impassioned case against school closure on their behalf. In each of these examples, students' identities as community insiders who were keenly attuned to the concerns, needs, and ways of their community and their identities as science and math learners not only were equally vital, but also fortified each other to bring about an authentic mode of engagement that had far-reaching impact (especially in the case of preventing school closure), both for the students themselves and for their communities. It was imperative that the girls had equal footing in both the world of math and in their community to be able to successfully prevent the impending school closure.

Finally, multivocality demands accountability to the multiple modes of communicating, interacting, and representing ideas that constitute the work of youth in science and math (Kress 1997). Flewitt, Nind, and Payler (2009) argue that "perceptions of individuals' literacy competence necessarily pivot on understandings of what literacy is," and that there are currently two competing interpretations: literacy as a "curricular goal" that focuses on the "development of skills-based reading and writing competences" and literacy as "as the development of shared meanings through diverse symbol systems in social contexts—literacy as woven into the fabric of daily practice" (pp. 212–213).

We argue that this idea can be extended to literacy in math and science and helps to explain both the difference in functional and critical math and science literacies and why and how such differences can be partly understood through the importance of the primacy of multivocality in and of more expansive hybrid spaces.

The heteroglossic nature of hybrid spaces not only elevated the voices of individual students in math and science, but also recruited community voices to contribute to the hybrid Discourse, and positioned broader participation as an important artifact of learning. Since the issues that students wanted to investigate across the stories presented were community-based instead of classroom-bound, the students ventured out of the classroom for field work in gathering data for their investigations, whether in the form of an informal community ethnography on UHIs or of gathering familial stories on salad traditions. New modes of engaging in science and math were created. In the cases of the urban heat islands, save our school, healthy eating, and math counterstories, students were not merely desk bound in the classroom practicing sums and learning scientific vocabulary, they engaged in ethnography and conducted interviews with members of their community. Students took photographs, made audio and video recordings, and collected authentic and current data from members of the community who were experiencing and living the issues they were exploring. Through engaging in ethnographic investigations, the students also recruited and gave voice to other members of their community. In so doing, the students enacted a democratic and critical process in their scientific and mathematical investigations into community issues that affect the lives of many. The students recognized that in order for data to be authentic and accurate, more than their own knowledge in these issues was required. Local expertise was actively sought as additional resources. Thus, multiple scripts were valued and necessary for the students' mathematical and scientific undertakings to be successful. The students drew from science or mathematical content and skills, their own experiences, and those of different community members, to frame their investigations and analysis meaningfully. As a result, not only were the hybrid Discourses enriched, the students' mathematical and scientific endeavors were broadened to include more stakeholders, elevating the authenticity and importance of the investigations students were undertaking.

Multivocality and identities for practice stand in stark contrast to the normative practices of school science and math. School science and math for too long has played out in isolation—isolation from other knowledge systems and from other people. Furthermore, multivocality has been critiqued as well, because not all vocalities have been equally empowered by normative social and cultural structures, limiting the ability of the practice to foster a meaningful negotiation of ideas. Yet we see, with imperfection, the degree to which the spaces of learning of the teachers and the youth in the stories of this text imposed multivocality as a means for holding each other accountable to the goals of critical mathematical and scientific literacy. In addition to adding their voices and perspectives in helping students frame and analyze their investigations, community members also played crucial roles in holding students accountable for their investigations. More than just knowledge acquisition to pass a test, in many of the stories, students had to accomplish larger goals that impacted others apart from themselves. The students had authentic audiences for whom they showcased their work in these hybrid spaces. As such, the scientific and mathematical investigations gained a deeper significance, and presented opportunities for the students to demonstrate critical math and critical science agencies.

Learning Outcomes in Hybrid Spaces

Gaining critical literacy in math and science, and demonstrating critical math and critical science agency, were key learning outcomes in hybrid spaces. As we described in chapter 2, critical science and math literacy is built on the three main ideas of transforming Discourses and practices, identities, and spaces for learning/doing science and math. Throughout the stories, we have seen how the learning communities have engaged in all three modes of transformation through creating and sustaining hybrid spaces.

By valuing multiple perspectives and recruiting other Discourses (including community and local Discourses as well as youth-based Discourses), the hybrid spaces described in chapters 3 through 6 redefined what math and science learning can look like. Specifically, these hybrid spaces redefined who can participate and do well in math and science, what counts as rigorous math and science, and what can be produced and accomplished in math and science. Although traditional math and science classes typically begin with teacher-identified content objectives to be learned before finally and faintly alluding to applications of such content, the approach taken in these hybrid learning spaces traced the reverse arc. Either students could decide what issues were pertinent to them now that could be investigated via science and math or, if the content topic was predetermined (e.g., at GET City), students could choose which aspects of the content were relevant to them and how they wanted to engage with the subject matter. Empowering students in this manner radically challenges the traditional modes of science and math—subjects deemed elitist and difficult, and often taught didactically to novices (students) by experts (teachers).

By focusing on students' interests, hybrid spaces make the barriers between minority students and the disciplines of science and math more porous, removing the school-mediated ways through which students gain access (or not) to science and math. Students were no longer learning the knowledge of the "other"; they were acquiring scientific and mathematical knowledge to critically make sense of important issues in *their community*, and were acting on their knowledge to bring about change. These hybrid spaces were more successful in fulfilling the agenda of science and math "for all" because students' interests, needs, concerns, and local contexts were foundational to the scientific and mathematical investigations. Such an approach deeply values local knowledge, and actively seeks out the daily contexts of how youth live, play, and learn for critical opportunities for them to learn science and math. Such a stance purposefully elevates the local expertise of youth as not being lesser to professional expertise. Creating and sustaining hybrid spaces is grounded in the belief that expertise takes different forms, and that there is value in multiple perspectives and multiple representations. How youth see and frame a problem will look different from how adults do so. How insiders and outsiders see problems will also vary. For example, the perspectives of the girls facing school closure will differ from that of an adult member of the school board advocating for school closure. The girls, owing to their identities as children, as students being forced to attend another school, as community members who will have to walk long distances to that other school, will naturally view their school closure in far different terms than will an adult school board member who views the 1.3 miles that separate the two schools as an insignificant distance. It may be insignificant for an adult, or for an adult who does not need to traipse 2.6 miles daily. Since they were living out the issue of impending school closure in their local context, the girls were uniquely qualified and positioned to respond to the unfolding of this community issue and to transform it.

The same can be said about all of the episodes of empowering science and math education that cut across the text; there is real engagement with science and math in ways that are responsive to and transformative of local context. While not all moments of empowering science and math education are about changing the local community (as, for example, the youth in GET City tried to do), they all do seek to transform the meaning, value, and practice of math and science in the moment, whether it be how to learn about healthy eating habits or about weather or mathematical representations. The stories of Mrs. Davis and of the students at Francis Middle School are grounded in experiences and perspective that give meaning to the science and math at hand while at the same time challenging the sterile and simple nature of how that science and math are framed for the purposes of schooling. Through their engagement in science and math, the students were active contributors to knowledge-in-the-making, instead of passive consumers of a "final form" of knowledge.

These hybrid spaces also challenged what counts as rigorous evidence of mathematical and scientific knowledge and achievements. Instead of the traditional pen-and-paper test and one final test score to quantify students' expertise in science and math, students showcased their expertise in science and math by creating artifacts that reflect their unique identities as youth and insider community members. Most of the chapters described youth creating digital movies tailored to inform and educate community members, peers, or stakeholders about issues that affect them all. In fact, we argue that this mode of reflecting on their scientific and mathematical knowledge is more rigorous then taking a pen-and-paper test. More was at stake than doing well at a school task. Instead of merely regurgitating content facts and figures, the students had to apply their content knowledge to the specifics of their local context. The students depended on their science and math knowledge to achieve the goals they had set out for themselves with regard to their communities. Without a firm grasp of the relevant mathematical and scientific principles, the youth would be limited in the making their case to their intended audience. In that sense, the stakes are much higher for the students to exhibit competence in mathematical and scientific content with the creation of these artifacts than it is for them to take a solitary pen-and-paper test.

The creation and sustenance of hybrid spaces by teachers and students in math and science is one approach toward affording students (especially minority students) an empowering learning environment. Figure 7.2 shows how the various aspects we have been discussing in this book come together. Explicitly valuing and inviting community, local, and youth-based Discourses to complement and make relevant mathematical and scientific Discourses create a hybrid space where the hybrid Discourse is heteroglossic. Students are positioned not as novices but as experts in the local context. Such hybridity supports and fosters new modes of engagement, values multiple identities and perspectives, and nurtures the creation of science and math artifacts that reflect students' varied interests in discipline content, in their communities and themselves. Teachers are positioned as co-inquirers who, together with stu-

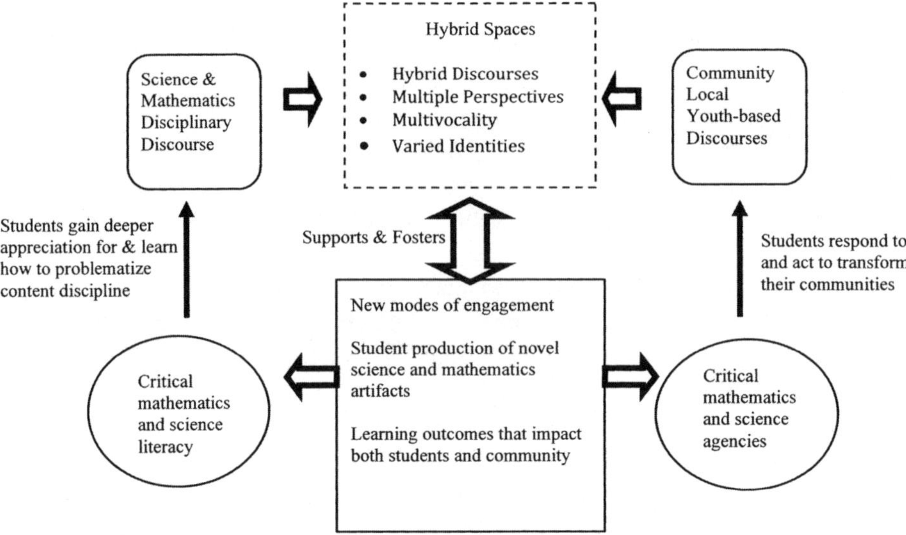

FIGURE 7.2. How hybrid spaces foster critical literacy and critical subject agency

dents, are invested in researching the issues, valuing the input and ideas of students. How the engagements take shape is organic as students and teacher solicit input from one another, from the disciplines of science and math, and from the community. This is an empowering process for students and secures their investment. As Angel reminds us in chapter 3, "It is like information that could involve *you*." Through the process, students gain critical literacy that helps them develop a deeper and more analytical understanding of the value of science and math, as well as to problematize the existing ideologies of science and math. Students are also able to respond to important community issues and take action because of their knowledge and skills in science and math, thereby demonstrating critical math and critical science agency. As Naisha from chapter 3 puts it so simply yet powerfully, "we *did* something with [math]."

Politics and Tensions in Expansive Hybrid Spaces

The empowering learning environments described in this book aspire to achieve the kind of emancipatory education championed by scholars like Freire (1973) and Giroux (1981), where critical knowledge gained exposes the layers of injustices in one's life, impelling one to take action toward liberatory social change. In short, in the Freirean and Girouxian perspective, there is a commitment toward rejecting oppression as a "fact of life" and the connections between critical knowledge and transformative action made ineluctable. Such a political stance surfaces tensions that must be considered. When asked what it was about her experiences with GET City that was most important to her, Janelle, a sixth grader, answered, "I'm a make-a-difference expert." Janelle's answer is reflective of how she has configured her science knowledge, practices, and identities at GET City into a personal conviction that she can act on her agency to do something. Janelle's statement also reminds us of the political aspects of hybrid spaces and the tensions that emerge in both the creation and the sustenance of hybrid spaces.

The premise of hybrid spaces rests on the assumption that it is important to question not just what students learn, but why, how, and for whom the learning of science and math makes a difference, as well as the nature of the difference. Creating and sustaining expansive hybrid learning spaces is not an easy or simple undertaking. On the contrary, it is fraught with political underpinnings and challenges, both in the arena of the classroom/learning environment, and in society when students enact critical science and critical math agency.

Let us go back to Janelle's statement. In order for her to be a "make-a-difference expert," she needed to have access to rigorous science content that is relevant to her life. She also needed to be informed about community issues and be able to bring these issues to the table at GET City sessions for discussions. It was incumbent upon the GET City teachers to explicitly solicit for student input on community issues, be intimately aware of the students' concerns and local contexts, and seize every opportunity to use these everyday experiences as entry points for students to learn science. Therefore, the teachers at GET City had to actively and consistently not position themselves as the authority figures, but purposefully cede power to students as the youth drew from their local expertise as community insiders. The process is complex and messy. Students and teachers bring multiple scripts and agendas to the table that have to be teased out and translated into concise, scientific, yet personalized tasks that will empower students and sustain their agency. There is no master narrative to follow in such hybrid spaces since the evolving hybrid Discourse builds on multiple perspectives organically recruited. Such a process is a marked departure from the traditional classroom lesson plan where the content storyline, lesson objectives, and tasks are neatly demarcated.

We also think it is important to raise the question of how teachers and youth learn to engage in the practice of critical mathematical and science literacy. One of the challenges posed by such an organic process is that it demands that teachers and students take up different positions and identities. While these positions may be welcomed and necessary for the work of empowering students to excel in science and math and develop critical literacy and critical agency, these are nonetheless novel positions and identities radically different from traditional teacher and student roles. Even as the teachers and students in these chapters embraced the hard work and struggles required to create and sustain hybrid spaces, they constantly grappled with the tendency to retreat into the more familiar teacher and student roles and to "do school," especially when the next steps forward in their student- and community-centered projects were unfolding in murky territory. Therefore, both teachers and students are required to occupy uncomfortable and risky spaces as they collectively create a more empowering hybrid space for learning. In order for the learning community to successfully create and sustain a hybrid space for empowering learning, both teachers and students have to resist the ingrained practices and attitudes of classroom routines that have been previously inscribed and normalized by traditional modes of instruction.

In the case of Mrs. Davis' teaching, we see a teacher who carefully modified the designated curriculum to scaffold more opportunities for student-centered Discourse. She assigned oral histories for homework, told her own stories and elicited those of the students, and used various scientific and cultural artifacts in ways that challenged the norm. We view these moments as her attempts to scaffold students in participating in new ways and to clearly announce to her students that doing science in her classroom operated under a set of norms and routines that differed from tradition. While we see a less explicitly scaffolded approach in Mrs. Tiller's classroom (chapter 1), we see the embodied work of teaching as implicitly challenging the norms for talking and doing science, making possible a moment for engaging in critical dialog on the complexity of the food environment. Cooking and eating French fries, while so simple, radically rewrites the physical and political space of the science classroom. Eating in the science classroom is against the rules, and savoring fries challenges the take-home message of healthy eating. Yet, together they enabled a more dynamic engagement with the text of science.

Classrooms can be high-stakes environments. They can control one's academic trajectory and one's social status. But the stakes are equally high for teachers. The loss of control and the existence of contemporary accountability measures play into how and why ways of being have become so highly structured for teachers and students. Yet, what the stories in this text reveal is that stepping outside these increasingly structured ways of being in schools increases student engagement and identity work in math and science. However, we also acknowledge the very real struggles involved by both teachers and students, in venturing beyond traditional roles and responsibilities. How can teachers and students continually engage in these struggles without incurring "burn-out"?

Beyond the immediate learning environment, enacting critical science and math agency also means that students engage in potentially subversive activism in resisting inequitable or harmful practices inflicted upon their communities. Such engagements are not without tensions. The middle school girls advocating against the closure of their school provide an example that highlights tensions inherent in the enactment of critical agency. While the girls were successful in persuading the school board to abandon the plans for school closure, they (and by extension their teachers) had to set themselves up against the higher authority figures of the school when making their case against the school board. The highly transparent and visible manner in which the students (and their teachers) opposed the school board and refuted their arguments is likely to put both students and teachers at risk for repercussions from the higher-ups.

Embedded in this last point is the idea that the goals of critical mathematical and scientific literacy are often in tension with the normative work of schools. Can or should the success of empowering classrooms be measured in standard ways? How do we encourage and applaud teachers and students for embracing critical literacy and enacting critical agency when these very acts may render them vulnerable to the political consequences that are often meted out by normative education systems? How do we sustain these efforts so that students do not merely acquire fragments of critical knowledge? These are uncomfortable yet necessary questions that we have to grapple with if we are serious about achieving the goals of science and math for all through the creation of more expansive hybrid spaces.

Moving Forward

We started this book with the desire to offer a concrete set of images of math and science hybrid spaces in action in urban science and math classrooms as well as out-of-school learning environments. While many have written about the need for creating such hybrid spaces in classrooms, especially in light of the increasing achievement gaps between white and minority students, we do not as yet have many images of what this hybrid space looks like, how it is connected to students' lives and what they need to learn, how it might be measured, and how it can fit into the current policy climate. Through this book, the authors have discussed what hybrid space is, how it is connected to the learning of school science and math, how it is constructed, what its multiple outcomes are, and why multiple outcomes matter in science and math education. In particular, this book drew upon a social justice framework and hybridity theories grounded in critical and sociocultural theories to offer an in-depth look at how authentic third or hybrid spaces are created and sustained in action.

We use the phrase "empowering learning environments" intentionally to capture a vision of education that engages youth in learning and using science and math as both a tool and a context for change. This means that one both views the world with a critical mindset and imagines how the world might be a more socially just and equitable place, and views oneself as a powerful scientific and mathematical thinker and doer. We have argued that an empowering science and math education is one where authentic and expansive hybrid spaces are created, which allow students to merge their worlds with the worlds of science and math education in support of learning and agency. We also paid special attention to the cultivation of student critical science and math agency as an essential outcome of student engagement in hybrid spaces. We discussed the importance of student agency as a pertinent hybrid-space learning outcome in fostering and strengthening a student's positive identity with school science and math. This has implications both for student performance in school science as well as their trajectory in science and math learning beyond middle school.

These stories have illustrated how hybrid spaces are expansive, and can be an approach to creating empowering math and science learning environments for urban youth. They have also revealed that creating and sustaining hybrid learning spaces takes collective effort from teachers and students, and that it is a messy, complex, and political affair. However, hybrid spaces also make science and math learning deeply meaningful for urban youth, and help them develop positive identities in math and science that can serve to sustain their interest and investment in their future science and math trajectory, so that minority students and girls would no longer be so severely underrepresented. It is our hope that the stories in this book will serve as helpful examples of how empowering hybrid spaces in math and science can be brokered for across different learning environments. As so vividly captured by Jeremy and Naomi in the quotes below, when equipped and empowered, urban youth are more than capable of quality scientific and mathematical achievements, and have the heart and confidence to actively use their mathematical and scientific knowledge to transform their communities into a more socially just world:

NAOMI: If I had a chance to talk to the governor, I won't be shy. I would tell her what a urban heat island is, and for all those who don't know what it is, it's just a place that doesn't have a lot of trees and has a lot of buildings and it's very, very hot.

JEREMY: I would tell the governor that urban heat islands is a place with very little trees . . . and the buildings, the black tar absorbs a lot of heat so it gets hotter in a heat island. I would want her to put rooftop gardens on the buildings so that it absorb carbon dioxide and . . . or make there be less cars driving around in the city so it's not as hot.

(12-year-old GET City youth Naomi and Jeremy, on what they would tell the governor of their state if they could show her their movie on urban heat islands)

References

Action for Healthy Kids. 2002. "Taking Action for Healthy Kids: A Report on the Healthy Schools Summit and the Action for Healthy Kids Initiative." Accessed November 3, 2011. http://www.actionforhealthykids.org/resources/.

Ahearn, L. M. 2001. "Language and Agency." *Annual Review of Anthropology.* 30:109.

Allexsaht-Snider, M. and Hart, L. 2001. "Mathematics for All: How Do We Get There?" *Theory into Practice* 40(2):93–101.

American Academy of Pediatrics. 2003. "Prevention of Pediatric Overweight and Obesity." *Pediatrics* 112(2):424–30.

American Association for the Advancement of Science (AAAS). 1989. "*Science for All Americans*." New York: Oxford University Press.

——. 2009. Benchmarks On-line, Project 2061. Accessed September 29, 2009. http://www.project2061.org/publications/bsl/online/index.php.

American Association of University Women Educational Foundation (AAUWEF). 1999. *Gaining a Foothold: Women's Transitions through Work and College.* Washington, DC: AAUWEF.

American Diabetes Association (ADA). 2000. "Type 2 Diabetes in Children and Adolescents." *Diabetes Care* 23(3):381–89.

Anderson, C. W. 2006. "Perspectives on Science Learning." In *Handbook of Research in Science Education*, edited by S. Abel and N. Lederman. Mahwah, NJ: Lawrence Erlbaum Associates.

Anderson, D. D., and E. Gold. 2006. "Home to School: Numeracy Practices and Mathematical Identities." *Mathematical Thinking and Learning 8*(3):261–86.

Anderson, G. L. 1989. "Critical Ethnography in Education: Origins, Current Status, and New Directions." *Review of Educational Research* 59:249–70.

Apple, M. W. 1992. "Do the Standards Go Far Enough? Power, Policy, and Practice in Mathematics Education." *Journal for Research in Mathematics Education* 23(5):412–31.

Atwater, M. M., J. Wiggins, and C. M. Gardner. 1995. "A Study of Urban Middle School Students with High and Low Attitudes Toward Science." *Journal of Research in Science Teaching* 32(6):665–77.

Barmby, P., P. Kind, and K. Jones. 2008. "Examining Changing Attitudes in Secondary School Science." *International Journal of Science Education* 30(8):1075–93.

Barone, T. 2000. *Aesthetics, Politics, and Educational Inquiry: Essays and Examples.* New York: Peter Lang.

Bell, P., B. Lewenstein, A. Shouse, and M. Feder, eds. 2009. *Learning Science in Informal Environments: People, Places and Pursuits.* Washington, DC: National Academy Press.

Behar, R. 1995. *Translated Woman: Crossing the Border with Esperanza's Story.* Boston: Beacon Press.

Bhabha, H. K. 1990. *Nation and Narration.* New York: Routledge.

——. 1994. *The Location of Culture.* New York: Routledge.

Black Eyed Peas. 2003. "Where Is the Love?" On *Elephunk.* [CD] Location: Interscope.

Boaler, J. 2002. "Paying the Price for 'Sugar and Spice': Shifting the Analytical Lens in Equity Research." *Mathematical Thinking and Learning* 4(2–3):127–44.

Boaler, J., and J. Greeno. 2000. "Identity, Agency, and Knowing in Mathematics Worlds." In *Multiple Perspectives on Mathematics Teaching and Learning,* edited by J. Boaler, 171–200. Westport, CT: Ablex.

Bourdieu, P. 1977. "Cultural Reproduction and Social Reproduction." In *Power and Ideology in Education,* edited by J. Karabel and A. H. Hasley, 487–511. New York: Oxford University Press.

Brickhouse, N. W. 1994. "Bringing In the Outsiders: Reshaping the Sciences of the Future." *Journal of Curriculum Studies* 26:401–16.

——. 2001. "Embodying Science: A Feminist Perspective on Learning." *Journal of Research in Science Teaching* 38(3):282–95.

Brickhouse, N. W., P. Lowery, and K. Schultz. 2000. "What Kind of Girl Does Science? The Construction of School Science Identities." *Journal of Research in Science Teaching* 37(5):441–58.

Brickhouse, N. W., and J. T. Potter. 2001. "Young Women's Scientific Identity Formation in an Urban Context." *Journal of Research in Science Teaching* 38(8):965–80.

Bridgeland, J., J. DiIulio, and K. Burke Morrison. 2006. *The Silent Epidemic: Perspectives of High School Dropouts.* Seattle, WA: Bill and Melinda Gates Foundation.

Brown, B. 2006. "'It Isn't No Slang That Can Be Said about This Stuff': Language, Identity, and Appropriating Science Discourse." *Journal of Research in Science Teaching* 43(1):96–126.

Brown, B., J.M. Reveles, and G. Kelly. 2005. "Scientific Literacy and Discursive Identity: A Theoretical Framework for Understanding Science Learning." *Science Education* doi:10.1002/sce.20069.

Brown, B. A. 2004. "Discursive Identity: Assimilation into the Culture of Science and Its Implications for Minority Students." *Journal of Research in Science Teaching* 41(8):810–34.

Brown, C. 2005. "Run It!" On *Run It!* [CD] Location: BMG/Jive.

Bruner, J. S. 1986. *Actual Minds, Possible Worlds.* Cambridge, MA: Harvard University Press.

———. 1996. *The Culture of Education.* Cambridge, MA: Harvard University Press.

Brunson, D., and J. Vogt. 1996. "Empowering Our Students and Ourselves: A Liberal Democratic Approach to the Communication Classroom." *Communication Education* 45:73–83.

Buckingham, S., D. Reeves, and A. Batchelor. 2005. "Wasting Women: The Environmental Justice of Including Women in Municipal Waste Management." *Local Environment* 10(4):427–44.

Buckwheat Boyz. 2000. "Peanut Butter Jelly Time." On *Buckwheat Boyz.* [CD] Location: Koch Records.

Burk, N. M. 2000. "Empowering At-Risk Students: Storytelling as a Pedagogical Tool." Paper presented at the Annual Meeting of the National Communication Association, Seattle, WA.

Buxton, C. 2010. "Social Problem Solving through Science: An Approach to Critical Place-Based Science Teaching and Learning." *Equity and Ethics in Education* 43(1):120–35.

Calabrese Barton, A. 1998. "Teaching Science with Homeless Children: Pedagogy, Representation and Identity." *Journal of Research in Science Teaching* 35:379–94.

———. 2003. *Teaching Science for Social Justice.* New York: Teachers College Press.

Calabrese Barton, A., E. Tan, and A. Rivet. 2008. "Creating Hybrid Spaces for Engaging School Science among Urban Middle School Girls." *American Education Research Journal* 45:68–103.

Campbell, P. F., and E. A. Silver. 1999. "Teaching and Learning Mathematics in Poor Communities." Report to the Board of Directors of the National Council of Teachers of Mathematics. Reston, VA: National Council of Teachers of Mathematics.

Carlone, H. B. 2004. "The Cultural Production of Science in Reform-Based Physics: Girls' Access, Participation, and Resistance. *Journal of Research in Science Teaching* 41:392–414.

Carspecken, P. 1996. *Critical Ethnography in Educational Research: A Theoretical and Practical Guide.* New York: Routledge.

Chazan, D. 2000. *Beyond Formulas in Mathematics Teaching: Dynamics of the High School Algebra Classroom*. New York: Teachers College Press.

Civil, M. 2007. "Building on Community Knowledge: An Avenue to Equity in Mathematics Education." In *Improving Access to Mathematics: Diversity and Equity in the Classroom*, edited by N. Nasir and P. Cobb, 105–17. New York: Teachers College Press.

Cobb, P., M. Gresalfi, and L. L. Hodge. 2009. "An Interpretive Scheme for Analyzing the Identities That Students Develop in Mathematics Classrooms." *Journal for Research in Mathematics Education* 40(1):40–68.

Cobb, P., and L. L. Hodge. 2002. "A Relational Perspective on Issues of Cultural Diversity and Equity as They Play Out in the Mathematics Classroom." *Mathematical Thinking and Learning* 4(2–3):249–84.

Conle, C. 2003. "An Anatomy of Narrative Curricula." *Educational Researcher* 32(3):3–15.

Connelly, F. M., and D. J. Clandinin. 1994. "Personal Experience Methods." In *Handbook of Qualitative Research*, edited by N. Denzin and Y. Lincoln, 413–27. London: Sage.

Coulter, C., C. Michael, and L. Poynor. 2007. "Storytelling as Pedagogy: An Unexpected Outcome of Narrative Inquiry." *Curriculum Inquiry* 37(2): 103–22.

Darling-Hammond, L. 1999. "Educating: The Academy's Greatest Failure or Its Most Important Future?" *Academe* 85(1):26–33.

Delgado, R. 1989. "Storytelling for Oppositionists and Others: A Plea for Narrative." *Michigan Law Review* 87:2411–41.

———. 1995. *Critical Race Theory: The Cutting Edge*. Philadelphia: Temple University Press.

Egan, K. 1988. *Teaching as Storytelling: An Alternative Approach to Teaching and the Curriculum*. London: Routledge.

Ellsworth, E. 1997. *Teaching Positions: Difference, Pedagogy, and the Power of Address*. New York: Teachers College Press.

Elmesky, R. 2005. "'I Am Science and the World Is Mine': Embodied Practices as Resources for Empowerment." *School Science and Mathematics* 105:335–42.

Empson, S. 2003. "Low-Performing Students and Teaching Fractions for Understanding:

An Interactional Analysis." *Journal for Research in Mathematics Education* 34(4):305–43.

Engeström, Y. 2001. "Expansive Learning at Work: Toward an Activity Theoretical Reconceptualization." *Journal of Education and Work* 14(1):133–56.

Enyedy, N., and J. Goldberg. 2004. "Inquiry in Interaction: Developing Classroom Communities for Understanding through Social Interaction." *Journal for Research in Science Teaching* 41(9):905–35.

Ernest, P. 2001. "Critical Mathematics Education." In *Issues in Mathematics Teaching*, edited by P. Gates. London: Routledge.

Esmonde, I. 2009. "Ideas and Identities: Supporting Equity in Cooperative Mathematics Learning." *Review of Educational Research* 79(2):1008–43.

Fine, M., ed. 1996. *Talking across Boundaries: Participatory Evaluation Research in an Urban Middle School*. New York: Bruner Foundation.

Flewitt, R., M. Nind, and J. Payler. 2009. "'If She's Left with Books She'll Just Eat Them': Considering Inclusive Multimodal Literacy Practices." *Journal of Early Childhood Literacy* 9(2):211–33.

Frankenstein, M. 1990. "Incorporating Race, Gender, and Class Issues into a Critical Mathematical Literacy Curriculum." *Journal of Negro Education* 59(3):336–47.

——. 1995. "Equity in Mathematics Education: Class in the World Outside of Class." In *New Directions for Equity in Mathematics Education*, edited by W. Secada, E. Fennema, and L. B. Adajian, 165–90. New York: Cambridge University Press.

——. 1997. "In Addition to the Mathematics: Including Equity Issues in the Curriculum." In *Multicultural and Gender Equity in the Mathematics Classroom*, edited by J. Trentacosta and M. Kenney. Reston, VA: National Council of Teachers of Mathematics.

Freire, P. 1970/1993. *Pedagogy of the Oppressed*. Rev. ed. New York: Continuum.

——. 1973. *Education for Critical Consciousness*. New York: Continuum.

Freire, P., and D. Macedo. 1987. *Literacy: Reading the Word and the World*. Westport, CT: Bergin and Garvey.

Frey, Glenn. 1993. "The Heat Is On." On *Glenn Frey Live*. Nashville: MCA Records.

Fusco, D., and A. Calabrese Barton. 2001. "Representing Student Achievements in Science." *Journal of Research in Science Teaching* 38(3):337–54.

Gaye, M. 1971. "Mercy Mercy Me (The Ecology)." On *What's Going On*. [CD] Location: Tamia.

Gee, J. P. 1999. *An Introduction to Discourse Analysis: Theory and Method*. London: Routledge.

Gellert, U., E. Jablonka, and C. Keitel. 2001. "Mathematical Literacy and Common Sense in Mathematics Education." In *Sociocultural Research on Mathematics Education: An International Perspective*, edited by B. Atweh, H. Forgasz, and B. Nebres, 57–73. Mahwah, NJ: Lawrence Erlbaum.

Gerrig, R. 1993. *Experiencing Narrative Worlds: On the Psychological Activities of Teaching*. Newhaven, CT: Yale University Press.

Gilbert, A., and R. Yerrick. 2001. "Same School, Separate Worlds: A Sociocultural Study of Identity, Resistance, and Negotiation in a Rural, Lower

Track Science Classroom." *Journal of Research in Science Teaching* 38(5): 574–98.

Giroux, Henry A. 1981. *Ideology, Culture and the Process of Schooling.* Philadelphia: Temple University Press.

——. 1983. "Ideology, Culture, and the Process of Schooling." In *The Hidden Curriculum and Moral Education: Deception or Discovery?*, edited by H. A. Giroux and D. E. Purpel. Berkeley, CA: Temple University Press.

——. 1988. *Schooling and the Struggle for Public Life: Critical Pedagogy in the Modern Age.* Minneapolis: University of Minnesota.

Giroux, Henry A., C. Lankshear, P. McLaren, and M. Peters. 1996. *Counternarratives: Cultural Studies and Critical Pedagogies in Postmodern Spaces.* New York: Routledge.

González, N., R. Andrade, M. Civil, and L. Moll. 2001. "Bridging Funds of Distributed Knowledge: Creating Zones of Practices in Mathematics." *Journal of Students Placed at Risk* 6(1–2):115–32.

González, N., L. Moll, and C. Amanti, eds. 2005. *Funds of Knowledge: Theorizing Practices in Households, Communities, and Classrooms.* Mahwah, NJ: Lawrence Erlbaum.

Goodman, E., and R. Whitaker. 2002. "A Prospective Study of the Role of Depression in the Development and Persistence of Adolescent Obesity." *Pediatrics* 110(3):497–504.

Gutiérrez, K. D. 2002. "Studying Cultural Practices in Urban Learning Communities." *Human Development* 45(4):312–21.

——. 2008. "Developing a Sociocritical Literacy in the Third Space." *Reading Research Quarterly* 43(2):148–64.

Gutiérrez, K. D., P. Baquedano-López, and C. Tejeda. 1999. "Rethinking Diversity: Hybridity and Hybrid Language Practices in the Third Space." *Mind, Culture and Activity* 6(4):286–303.

Gutiérrez, K. D., and B. Rogoff. 2003. "Cultural Ways of Learning: Individual Traits or Repertoires of Practice." *Educational Researcher* 32(5):19–25.

Gutiérrez, K. D., B. Rymes, and J. Larson. 1995. "Script, Counterscript, and Underlife in the Classroom: James Brown versus Brown v. Board of Education." *Harvard Educational Review* 65(3):445–71.

Gutiérrez, R. 2002. "Enabling the Practice of Mathematics Teachers: Towards a New Equity Research Agenda." *Mathematical Thinking and Learning* 4(2–3):145–87.

——. 2007. "(Re)defining Equity: The Importance of a Critical Perspective." In *Improving Access to Mathematics: Diversity and Equity in the Classroom*, edited by N. Nasir and P. Cobb. New York: Teachers College Press.

Gutstein, E. 2003. "Teaching and Learning Mathematics for Social Justice in an Urban, Latino School." *Journal for Research in Mathematics Education* 34(1):37.

——. 2006. *Reading and Writing the World with Mathematics: Toward a Pedagogy for Social Justice.* New York: Routledge.

——. 2007. "'And That's Just How It Starts': Teaching Mathematics and Developing Student Agency." *Teachers College Record* 109(2):420–48.

——. 2010. "The Common Core State Standards Initiative: A Critical Response." *Journal of Urban Mathematics Education* 3(1):9–18.

Gutstein, E., P. Lipman, P. Hernández, and R. Reyes. 1997. "Culturally Relevant Mathematics Teaching in a Mexican-American Context." *Journal for Research in Mathematics Education* 28(6):709–37.

Gutstein, E., J. A. Middleton, and J. T. Fey. 2005. "Equity in School Mathematics Education: How Can Research Contribute?" *Journal for Research in Mathematics Education* 36(2):92–100.

Gutstein, E., and B. Peterson. 2005. *Rethinking Mathematics: Teaching Social Justice by the Numbers.* Milwaukee: Rethinking Schools.

Halliday, M. A. K. 1993. "Some Grammatical Problems in Scientific English." In *Writing Science: Literacy and Discursive Power,* edited by M. A. K. Halliday and J. R. Martin, 69–85. Pittsburgh: University of Pittsburgh Press.

Haraway, D. 1989. *Primate Visions: Gender, Race and Nature in the World of Modern Science.* New York: Routledge.

Harding, S. 1991. *Whose Science? Whose Knowledge? Thinking from Women's Lives.* Ithaca: Cornell University Press.

Hodge, L. 2006. "An Orientation on the Mathematics Classroom That Emphasizes Power and Identity: Reflecting on Equity Research." *The Urban Review* 38(5):373–85.

Hogan, K., and C. Corey. 2001. "Viewing Classrooms as Cultural Contexts for Fostering Scientific Literacy." *Anthropology and Education Quarterly* 32(2):214–44.

Hogg, M. 1995. "To Huff and Puff: There's More to Storytelling than the 'Three Little Pigs'!" Paper presented at the Central States Communication Association Conference, Indianapolis, IN.

Holland, D. 2003. "People in Activity: A Cultural Historical Approach to Identity, Agency and Social Change." Paper presented at the SIG-CHAT business meeting at the Annual Conference of the American Educational Research Association, Chicago, IL.

Holland, D., D. Skinner, L. J. William, and C. Cain. 2001. *Identity and Agency in Cultural Worlds.* Cambridge, MA: Harvard University Press.

Hopkins, R. 1994. *Narrative Schooling: Experiential Learning and the Transformation of American Education.* New York: Teachers College Press.

Ingersoll, R. M. 1999. "The Problem of Underqualified Teachers in American Secondary Schools." *Educational Researcher* 28(2):26–37.

Jurow, A. S., H. Rogers, and J. Y. Ma. 2008. "Expanding the Disciplinary Expertise of a Middle School Mathematics Classroom: Re-Contextualizing Student

Models in Conversations with Visiting Specialists." *Journal of Learning Sciences* 17:338–80.

Kafai, Y. B., and C. C. Ching. 2001. "Affordances of Collaborative Software Design Planning for Elementary Students' Science Talk." *Journal of the Learning Sciences* 10(3):323–63.

Kaswom, C. 1993. "An Alternative Perspective on Empowerment of Adult Undergraduates." *Contemporary Education* 64:162–65.

Kellas, J. K. 2006. "Family Ties: Communicating Identity through Jointly Told Family Stories." *Communication Monographs* 27(4):365–89.

Kelly, R. 2001. "The World's Greatest." On *Ali.* [CD] Location: Zoomba Recording.

Kimura, M. 2008. "Narrative as a Site of Subject Construction." *Feminist Theory* 9(1):5–24.

Koch, P., I. Contento, and A. Calabrese Barton. 2007. "Choice, Control and Change: Linking Food and the Environment." Teachers College Columbia University Center for Food and Environment website. http://www.tc.edu/life/choice.html.

Kress, G. 1997. *Before Writing: Rethinking the Paths to Literacy.* London: Routledge.

Kurth, L. A., C. A. Anderson, and A. S. Palincsar. 2002. "The Case of Carla: Dilemmas of Helping All Students to Understand Science." *Science Education* 86(3):287–313.

Ladson-Billings, G. 1997. "It Doesn't Add Up: African American Students' Mathematics Achievement." *Journal for Research in Mathematics Education* 28(6):697–708.

Lave, J., and E. Wenger. 1991. *Situated Learning: Legitimate Peripheral Participation.* New York: Cambridge University Press.

Lee, C., and Y. Majors. 2003. "'Heading up the Street': Localised Opportunities for Shared Constructions of Knowledge." *Pedagogy, Culture and Society* 11(1):49–69.

Lee, O. 2002. "Science Inquiry for Elementary Students from Diverse Backgrounds." In *Review of Research in Education, vol. 26, edited by* W. G. Secada, 23–69. Washington, DC: American Educational Research Association.

——. 2005. "Science Education and English Language Learners: Synthesis and Research Agenda." *Review of Educational Research* 75(4):491–530.

Lee, O., and S. H. Fradd. 1998. "Science for All, Including Students from Non-English-Language Backgrounds." *Educational Researcher* 27(4):12–21.

Lee, O., and A. Luykx. 2006. *Science Education and Student Diversity.* New York: Cambridge University Press.

——. 2007. "Science Education and Student Diversity: Race/Ethnicity, Language, Culture, and Socioeconomic Status." In *Handbook of Research in Sci-*

ence Education, 2nd ed., edited by S. K. Abell and N. G. Lederman, 171–97. Mahwah, NJ: Lawrence Erlbaum.

Lemke, J. L. 1990. *Talking Science: Language, Learning and Values.* Norwood: Ablex Publishing Company.

Licón Khisty, L. 1997. "Making Mathematics Accessible to Latino Students: Rethinking Instructional Practices." In *Multicultural and Gender Equity in the Mathematics Classroom: The Gift of Diversity,* edited by J. Trentacosta and M. Kenney. Reston, VA: National Council of Teachers of Mathematics.

Lindsay, G. 2001. "Nothing Personal? Narrative Reconstructions of Registered Nurses' Experience in Health Care Reform." PhD diss., University of Toronto, ON.

Lineham, C., and J. McCarthy. 2001. "Reviewing the 'Community of Practice' Metaphor: An Analysis of Control Relations in a Primary School Classroom." *Mind, Culture and Activity* 8(2):129–47.

Little Bear, L. 2000. "Jagged Worldviews Colliding." In *Reclaiming Indigenous Voice and Vision,* edited by M. Battiste, 77–85. Vancouver: University of British Columbia Press.

Livo, N. J., and S. A. Rietz. 1986. "*Storytelling: Process and Practice.*" Littleton, CO: Libraries Unlimited.

Martin, D. 2000. *Mathematics Success and Failure among African-American Youth: The Role of Sociohistorical Context, Community Forces, School Influence and Individual Agency.* Mahwah, NJ: Lawrence Erlbaum.

——. 2006a. "Mathematics Learning and Participation as Racialized Forms of Experience: African American Parents Speak on the Struggle for Mathematics Literacy." *Mathematical Thinking and Learning* 8(3):197–229.

——. 2006b. "Mathematics Learning and Participation in African American Context: The Co-construction of Identity in Two Intersecting Realms of Experience." In *Diversity, Equity, and Access to Mathematical Ideas,* edited by N. Nasir and P. Cobb, 146–58. New York: Teachers College Press.

McFarlane-Alvarez, S. L. 2007. "Trinidad and Tobago Television Advertising as Third Space: Hybridity as Resistance in the Caribbean Mediascape." *Howard Journal of Communications* 18(1):39–55.

Mellin-Olson, S. 1987. *The Politics of Mathematics Education.* Dordrecht, Holland: Kluwer.

Miller, P. J., G. E. Cho, and J. R. Bracey. 2005. "Working-Class Children's Experience through the Prism of Personal Storytelling." *Human Development* 48(3):115–35.

Mims. 2007. "This Is Why I'm Hot." On *Music Is My Savior.* [CD] New York: Capital Records.

Moje, E. B. 2007. "Developing Socially Just Subject-Matter Instruction: A Review of the Literature on Disciplinary Literacy." In *Review of Research In*

Education, edited by L. Parker, 1–44. Washington, DC: American Educational Research Association.

Moje, E. B., K. M. Ciechanowski, K. Kramer, L. Ellis, R. Carrillo, and T. Collazo. 2004. "Working toward Third Space in Content Area Literacy: An Examination of Everyday Funds of Knowledge and Discourse." *Reading Research Quarterly* 39(1):38–70.

Moje, E. B., C. Tehani, R. Carillo, and R. W. Marx. 2001. "Maestro, What Is 'Quality'?: Language, Literacy, and Discourse in Project-Based Science." *Journal of Research in Science Teaching* 38(4):469–98.

Moll, L., and R. Ruiz. 2002. "The Schooling of Latino Children." In *Latinos: Remaking America*, edited by M. M. Suárez-Orozco and M. M. Páez. Berkeley: University of California Press.

Moschkovich, J. 2005. "Using Two Languages When Learning Mathematics." *Educational Studies in Mathematics* 64(2):121–44.

Muenzing, M., and L. Anziotti. 1990. "The Power." On *World Power*. [Recorded by Snap!] Location: Ariola Records.

Nasir, N. S., and V. Hand. 2008. "From the Court to the Classroom: Opportunities for Engagement, Learning, and Identity in Basketball and Classroom Mathematics." *Journal of the Learning Sciences* 17(2):143–79.

Nasir, N. S., V. Hand, and E. V. Taylor. 2008. "Culture and Mathematics in School: Boundaries Between Cultural and Domain Knowledge in the Mathematics Classroom and Beyond." *Review of Research in Education* 32(1):187–240.

National Assessment of Educational Progress (NAEP). 2005. *NAEP 2004 Trends in Academic Progress: Three Decades of Student Performance in Reading and Mathematics*. Alexandria, VA: National Center for Education Statistics.

National Center for Education Statistics (NCES). 2006. *Education Statistics Quarterly* 6, no. 4 (2004). NCES 2006–613. Washington, DC: NCES.

National Research Council (NRC). 1989. *Everybody Counts: A Report to the Nation on the Future of Mathematics Education*. Washington, DC: National Academy Press.

——. 1996. *National Science Education Standards*. Washington, DC: National Academy Press.

New London Group. 1996. "A Pedagogy of Multiliteracies: Designing Social Futures." *Harvard Educational Review* 66(1):60–92.

Newman, R. 2001. "Making Environmental Politics: Women and Love Canal Activism." *Women's Studies Quarterly* 29(1):51–64.

Nieto, S. 1999. *The Light in Their Eyes: Creating Multicultural Learning Communities*. New York: Teachers College Press.

Noddings, N. 1993. "Politicizing the Mathematics Classroom." In *Math Worlds: Philosophical and Social Studies of Mathematics and Mathematics Educa-*

tion, edited by S. Restivo, J. P. Van Bendegem, and R. Fischer. New York: SUNY Press.

Oakes, J. 1990. *Multiplying Inequalities: The Effects of Race, Social Class, and Tracking on Opportunities to Learn Mathematics and Science*. Santa Monica: RAND.

——. 2005. *Keeping Track: How Schools Structure Inequality*. 2nd ed. New Haven: Yale University Press.

Oakes, J., R. Joseph, and K. Muir. 2003. "Access and Achievement in Mathematics and Science: Inequalities That Endure and Change." In *Handbook of Research on Multicultural Education*, edited by J. A. Banks and C. A. M. Banks, 69–90. San Francisco: Jossey-Bass.

Olitsky, S. 2006. "Facilitating Identity Formation, Group Membership, and Learning in Science Classrooms: What Can Be Learned from Out-of-Field Teaching in a Urban School?" *Science Education* 91:201–21.

Page, R. 1990. "Games of Chance: The Lower-Track Curriculum in a College-Preparatory High School." *Curriculum Inquiry* 20(3):249–64.

Peterson, B. 1994. "Math and Media: Bias Busters." In *Rethinking Our Classrooms: Teaching for Equity and Social Justice*, edited by B. Bigelow, L. Christensen, S. Karp, B. Miner, and B. Peterson. Milwaukee: Rethinking Schools.

——. 1999. "Teaching Math across the Curriculum." In *Education Is Politics: Critical Teaching across Differences, K-12*, edited by I. Shor and C. Pari. Portsmouth, NH: Heinemann.

Pew Hispanic Center. 2006. "A Statistical Portrait of Hispanics at Mid-decade." http://pewhispanic.org/reports/middecade/.

Pickering, A. 1995. "*The Mangle of Practice*." Chicago: University of Chicago Press.

Poindexter, B. 1987. "Hot Hot Hot." On *Buster Poindexter*. [CD] Nashville: RCA Records.

Powell, A. and M. Frankenstein, eds. 1997. *Challenging Eurocentrism in Mathematics Education*. New York: SUNY Press.

Proposition 203. 2000. "English for the Children." Arizona voter initiative.

Pruyn, M. 1999. "*Discourse Wars in Gotham-West: A Latino Immigrant Urban Tale of Resistance and Agency*." Boulder, CO: Westview Press.

Rahm, J. 2008. "Urban Youths' Hybrid Identity Projects in Science Practices at the Margin: A Look Inside a School-Museum-Scientist Partnership Project and an Afterschool Science Program." *Cultural Studies of Science Education* 3(1):97–121.

Reyes, L. H., and G. M. A. Stanic. 1988. "Race, Sex, Socioeconomic Status, and Mathematics." *Journal for Research in Mathematics Education* 19(1):26–43.

Rihanna. 2007. "Umbrella." On *Good Girl Gone Bad*. [CD] Los Angeles: Westlake Recording Studios.

Rimes, LeAnn. 2000. "Please Remember." On *Coyote Ugly*. [CD] Location: Curb Records.

Rosebery, A., B. Warren, and F. Conant. 1992. "Appropriating Scientific Discourse: Findings from Language Minority Classrooms." *Journal of the Learning Sciences* 2(1):61–94.

Roth, W.-M. 2006. "Bricolage, Métissage, Hybridity, Heterogeneity, Diaspora: Concepts for Thinking Science Education in the 21st Century." *Cultural Studies of Science Education* 1(1):1–42.

Roth, W.-M., and G. M. Bowen, 1995. "Knowing and Interacting: A Study of Culture, Practices, and Resources in a Grade 8 Open-Inquiry Science Classroom Guided by a Cognitive Apprenticeship Metaphor." *Cognition and Instruction* 13(1):73–128.

Rountree, K. 2007. "Archaeologists and Goddess Feminists at Çatalhöyük: An Experiment in Multivocality." *Journal of Feminist Studies in Religion* 23(2):7–26.

Ryder, J. 2001. "Identifying Science Understanding for Functional Scientific Literacy." *Studies in Science Education* 36:1–44.

Sanchez, C. 2009. "Learning about Students' Culture and Language through Family Stories Elicited by Dichos." *Early Childhood Education Journal* 37(2):161–69.

Schleppegrell, M. J. 2001. "Linguistic Features of the Language of Schooling." *Linguistics of Education* 12(4):431–59.

Schneider, R. M., J. Krajcik, R. Marx, and E. Soloway. 2001. "Performance of Students in Project-Based Science Classrooms on a National Measure of Science Achievement." *Journal of Research in Science Teaching* 38(7):821–42.

Schoenfeld, A. H. 2002. "Making Mathematics Work for All Children: Issues of Standards, Testing, and Equity." *Educational Researcher* 31(1):3–15.

Secada, W. G. 1989. "Educational Equity Versus Equality of Education: An Alternative Conception." In *Equity and Education*, edited by W. G. Secada, 68–88. New York: Falmer.

——. 1992. "Race, Ethnicity, Social Class, Language, and Achievement in Mathematics." In *Handbook of Research on Mathematics Teaching and Learning*, edited by D. A. Grouws, 623–60. New York: Macmillan.

Sewell, W. H. 1992. "A Theory of Structure: Duality, Agency, and Transformation." *American Journal of Sociology* 98(1):1–29.

Shamos, M. H. 1995. *The Myth of Scientific Literacy*. New Jersey: Rutgers University Press.

Sharma, A. 2008. "Making (Electrical) Connections: Exploring Student Agency in a School in India." *Science Education* 92(2):217–319.

Shor, I. 1992. *Empowering Education*. Chicago: University of Chicago Press.

——. 1996. *When Students Have Power: Negotiating Authority in a Critical Pedagogy*. Chicago: University of Chicago Press.

Skovsmose, O. 1994a. "Towards a Critical Mathematics Education." *Educational Studies in Mathematics* 27(1):35–57.

———. 1994b. *Towards a Philosophy of Critical Mathematics Education*. Dordrecht, Holland: Kluwer.

Soja, E. W. 1996. *Thirdspace: Journeys to Los Angeles and Other Real and Imagined Places*. Malden, MA: Blackwell.

Solorzano, D., and T. Yosso. 2001. "Critical Race and LatCrit Theory and Method: Counterstorytelling Chicana and Chicano Graduate School Experiences." *International Journal of Qualitative Studies in Education* 14(4): 471–95.

Spade, J. Z., L. Columba, and B. E. Vanfossen. 1997. "Tracking in Mathematics and Science: Courses and Course-Selection Procedures." *Sociology of Education* 70(2):108–27.

Spencer, H. 1859. *Education: Intellectual, Moral, and Physical*. New York: J. B. Alden.

Stanley, W. B., and N. W. Brickhouse. 1994. "Multiculturalism, Universalism and Science Education." *Science Education* 78(4):387–98.

Stevens, R. 2000. "Who Counts What as Math? Emergent and Assigned Mathematics Problems in a Project-Based Classroom." In *Multiple Perspectives on Mathematics Teaching and Learning*, edited by J. Boaler, 105–44. Westport, CT: Ablex Publishing.

Stinson, D. W. 2008. "Negotiating Sociocultural Discourses: The Counter-Story of Academically and Mathematically Successful African American Male Students." *American Educational Research Journal* 45(4):975–1010.

Supremes. 1965. "Stop! In the Name of Love!" On *Stop! In the Name of Love!* [CD] Detroit: Motown.

Surgeon General. 2001. *Surgeon General's Call to Action to Prevent and Decrease Overweight and Obesity*. Rockville, MD: US Department of Health and Human Services, Public Health Service.

Tan, E., and A. Calabrese Barton. 2008. "From Peripheral to Central, the Story of Melanie's Metamorphosis in an Urban Middle School Science Class." *Science Education* 92(4):567–90.

Tate, W. 1994. "Mathematics Standards and Urban Education: Is This the Road to Recovery?" *Educational Forum* 58(4):380–90.

———. 1995. "Returning to the Root: A Culturally Relevant Approach to Mathematics Pedagogy." *Theory into Practice* 34(3):166–73.

———. 1997. "Critical Race Theory and Education: History, Theory, and Implications." In *Review of Research in Education*, edited by M. Apple, 195–247. Washington, DC: American Educational Research Association.

———. 2001. "Science Education as a Civil Right: Urban Schools and Opportunity-to-Learn Considerations." *Journal of Research in Science Teaching* 38(9):1015–28.

Temptations. 1968. "Wish It Would Rain." On *Wish It Would Rain*. [CD] Detroit: Michigan.

Trueba, H. T. 1999. "Critical Ethnography and a Vygotskian Pedagogy of Hope: The Empowerment of Mexican Immigrant Children." *Qualitative Studies in Education* 12(6):591–614.

Turner, E. E. 2003. "Critical Mathematical Agency: Urban Middle School Students Engage in Significant Mathematics to Understand, Critique, and Act Upon Their World." PhD diss., University of Texas, Austin.

Turner, E. E., and B. T. Font Strawhun. 2007. "Problem Posing That Makes a Difference: Students Posing and Investigating Mathematical Problems Related to Overcrowding at Their School." *Teaching Children Mathematics* 13(9): 457–63.

Turner, E. E., M. Varley Gutiérrez, K. Simic-Muller, and J. Díez-Palomar. 2009. "'Everything Is Math in the Whole World': Integrating Critical and Community Knowledge in Authentic Mathematical Investigations with Elementary Latina/o Students." *Mathematical Thinking and Learning* 11(3):136–57.

Tzou, C., G. Scalone, and P. Bell. 2010. "The Role of Environmental Narratives and Social Positioning in How Place Gets Constructed for and by Youth: Implications for Environmental Science Education for Social Justice." *Equity and Ethics in Education* 43(1):105–19.

Urrieta, L. 2007. "Identity Production in Figured Worlds: How Some Mexican Americans Become Chicana/o Activist Educators." *Urban Review* 39(2):117–44.

Valenzuela, A. 1999. *Subtractive Schooling: US-Mexican Youth and the Politics of Caring*. Albany: State University of New York Press.

——. 2005. *Leaving Children Behind: How Texas-Style Accountability Fails Latino Youth*. New York: SUNY Press.

Valero, P. 2002. "The Myth of the Active Learner: From Cognitive to Socio-Political Interpretations of Students in Mathematics Classroom." Paper presented at the 3rd International Mathematics Education and Society Conference, Copenhagen.

Varenne, H., and R. McDermott. 1998. *Successful Failure: The School That America Builds*. Boulder, CO: Westview Press.

Varley Gutiérrez, M. 2009. "'I Thought This U. S. Place Was Supposed to Be about Freedom': Young Latinas Speak to Equity in Mathematics Education and Society." PhD diss., University of Arizona, Tucson.

Vásquez, O. A. 2003. *La Clase Mágica: Imagining Optimal Possibilities in a Bilingual Community of Learners*. Mahwah, NJ: Lawrence Erlbaum.

Vélez-Ibá–ez, C., and J. Greenberg. 2005. "Formation and Transformation of Funds of Knowledge." In *Funds of Knowledge: Theorizing Practices in Households, Communities, and Classrooms*, edited by N. González, L. Moll, and C. Amanti. Mahwah, NJ: Lawrence Erlbaum.

Wade, P. 2005. "Hybridity Theory and Kinship Thinking." *Cultural Studies* 19(5):602–21.

Warren, B., C. Ballenger, M. Ogonowski, A. Rosebery, and J. Hudicourt-Barnes. 2001. "Rethinking Diversity in Learning Science: The Logic of Everyday Sense-Making." *Journal of Research in Science Teaching* 38(5):529–52.

Warren, B., and A. Rosebery. 1995. "Equity in the Future Tense: Redefining Relationships among Teachers, Students and Science in Linguistic Minority Classrooms." In *New Directions for Equity in Mathematics Education*, edited by W. Secada, E. Fennema, and L. Adajian, 298–328. New York: Cambridge University Press.

Warren, B., M. Ogonowski, and S. Pothier. 2005. "Everyday and Scientific: Rethinking Dichotomies in Modes of Thinking in Science Learning." In *Everyday Matters in Science and Mathematics: Studies of Complex Classroom Events*, edited by R. Nemirovsky, A. Rosebery, J. Solomon, and B. Warren, 119–48. Mahwah, NJ: Lawrence Erlbaum.

Wenger, E. 1998. *Communities of Practice: Learning, Meaning, and Identity.* Cambridge: Cambridge University Press.

Wertsch, J. V. 1991. *Voices of the Mind: A Sociocultural Approach to Mediated Action*. Cambridge, MA: Harvard University Press.

Wiest, L. R. 2001. "Teaching Mathematics from a Multicultural Perspective." *Equity and Excellence in Education* 34(1):16–25.

Wilkinson, J. 1847. *Science for All: A Lecture*. London: William Newberg.

Index

The letter f *following a page number denotes a figure. The letter* t *denotes a table.*